Given By

Harold & Helen Michel

In Memory
Of

David Michel

The Western Hero in Film and Television
Mass Media Mythology

Studies in Cinema, No. 10

Diane M. Kirkpatrick, Series Editor

Associate Professor, History of Art
The University of Michigan

Other Titles in This Series

No. 8   *The Baudelairean Cinema: A Trend within the American Avant-Garde*   Carel Rowe

No. 9   *Visions of War: Hollywood Combat Films of World War II*   Kathryn Kane

No. 11   *Mass Media in Mobilization Regimes: The Case of Balkan Cinema*   Michael J. Stoil

No. 12   *The Rhetoric of Filmic Narration*   Nick Browne

No. 13   *From Formalization to Brecht: The Development of a Political and Aesthetic Sensibility in Cahiers du Cinema*   George Lellis

No. 14   Casablanca *and Other Major Films of Michael Curtiz*   Sidney Rosenzweig

No. 15   *Hollywood Film Genre as Ritual: A Theoretical and Methodological Inquiry*   Thomas G. Schatz

No. 16   *Donald Duck Joins Up: The Walt Disney Studio During World War II*   Richard Shale

No. 17   *The High Noon of American Films in Latin America*   Gaizka S. de Usabel

The Western Hero in Film and Television
Mass Media Mythology

by
Rita Parks

UMI RESEARCH PRESS
Ann Arbor, Michigan

Produced and distributed by
UMI Research Press
an imprint of
University Microfilms International
Ann Arbor, Michigan 48106

Library of Congress Cataloging in Publication Data

Parks, Rita.
The Western hero in film and television.

(Studies in cinema ; no. 10)
Revision of thesis (Ph.D.)–Northwestern University,
1974.
Bibliography: p.
Includes index.
1. Western films–History and criticism. 2. Westerns
(Television programs)–History and criticism.   I. Title.
II. Series.

PN1995.9.W4P33 1982 791.43'09'093278   81-21826
ISBN 0-8357-1287-7   AACR2

Contents

Acknowledgments   *vii*

Introduction   *1*

1   Historical and Mythical Roots   *7*
      The Westward Movement in History
      History into Myth

2   The Materials of Myth   *21*
      The Question of Genre
      The Western Hero and the Mythmakers

3   Cinema: The Myth as Epic   *79*
      The History: How the West Was Done
      The Film Mythmaker: The Way It Should
          Have Been
      The Film Western: A Song of Arms and
          The Man

4   Television: The Myth as Pastoral   *125*
      Electronic Aesthetics: A Question of Identity
      Transition to Television: Small-Scale Saga
          of the Hero Reborn
      Television Types: "Who Was That Masked Man?"
      The Saddle-Soap Formula: "Television Westerns
          Drive Me Nuts!"
      The Electronic Mythmakers: God Has Not
          Permitted Us To Know What Will Sell
      The Television Western: At Home on the
          Twenty-Five-Inch Range

Conclusion   *155*

Appendix A: Television Westerns   *159*

Appendix B: Writer Guidelines for *Bonanza*   *163*

Notes   *165*

Bibliography   *181*

Index   *187*

Acknowledgments

It is with pleasure that I acknowledge my gratitude to Dr. Martin Maloney, scholar and humanist. As scholar he not only shared his knowledge but was constantly learning. As humanist he had from the beginning shown me that what is of the people—popular—is a culture true and beautiful and good and, most of all, worthy of study.

I am also grateful to: the speech faculty of Northwestern University for sharing freely their unique approaches to mass media art and thus helping to shape my research there; those who encouraged my exploration into the West and its heroes; my religious community, the Sisters of Mercy, for encouragement and support; and my friends, whose remarkable sense of timing told them when it was a time to weep and a time to laugh, a time to mourn and a time to dance, a time to be silent and a time to speak.

Introduction

Dating from the writing of de Tocqueville and Crèvecoeur and continuing through the present moment, the character of the enigmatic American has been the subject for not always enlightening, but surely fascinating debate by historians, sociologists, psychologists, anthropologists, and philosophers both foreign and native to American soil.

The reasons are not at all surprising. Less than four hundred years after the beginnings of European colonization, barely two hundred years after the first trembling steps taken toward sovereignty as a nation, the United States of America has climbed to the summit of world power and is struggling for equal footing with nations whose history extends back into the unchronicled darkness of ancient times. Upstart Americans, however they may be characterized by those who study them, are metaphoric examples of the current generation gap discussion: Europe, though not all that far removed from its child in time, is unable to understand this United States, which seems to slight the values and culture of its parent and even speaks a different language—"American."

To speak collectively of the American, however, is to speak in generalizations which undoubtedly can be refuted by specific instances. But the specifics do not make the generalizations any less true, even though the general may be less factual.

Indeed, it is one of the basic assumptions of this study that what is true— that is, internally consistent—often goes beyond what is factual to create a reality more genuine than the facts can hope to produce. Furthermore, it is this apparent paradox between history and myth that may very likely have produced one of the most enduring and popular phenomena of American cultural history, letters, and—in the present time—mass media entertainment. The historical fact is the existence of the Man of the West; the legend is the myth of the Western hero.

The Western hero is a subject whose roots are in history, whose image has been transformed into myth, and whose chief function for the contemporary audience is to provide popular entertainment. Moreover, he has enjoyed a long and popular life as a mass culture hero. Born in print in the 1830s, he was reborn with the birth of film at the turn of the century and almost fifty years later provided one of the first staples of the infant medium of television. Such an ancestry spans both time and media; it also crisscrosses the thin line between fact and fiction, history and myth. Finally, the popularity of this culture hero—together with that of his counterpart who rides the urban range (the gangster, the private eye, the cop)—points toward insights into the problem of reality versus art (or artifice) in both film and television.

Age, versatility, and popularity qualify the Western hero as subject for the study of what Americans are likely to expect of those to whom they give their adulation as popular heroes. From Cooper tales to television reruns, Americans have been intrigued by the Western hero in whatever form the mythmakers have chosen to present him. Yet the constantly changing face of this hero is indicative of several aspects of popular culture that are characteristic both of audience expectations and media willingness to please.

For popular entertainment, audiences require the fulfillment of a code almost as rigid as that of the legendary West: the hero must be romantic, yet familiar; he must provide a reflection of the audience's own taste in life style, morality, and attitudes toward situations encountered; and he must be able to furnish escape entertainment without too much challenge to the intellect or imagination. Not a very happy prospect, nor a challenging one to the writer, producer, director, or actor who seeks to create a work of art in the Western genre. Yet the image of the West and the Western hero have been portrayed with varying degrees of artistry in both film and television during the past seventy years. Through those years, and from film to television, changes have been wrought in the image of the Man of the West—changes that are at times a blatant, at other times a subtle reflection of the shifting values of the society and audience which help to create and sustain him.

Although all narrative or story-telling art reflects the society in which the artist lives, mass media art has the additional problem of being a product as well. It is the end result of a vast and complex industry which must turn a profit as well as produce a "reflection of life." Indeed, the creative person frequently feels that the film and television industry does live by bread alone, and perhaps is more right than paranoid in this assessment. But the artist's lot notwithstanding, this interplay between art and commerce peculiar to the film and television industry does create both problems and possibilities for the message that each medium communicates. The exigencies of the industry will influence the content of the communication while the nature of the medium will modify the form of that communication. Thus, the so-called "popular entertainments" of film and television shape their content according to the nature and scope of their unique form—just as liquid is shaped by the vessel which holds it. The fact of this enforced content and form will, in turn, help to develop an aesthetic of mass media as something other than the presentation of a "filmed novel" or a "televised short story."

Film and television are both media that reflect some of the complexities of contemporary communication. First, both are purveyors of a staggering variety of facts and fictions, realities and fantasies for their audiences. Second, films and television programming are products of a complex organizational effort rather than the individual work of an artist creating alone. Third, the environment in which the audience receives these media is multisensed and generally social, while other and older types of communication (such as print) tend to focus on a single sense and are designed chiefly for individual participation.

Each of these factors in the film and television media tends to increase the complexity of the communication process. Such complexity, in turn, multiplies the possibilities for ambiguity in the resulting message. It is useful, then, for the audience to understand the factors which produce such ambiguity in order to comprehend better the nature of the medium through which they receive such and so many messages. The clearer the understanding, the better able the audience will be to manage the complex messages that constantly bombard them through the mass media. From such an understanding can flow realistic attitudes toward those media which often present a subtle and confusing amalgam of fact and fiction.

Therefore, the manner in which form and content are fused in film and television entertainment can provide insights into the aesthetics of these media as well as giving indications of how and why certain types of programming and characters have enjoyed long-standing popularity. The Western genre as a distinctive type and the figure of the Western hero as a specific focus can provide concrete material with which to work.

American films and television have provided their viewers with several types of cultural heroes. Besides the Man of the West, the audience can choose from types like the urban cop or private eye, the family man, the man on the run, the professional (doctor, lawyer, journalist), and others. The Western hero is the subject of this study for several reasons. First, he—together with the historical-political figure, the tall-tale folk hero, and the self-made "little" man—has held a traditional place as one of America's oldest and most basic popular heroes. Second, he has appeared in both film and television from their beginnings up to the present time. Third, there is a large body of literature and videature available for examination of his changing image. Fourth, the Western genre seems to be "set"; that is, it seems to have completed a cycle of beginning, growth, and development, "golden age," and decline. And although such a state does not necessarily portend imminent death, the Western genre in film and television is at a point where some assessment is due.

The purpose of this investigation is, therefore, to examine the creation and development of the Western hero as he evolves from an historical figure to a mass media myth. The study will examine both the generic constants and the artistic variables in the figure of the hero as portrayed both in film and on television, and the movement of the hero between the two media. The result can provide certain insights into both the nature of this American popular culture hero and the nature of mass media as well.

In such a study, several questions present themselves. What are the roles of history and myth in the shaping of the American experience? Who are the mythmakers and how do they transform fact into fiction? What changes take place in the figure of the hero as he moves from history to myth and from one medium to another? What characteristics account for the enduring popularity of mass media heroes in general and the Western hero in particular? What might this indicate about mass media communication? What problems are presented for the audience by film and television in presenting myth, fiction, and art (or artifice) through media which simulate history, fact, and reality? What attitudes seem useful or necessary to an audience in enabling them to manage successfully the mixed messages that film and television provide?

These and other questions are approached through analysis of the myth-making process by which the historical person is transformed into a media persona. An essential element of this process is an examination of the role of both the creator of the image (the writer, director, and others) and the image created (the actor or personality). In a few significant instances, both creator and image created will be the same person.

There are also problems associated with such a study of the Western genre and Western hero. Where, in fact, is "the West?" Depending upon the historical period referred to, it can be: the area where Cooper placed his Leatherstocking Tales; the trans-Allegheny territory whence emerged Daniel Boone; the Mississippi and Ohio valley that provided routes for the trappers of the fur trade; the earliest settled region of the Spanish Southwest; the California territory; the northern and Oregon trails blazed by Lewis and Clark, Fremont and Carson; the deserts and high country of Utah, Nevada, and Colorado; The Texas cattle country; or the last-settled "sea of grass" of the Great Plains. At a specific historical moment, the West could be—and was—located in each of these territories. The historians and mythmakers have followed all of these trails, and it will be necessary to retrace many of them before finally settling in an area that is more mythical than geographical, more symbolic than real.

A corollary of the geographic problem is the difficulty of sketching with any degree of accuracy the composite image of the Man of the West. Corresponding to his habitat and moment in history he may be a mountain man, a soldier or scout, an outlaw or lawman, a gunfighter. Complicating the matter still further, he may be an historical character, a fictional or mass media creation, or a personality who has taken on a mythic or heroic persona as the result of his acting out of the Western myth. Again, the most useful approach will explore the characteristics of several of these heroes in order to generalize about the image of the Man of the West as he evolves from mountain man to mass media myth.

There is another problem that arises from the mythologizing of history. Very simply, it is the blurring of the distinction between fact and fiction in the constant retelling of the story of the United States. It will therefore be necessary to discuss history and myth as both shapers and products of the American experience. Such an examination can help to assess the roles played by historic fact and artistic imagination in the development of the American character and, in a larger sense, in the intellectual and emotional life of humanity.

Still another problem that must be faced is the fact of the less than distinguished reputation of the Western genre. In whatever form, Westerns are still considered pure escapist fare for the majority of readers, filmgoers, and television audiences. This view has encouraged further stereotyping of the genre to the point that the Western has been neglected in the area of serious criticism until very recent years. This study seeks to examine the genre as it has evolved; at the same time it attempts to avoid the extremes of either the chilling condescension of elitist criticism or the indiscriminate enthusiasm of an all-embracing worship of nostalgia, camp, or pop.

Although not the most important, possibly the most difficult problem of all presents itself in this attempt to help correct critical neglect and balance critical extremes. The question becomes one of how to select among the multitude of examples of the Western genre in each medium. Should attention be given to all media; print, theatre, radio, film, television? Should selections be limited to the outstanding artistic contributions to the genre, or should more typical (but possibly less artistic) work be studied? What about significant works which stand as landmarks in the evolution of the form? And what attention, if any, should be given to those works which reflect the change in audience expectations from one period to another? Then, too, there is the very practical problem of limitations of time and space in treating such a wide spectrum of material, characters, and creators.

To attempt to assess the contributions of all media that have produced work in the Western genre would require a study of formidable proportions. Attention will be given here to the media of film and television; in particular, to changes that have occurred in the genre from one medium to the other. Following a roughly chronological format, the study will pinpoint outstanding contributions among typical as well as significant examples in the movement of the genre through film and television. The role played by audience expectations in the development of the Western tends to follow the chronology insofar as such changes reflect changes in the sociocultural lives of Americans moving from one era to the next.

Finally, any critical analysis must run the risk of becoming subjective, opinionated, and narrow in its interpretation of data. Such dangers cannot be dismissed but they can be diminished. The conclusions of a study employing the historical-critical methodology will be as sound as the careful selection and analysis of the materials that lead to those conclusions.

The culture of a people—its values, consciousness of self, community spirit, sense of the past and expectation of the future—is a diffuse and slippery concept to grasp for at best. In the case of the North American nation, barely two hundred years old (and in some opinions not old enough to develop even the rudiments of a national consciousness), the concept of culture is even more difficult to grasp, let alone define. However, the myth of the American West and its heroes—complex in its depiction of the antinomies of frontier and civilization, individualism and community, primitivism and progress, savagery and law—does provide strong and specific themes for the artist. These, in turn, can help to illuminate the elusive nature of the American experience. Ralph Waldo Emerson pointed the way in the 1830s when he observed that the outcasts, the pioneers, and the empire builders knew indeed where to begin to discover America. Europe, Emerson said, extended to the Alleghenies; America lay beyond.

1

Historical and Mythical Roots

The Westward Movement in History

If, indeed, America did lie beyond the Alleghenies, it did not take the colonial Europeans long to discover it. For European they were—these thirteen little colonies that clung so precariously to the Atlantic coastline prior to the War of Independence. After that astonishing victory it remained to be seen whether they could be as tenacious in clinging to one another to form a new body of united states. European by politics, religion, and cultural heritage, the new independents found themselves citizens of possibly the most bewildered and dazed of emerging nations as they gazed about at what they had won as the spoils of war.

Not since the exploding of the horizons of the mind during the Renaissance had such possibilities presented themselves for seemingly endless movement across new frontiers. It was a wildest dream come true. The infant American discovered a unique milieu that Europeans had not experienced for centuries: a virgin land that stretched to what might well be infinity—with the possibilities seemingly infinite as well. It was a place to become what one could not be in one's present state. It offered the outcast escape from the oppressive strictures of the law; it provided the explorer uncharted regions to challenge; it gave the settler the chance of a fresh start; it promised the entrepreneur unclaimed goods to gain the opportunity to turn a handy profit or to establish a personal empire.

The Land

Thus the post-Revolution migration began. The emigrants trickled through the Cumberland Gap and the mountains of Pennsylvania into the new territory, leaving behind them whatever or whomever it was they were escaping, for if the westward movement meant anything, it meant escape. But escape to what? The Ordinance of 1785 and the Northwest Ordinance of 1787 were the first of a series of government enticements to populate the unknown western lands. Bernard DeVoto, writing for *Harper's Magazine* in the aftermath of the Great Depression, refers to a sardonic joke about the government's encouragement to western emigrants through the early land grant acts. The land grants, so the joke goes, were simply the federal government's bet with the emigrants that before they could conquer the land they would themselves be conquered by it.[1] Federal inducements, however, did bolster the courage and help supply the incentive for those who were on the verge of joining the movement. It also put ideas into the hands of those who were heretofore, complacent homebodies.

It was not until after the turn of the nineteenth century, however, that the trickle of emigrants widened into a flood, pouring into the middle and southern territories between the Alleghenies and the Mississippi River. The trappers, hunters, and scouts penetrated much farther. In 1804 Lewis and Clark started their trek across the western plains. By 1807 Zebulon Pike's party had crossed the western mountains, later known as the Rockies. In 1811 and 1812 John Jacob Astor was establishing outposts for his fur trade on the far Pacific coast—a venture that burgeoned into one of the most lucrative enterprises of those early days and which made Astor one of the first of the American empire builders.

These, however, were the adventurers, the people of extraordinary courage who dared the deep plunge into the western wilderness. Furthermore, they did not represent that idealistic agrarian figure—the humble yet noble tiller of the soil apotheosized by Thomas Jefferson as the ideal American and the virtual image of democracy. Those who approximated that description attempted more modest—but still hazardous—distances to settle the closer frontiers of the Northwest and Southwest territories.

Thus, in the years after the War of 1812 the settlements from the Great Lakes in the north through Louisiana in the south caused the American population center to shift westward. Nye and Morpugo, in their brief review of that period, state that when Washington was inaugurated

> less than six per cent of the country's population lived west of the Allegheny-Appalachian mountain ranges. By 1820 the figure stood at twenty-seven percent and was still growing; Ohio's population exceeded that of Massachusetts, while Louisiana and Missouri, the most western of the new states, had more than fifty thousand inhabitants.[2]

The statistics of the western migration provoke pertinent questions for developing historical background in an examination of the individuals who descended from these early wanderers and who were—if America really did lie beyond the Alleghenies—among the first Americans. Three questions in particular play an important part in penetrating to the heart of the myth that was even then developing. Who were the settlers? Why were they drawn westward? What did they find?

Important to historians, these questions are equally vital to the story-teller as well. They are, in fact, the stuff of which myths are made; they are the basic material of the story-teller's art: character, motivation, and action. Who is the protagonist, why does that character act, and what happens?

The People

Romantics, realists, and pragmatists have all identified the people who settled the first American frontier and who, by a repetition of basically the same pattern, were to push farther and farther into the wilderness until the census of 1890 declared that for the citizens of the United States there were no more American worlds to conquer.

Frederick Jackson Turner, whose Frontier Thesis has encouraged increased scholarship on the part of both his disciples and his opponents, quoted John Mason Peck's *A New Guide for Emigrants to the West* (1837) in order to account for the types of persons who were drawn westward. Peck spoke of the pioneer as the first emigrant who, with a horse, a cow, and a few swine, struck out to settle a plot of land, gather a few neighbors, and perhaps create a new state. Then, when "the range is somewhat subdued, and hunting [becomes] a little precarious, or, which is more frequently the case, till neighbors crowd around, roads, bridges, and fields annoy him, and he lacks elbow room," the pioneer deserts the area to begin the same process elsewhere.

Following the pioneer, Peck says, are those who purchase land and throw up the first structures that indicate permanence—primitive schoolhouses, mills, and civic buildings. This second group is forced farther west by the "men of capital and enterprise," who add elements of stability and complexity to the new civilization:

> The small villages rise to spacious towns or cities; substantial edifices of brick, extensive fields, orchards, gardens, colleges and churches are seen. Broadcloths, silks, leghorns, crapes, and all the refinements, luxuries, elegancies, frivolities and fashions, are in vogue. Thus wave after wave is rolling westward:—the real *el dorado* is still farther on.[3]

In contrast to Peck's somewhat romantic account, J.F. McDermott's revisionist version of the same movement is hard-nosed and pragmatic:

> It was the men of capital and enterprise who came first. . . . The focus was on business. Daniel Boone was not the restless, romantic hero pictured so graphically by Timothy Flint "on foot and alone, with no companion but his dogs, and no friend but his rifle, making his way over trackless and unnamed mountains and immeasurable forests until he explores the flowering wilderness of Kentucky"—he was the agent of a land company planning a real estate development. He did not eventually leave Kentucky because he lacked elbow room but because through business ignorance he lost the stake in life he had acquired as land agent.[4]

McDermott's study, *The Frontier Re-examined,* focuses upon the prime importance of business in the development of the West and although this fact certainly influences his interpretation of the material, his assessment of the historical Boone is in basic agreement with the facts—however unromantic those facts may be.

Nye and Morpugo synthesize the five main types who went west, as generally identified by both contemporary observers and later historians. For the most part, the order of migration was the same. The explorers, "half-Indian, half-adventurer," came first. Driven by their own curiosity, they returned with wondrous tales that whetted the curiosity of anyone who would listen. The explorers' assurances of game in abundance brought the hunter and trapper, "living by his rifle and bringing his skins back to some trading outpost, there to stand mute and uncomfortable until he had received his salt, powder, and bullets and could disappear into the wilderness again." After the trapper came the pioneer farmer who cleared, built, and moved on, to be replaced by the settler with sturdier buildings, more enterprising use of the land, and a deeper-rooted sense of community continuity. In 1840,

> there were men in Michigan and Wisconsin who had moved five times, each time farther west; Lincoln's father liked to tell (with typical Western hyperbole) about a family that moved so often that the chickens were trained to walk to the wagon, lie down, and put their feet up to be tied for the trip.[5]

Finally, say Nye and Morpugo, the last to arrive were the men of capital and professional skill, "the men who rounded out the social, political, and economic society, the men who stayed." And with the coming of the stabilized community "the cycle was complete, but beginning all over again somewhere to the west, a cycle accomplished with incredible speed. Some of the first settlers of Chicago were still alive when it had become one of the nation's five largest cities."[6]

Whatever view the observer may wish to take concerning who settled the frontier and in what order, two characteristics remain common to almost every interpretation of the westward movement. First, emigrants went west with the desire to better their lot in some way (although many were bitterly disappointed, some were physically or mentally crushed, and others were ultimately destroyed). Second, almost everyone pulled up roots at least once and moved still farther west. The American emigrants possessed an independent and enterprising spirit, it is true; but they were, in turn, possessed by a restlessness that rarely permitted them to sink their roots very deeply into any given plot of land or place of work. Furthermore, emigrants' traits of enterprising independence and restlessness seem to have intensified in the American people, rather than having been satisfied. The foreigner looking at Americans today speaks with a mixture of amazement and faint disdain of their cheerful but determined aggressiveness and frenzied—almost obsessive—mobility.

Also relevant to the examination of the Western hero are two other facts which are obvious in the descriptions of those who moved westward. First, there is a consensus among historians about the chief types of emigrants, and these are the same types who will appear in both the written and visual story-telling of the West. Second, in categorizing emigrants by profession, character, physical characteristics and other factors, historians are preparing for the story-teller's art by developing a composite (and thus, fictional) image of the emigrant to the West—an image that is historically nonexistent but virtually true.

Historians have described the composite emigrant as a "self-reliant individualist," politically intransigent yet holding strong feelings of group responsibility; as a materialist, suspicious of the artist, the specialist, and the intellectual; as an undisciplined individual who made independent decisions regarding law and order and the proper execution of punishment for those who seemed to deserve it.

It was, therefore, not at all surprising during those remarkably few years of westward expansion that the Eastern establishment took a dim view of the exuberant, exasperating, explosive Westerner. Nye records the opinion of a traveler to the West in 1810 who warns that the folk of the frontier regions are those "who cannot live in regular society. They are all too ideal, too passionate, too prodigal and too shiftless to acquire either property or character."[7] An almost limitless territory being rapidly populated with unstable mavericks (a word coined during the opening of the West by the Westerners themselves) presented political implications that were not lost upon Eastern minds. Such people, they felt, were dangerous.

Yet the enterprising saw the West differently. The entrepreneurs, the gamblers glimpsed future wealth and power in the first small returns invested in the furs and railroads which later grew into trading empires and transportation monopolies. These were the speculators who grub-staked the prospectors in 1848 into the long-shot boom-and-bust mining claims that provided more promise than profit. These were the investors who for the most part stayed in the East, but ultimately came to own the West. They also came to own the people of the West—those who set the traps, laid the ties, mined the claims, and worked the land that Daniel Webster had branded "The Great American Desert." The Westerner became the pawn of the East in the securing of America's "manifest destiny."

But these two views of the West—the political and the pragmatic—were not the only images abroad in expansionist thought. There was also the more idealistic view of the eighteenth-century philosophers and dreamers who envisioned the western lands as the spawning ground of the agrarian ideal: blissful husbandry, the virtuous, enlightened simplicity of tilling the soil, the pastoral image of perfect union of land and farmer, in peace with God and humanity.

This concept was closely aligned with an equally classic myth of the land itself—that of the Edenic Garden. Fruitful, inviting, and idyllic, the distant and untouched West enticed with an aura of hidden riches both material and spiritual. Here a nation could live in joyous contentment, drawing sustenance, wealth, and comfort from a cooperative and fruitful earth. But whether one subscribed to the empire or the agrarian image of the West, it was difficult to separate an image of the Westerner from a discussion of the land which, like its inhabitant, was still very much an unknown factor. It is of such unknowns that dreams are made. The seekers—be they politicians, merchants, adventurers, or philosophers—created this virgin land in the image of their own personal fears, hopes, or dreams. Even before the actual territory was penetrated beyond its fringes, the mythic land was beginning to appear.

Bernard DeVoto speaks of the West as a land of strangeness, resulting chiefly from its lack of rain. Drought, poisonous animals and minerals, stubborn and rocky terrain all contributed to the Westerners' never-ending struggle to make the land less hostile and more like the world they had known.[8] And in spite of the great urban centers, the tamed and fenced and cultivated prairies, the arteries of irrigation through the deserts, the land remains strange today. Within minutes, one can move from basin to plateau, from almost tropical valleys to peaks fourteen inches deep in snow. Travelers can relax in a luxury hotel and read in their newspapers of the death by exposure of a less fortunate person who lost his way in the desert thirty miles to the east. It is small wonder that, in a land of such contrasts and capricious fortune, those who would venture into it to master it would oftentimes be mastered by it.

Such a land invites legend. It can captivate even those who might consider themselves above romanticizing. Turner affirmed the victory of land over settler in near-romantic terms when he wrote in his essay "The Significance of the Frontier in American History" that the wilderness

> finds him [the colonist] a European in dress, industries, tools, modes of travel, and thought. It takes him from the railroad car and puts him in the birch canoe. It strips off the garments of civilization and arrays him in the hunting shirt and the moccasin. It puts him in the log cabin of the Cherokee and Iroquois and runs an Indian palisade around him. Before long he has gone to planting Indian corn and plowing with a sharp stick; he shouts the war cry and takes the scalp in orthodox Indian fashion. In short, at the frontier the environment is at first too strong for the man. He must accept the conditions which it furnishes, or perish, and so he fits himself into the Indian clearings and follows the Indian trails. Little by little he transforms the wilderness, but the outcome is not the old Europe,... [instead, it is] a steady growth of independence on American lines.[9]

The frontier of Turner's writing is the trans-Appalachian territory, but the process of "Americanization"—by which the adventurer attempted an uneasy truce with the land—was repeated from the Alleghenies to the Sierras and from the Montana Rockies to the Arizona deserts and the dry Texas flatlands. The European became the frontiersman or the Daniel Boone. Moving deeper into the wilderness as scout, hunter, or trapper, he became the mountain man or the Kit Carson. Warring with the Spaniards and Indians in the Southwest and pointing his herds north from Texas he became the lawman, the gunman, or the cowboy—each with his real-life counterpart in men like Wyatt Earp or James Butler Hickok or William Bonney or Eugene Manlove Rhodes, but each more real as type than as historical entity.

History into Myth

If, as it is said, poetry is more real than history, the literary and iconographic poetry about the American West may rightfully share a place with historical chronicle in depicting the American Western experience.

History is, after all, an interpretation of the human race's movement through time. Poetry is a metaphoric vision of that same journey. Both are seen from the perspective of an individual—the historian or artist—and both employ the mythology essential to the telling of the tale. But in the poetic vision the artist, able to play with the facts of history, approaches the material with a freedom of form not allowed the chronicler. By treating the facts of history as ever subordinate to the recounting of the myth, the artist can achieve a sense of the human experience that the historian cannot provide. It is not a matter of one approach being superior to the other; rather, the function of each is simply different. The artist approaches material with the express purpose of creating metaphor—of bending reality without breaking it—to display another facet of that reality. It is the nature of literature (verbal or visual or both) to fictionalize fact in the process of changing it into art. And in the instance of the Western experience, it would be rash indeed to insist that history is betrayed by its being transformed into myth.

At this point, however, some clarification is in order, chiefly of the meaning of "myth" and "myth of the West" in the context of this study. Following this, the form and content of the Western myth will be examined through three categories: the question of genre, the central concept of the Western hero, and the phenomenon of the mythmaker.

The Meaning of Myth

John Cawelti, in his essay on the Western as a form of popular culture, argues that the word "myth" has all too many and varied meanings: myth as describing false belief, myth as simply describing belief, or myth as synonomous with archetypal pattern.[10] When no distinctions are made, such meanings tend to confuse rather than clarify discussion. In this study, however, myth is not used in the pejorative sense of untruth, although it may frequently refer to descriptions and narrative that are not factually or historically accurate. Rather, it refers to the portrayal of human experience by means of story or symbol. Writing of this meaning, Northrop Frye explicates Aristotle by defining *mythos* as "a secondary imitation of an action, which means, not that it is at two removes from reality, but that it describes typical actions, being more philosophical than history."[11] In this manner myth may be true in a philosophical sense, yet remain factually inexact.

Furthermore, myth is an attempt to explain some theme, belief, or phenomenon in human experience that cannot be articulated because the "language" necessary is beyond the ability of the narrator to put into logical discourse. Instead, the myth expresses the particular truth to be conveyed about human experience by telling a story (verbally or visually or both). Thus, by a nonlogical—or extralogical—mode of communication, the myth portrays what logical discourse cannot express. At the same time, the manner of recounting the myth indicates something about the teller as well as about the listener—about the artist's world view as well as that of the audience.[12]

Myth, then, refers here to a metaphoric depiction of human experience. That depiction's historical accuracy is of much less import than its ability to convey the human condition as it is perceived at a specific point in time. Moreover, such mythic representations or narratives will frequently include archetypal elements—patterns of character, action, or structure that have recurred in verbal and visual story-telling since ancient times. Cawelti notes that such archetypal patterns are more complicated than the simple theme or belief forms of myth; archetypal approaches to the study of literature, film, and television indicate that his point is well taken. This complexity is latent but no less real in one of the apparently unsophisticated popular culture entertainments available in literary and visual form—that is, the depiction of the American Western experience.

Myth and Archetype: The Ancient Roots

The mythology of the American West, however, is neither original nor unique. Stemming from a rich European folkloric background and based upon Greek classical tradition, the mythology of the American nation is deeply rooted in the more primitive story-telling expressed in tribal rite and cult. These ancient roots—spreading from tribe to culture to continent—provided the new nation with stories, characters, and themes that later helped to form the folklore tradition of the Americans.

Side by side with this complex derivation of primitive myths, however, there existed for Americans another formative strain in the folklore of the American Western experience. More direct than the European tradition, the myth and ritual of the original inhabitants of the new land enriched and further specified the body of folklore that Americans claim as their own. Indeed, it is difficult to determine where the European tradition ends and the native American contribution begins, so intertwined are the basic myths and archetypal materials.[13]

It is equally difficult to speak of the content of either tradition without centering the discussion upon the character of the heroes and heroines. These recurring characters, of course, are the personification of humankind in its journey up through the slowly developing world of consciousness.

Before human beings developed the ability to express verbally their wonder, fears, and hopes about themselves and their world, they were depicting stories about it on the stone walls of caves in Altimira and Dordogne. The drawings were chiefly of the hunt—representations of animals, weapons, and those who braved danger and death as heroes have done from that time to this. The seasonal myths of the Syrian and Mesopotamian cultures attempted to explain the birth-death-rebirth cycle of nature by centering upon the hero Osiris, whose sacrifice of himself brought new life to his people at the price of his own death.

The story of the Greek heroine Persephone, restating the Osiris myth, was one tale among many for the ancient peoples of the Aegean peninsula. Indeed, the entire geneaology of Hellenic legend is rich with stories of heroes set in the context of developing natural science, theology, psychology, and sociology. From the battle of the Titans to the siege of Troy, the Greek heroes struggled with gods of good, evil, and mixed natures, were overcome, yet in the end emerged victorious.[14] Within the specific and exciting context of the tales, the more generic myths were expressed as thematic beliefs of the culture: the struggle for power between father and son, the role of woman as both virtuous and seductive, the crime of hubris, the sins of the fathers being visited upon the sons, the questing and testing of the hero, the savior rising out of nowhere to come to the aid of those in need.

Judaeo-Christian tradition provides still other examples of the mystical, cosmological, sociological, and psychological aspects of the stories of heroes and heroines. From the first human beings, Adam and Eve, through Abraham and Sarah, Isaac and Rebecca, Jacob, Rachel and Leah, the prophets, Jesus, the apostles, martyrs, and saints—each story focuses upon the protagonist's mission and ultimate victory over enemies, even though that victory be achieved only in death.[15]

With cultural variations, the Nordic and Icelandic sagas, the East Indian Vedas, the medieval legends all employ the basic archetypal images, characters, and tales emphasizing details of the hero's mysterious birth, his initiation into the heroic fellowship or brotherhood, his quest and trial, and his resulting immortality. The parallels with the American Western hero are unmistakable, even to the addition that some critics have noted of the venture into a mysterious wilderness replete with strange phenomena of nature and a bestiary of exotic and—at times—magical creatures who aid or threaten the hero's quest.

Schooled both formally and informally in this rich and complex tradition of myth and archetype, American colonists were confronted upon their arrival in the new land with a variety of cultures that proffered their own body of legend ranging from vague fragments to the ritual and cult that follows upon highly developed myth. They drew from both, since they had need of a mythic tradition to sustain them through the delicate and dangerous process of bringing a nation into social, political, and ideological being.

In his discussion of mythological themes in creative literature and art, Joseph Campbell lists the function of myth in four categories that respond to basic human needs: the mystical or metaphysical, the cosmological, the sociological, and the psychological. The mystical or metaphysical function responds to the need of reconciling the human with the divine, of providing means to make contact with the deity. The cosmological function helps people form an image of the universe in which they live that is consistent with the science of their time. The sociological function provides a means of validating and maintaining a specific social and moral order in the community. Finally, the psychological function of myth offers guidelines to steer the individual through the "dependency of childhood, the responsibility of adulthood, the wisdom of old age, and the ultimate crisis of death."[16]

Campbell's categories indicate with both flexibility and precision a basic reference point from which to view human beings, whether they are squatting fearfully in the flickering of a primitive campfire or uneasily sipping a martini before a glowing television tube. The myths created and sustained within the warming circle of both those lights respond to the deepfelt needs of those who gather there for courage, consolation, or wonderment.

Furthermore, Campbell's functions of myth are operative in the forming and preserving of American culture no less than in the culture of other civilizations both primitive and sophisticated. While the American Revolution provided political and ideological heroes for the people, the American Western experience offered social and cultural heroes who—though less real than the revolutionaries—often became the mythical embodiment of what Americans wanted to believe about themselves and their national character. Those basic beliefs—modified in form by the fashion and need of the times—are still operative in films and television today. The heartening tales told of heroes reflect and reinforce the human spirit as well as the life of the community.

It is in this sense that the body of myth associated with the American Western experience reflects ancient archetypes and reinforces present myths. American mythology is, however, less certain of its assurances for the future.

Myth and Archetype: The American Western Experience

In the initial issue of *The American West,* which began publication in the winter of 1964, Gale McGee, United States Senator from Wyoming, offered the following preface:

There is no area of the country with a history more interesting and more distorted in the public mind than the American West. The struggles of the pioneer American to conquer the last frontier have caught and retained the imagination of the public to such an extent that a veritable mythology has developed around the Old West until dreams and reality have become all but indistinguishable....

Perhaps in this mixture of dreams and reality lie the richness and beauty—as well as the complexity and ambiguity—of the myth of the West. In the opinion of one of the most extraordinary and controversial interpreters of the American West in literary history, Bernard DeVoto,

The West is the loveliest and most enduring of our myths, the only one that has been universally accepted. In that mythology it has worn many faces. It has meant escape, relief, freedom, sanctuary. It has meant opportunity, the new start, the saving chance. It has meant oblivion. It has meant manifest destiny, the heroic wayfaring, the birth and fulfillment of a race. It has, if you like, meant what the fourth house of the sky has meant in poetry and all religions—it has meant Death. But whatever else it has meant, it has always meant strangeness. That meaning may serve to reconcile the incompatibles.[17]

Elsewhere, DeVoto develops the idea of this strange and paradoxical land and offers an explanation of how and why the emigrants to the West responded to it:

All men find out they are fools. In the West, necessarily, they made that discovery with the dramatic violence inherent in the country. The by now tired symbol is the covered wagon that heads west lettered "Pike's Peak or Bust" and comes back lettered "Busted, by God!"...[P]art of the Western consciousness is the self-derision of a man who has shot the moon and missed.[18]

The only step left for the man who has shot the moon and missed is to make fun and fable out of the land he couldn't lick. From such quixotic desperation came first, embellishments of history and historical characters, then tall tales, and finally a full-blown body of legend. And while legend grew in the simple folk culture of the western emigrant who lived in the midst of the tall tale land, Easterners, backed by the classical mythology they preserved from European philosophy, art, and letters, applied it freely to the westen lands they had never seen. Thus "high" and "low" culture mixed (as they inevitably do): one, a syndrome of European heritage; the other, a symptom of the nascent American experience. The classical mythology of the Eastern seaboard combined with the folk legends of the West to produce a body of myth that both grew out of and helps to explain the American Western experience.

Although based in history, American Western mythology is not real in an historical sense. Rather, as James K. Folsom notes, it concerns itself with the presentation of the meaning which underlies the superficial facts of history, a meaning equally far from the recitation of events and the evocation of striking historical personalities. It celebrates not history but the themes of history; it sings "another golden age," a story about history but not of it, and the explanation it gives of history is an explanation in terms of myth.[19]

It is not at all surprising, then, to discover mythic analogies in critical analysis of the Western experience: the rancher-nester war as a repetition of the rivalry between Cain and Abel; the prairie schooner plowing through the plains like the ship of Ulysses sailing from Troy; the lonely gunfighter as a suffering god doing the killing for the community and then moving on as an exiled scapegoat, or the knight-errant on an unending quest. And last, but not least certainly, there is the myth of the Edenic Garden and the return to innocence.[20]

There are, however, various levels at which these and other analogies operate in the verbal and visual depiction of the West, and the mythic force will vary, obviously, with a particular artist's use of the basic themes.[21]

Myth into Formula: American Folklore

Continuing his clarification of the various uses of myth in the Western form, Cawelti distinguishes between myth and formula, and then further qualifies formula through the categories of "convention" and "invention." Before defining formula, he states an underlying assumption that all cultural products contain a mixture of two elements: conventions and inventions.

> Conventions are elements which are known to both the creator and his audience before-hand—they consist of things like favorite plots, stereotyped characters, accepted ideas, commonly known metaphors and other linguistic devices, etc. Inventions, on the other hand are elements which are uniquely imagined by the creator such as new kinds of characters, ideas, or linguistic forms.[22]

Conventions and inventions are the two poles of a continuum, Cawelti adds, and most works of art contain a mixture of both. Therefore, while conventions represent images and meanings that are familiar and shared in a particular culture, "inventions confront us with a new perception or meaning which we have not realized before." A formula, then, is a "conventional system for structuring cultural products. It can be distinguished from invented structures which are new ways of organizing works of art," and thus formula and inventive structure become analogous to the two poles of the convention-invention continuum.

With myth, then, as a generic category describing basic and universal themes in some kind of narrative form, formula is a subcategory representing the specific "way in which a particular culture has embodied both mythical archetypes and its own preoccupations in narrative form." And although the Western, the gangster story, the spy thriller all share the basic element of adventure, distinctions can be made among them which justify placing each (as is commonly done) in the specific genre categories just noted. For example, Cawelti notes,

> A Western that does not take place in the West, near the frontier, at a point in history when social order and anarchy are in tension, and that does not involve some form of pursuit, is simply not a Western. A detective story that does not involve the solution of a mysterious crime is not a detective story. This greater specificity of plot, character, and setting reflects a more limited framework of interests, values, and tensions that relate to culture rather than to the generic nature of man.[23]

It is beyond the scope of this study to analyze the differences among the generally accepted genres. Instead, categorizing what seem to be salient characteristics of the Western form will provide concrete material with which to work on the later examination of the genre as depicted by mass media storytellers. Cawelti's treatment of the concepts of myth and formula has been emphasized here because he lays the groundwork for establishing such categories, making useful distinctions between the various ways in which mythic elements can operate in the Western form. Such distinctions point toward clearer insights into the role of the Western for film and television audiences. More immediately, these distinctions provide an introduction for the discussion of the Western as a specific and widely recognized example of the controversial concept of genre.

2

The Materials of Myth

The Question of Genre

Ever since the showdown between film critics Andrew Sarris and Pauline Kael in the early sixties,[1] almost everyone with anything to say about film has entered the hot debate over the issue of auteur criticism. Like all polemic, such airing of views is both useful and detrimental to the cause of criticism. While at times controversy only serves to entrench opponents more firmly in their views, it can also afford the occasion for fuller development of a topic and deeper insights into the area in question. This is particularly true when several others join the fray in reacting to the original argument. The auteur theory is a case in point, and genre study—what seems to be an enriching dimension in critical analysis— is generally but inaccurately placed in opposition to the auteur theory.

As an alternative approach to the study of a body of films, the possibility of classifying them with reference to genre was given much attention by Jim Kitses in his 1969 publication, *Horizons West*. And in 1970, the editors of the British *Screen* devoted much of the magazine space to a discussion of genre criticism centering, as did the Kitses study, chiefly upon the Western.

In *Horizons West* Kitses begins by noting the gains resulting from the emergence of the auteur theory: "the beginnings of a systematic critical approach; the foundation for a subject with its own body of knowledge; the great task of re-evaluation of the American cinema under way." But acknowledging the danger of a "cult of personality" inherent in too worshipful an attitude toward auteur criticism, Kitses cites the study of genre as a means "to avoid this pitfall and build a body of film scholarship that is both vigorous and educationally valid." He then ends the chapter on authorship and genre by concluding that the one can enrich the other:

> The western is not just the men who have worked within it. Rather than an empty vessel breathed into by the film-maker, the genre is a vital structure through which flow a myriad of themes and concepts. As such the form can provide a director with a range of possible connections and the space in which to experiment, to shape and refine the kind of effects and meanings he is working towards. We must be prepared to entertain the idea that *auteurs* grow, and that genre can help to crystallize preoccupations and contribute actively to development.[2]

Kitses' discussion of the Western and its conventions will be referred to later, but it should be noted here that Kitses proposes the combined study of authorship and genre as a fruitful approach to film criticism.

The four views presented in *Screen,* however, do not all share Kitses' vision of a viable union between auteur and genre criticism. And although the resolution of the auteur-genre controversy is extraneous to this study, some points made by each of these writers (not intended as summaries or complete critiques of their views) will point up certain aspects of authorship and genre that may be useful in looking at the Western.

Tom Ryall's "The Notion of Genre" appears as the first of the four articles in *Screen.* An advocate of genre criticism, Ryall deplores what he calls the current emphasis on directors as the critical center of film study. He asserts that this focus shifts "awareness away from the positive role of genre in the American cinema." Instead, Ryall stresses the importance of the relationship between the film maker, the genre, and the audience.

> A crucial notion in any definition of genre, must be that the genre film is one which exhibits a relationship with other examples of the genre. This also implies a consciousness of this relationship on the part of the man who makes the film, and on the part of the audience who go to see it. If we consider the Western, the relationship will be in terms of a *complex* of basic material or subject matter, of thematic preoccupations and of iconographical continuity. This complex provides the director of genre films with a basic "given" to work upon and it also provides an audience with a set of expectations which they will carry to the film.[3]

Ryall therefore establishes the three chief elements of the genre as: (1) basic subject matter (the westward movement and establishment of civilization in the wilderness), (2) thematic preoccupations (which he states are too numerous to note briefly, but which frequently arise out of the subject matter), and (3) iconography (which he feels acquires certain connotations through continued and consistent usage). These categories, though somewhat vague and incomplete, may be acceptable as far as they go. Ryall's third element, however, offers a useful tool for the exploration of film and television Westerns. Then, too, Ryall's notion of genre as providing the director with certain "givens" and the audience with specific expectations widens the scope of genre study from structural, textual, or even iconographic criticism and expands it into the broader areas of its communicative, sociological, and psychological aspects as well. Granted, such broadening of scope can add to the confusion by becoming so diffuse that it is rendered useless. Nonetheless, it seems that the exploration of other dimensions ultimately may serve the best interests of the critic, the artist, and the audience.

Edward Buscombe's article, "The Idea of Genre in the American Cinema," follows Ryall's in the same issue of *Screen.* Buscombe notes that literary criticism tends to avoid the problem of genre because it leads to the prescription of rules and regulations which are restrictive to artistic freedom of creation. He thinks this need not be so:

> One does not have to set up a Platonic ideal, to which all particular examples try vainly to aspire, nor even to say that the closer any individual film comes to incorporating all the different elements of the definition, the more fully it will be a Western, or gangster picture, or musical.[4]

In seeking to avoid prescription in both form and content, Buscombe makes two points: First, he agrees with Ryall's rejection of an "ideal" form of the genre as rigid and untenable,[5] yet in the course of his article Buscombe tends to set up such an ideal. Second, he argues against being prescriptive in establishing too rigid a set of categories, yet in citing certain visual criteria as the framework of the story—i.e., setting, clothes, tools of the trade, and physical objects— Buscombe implies a critical judgment by seeing these as more than a mere framework; they also affect what sort of story it will be. In setting up these visual criteria, however, Buscombe does affirm Ryall's point tht iconography is a basic element to be considered in the study of the Western genre film.

An interesting point in Buscombe's discussion is his ambiguous use of the term "history" in assessing its importance in genre study.

> If one looks at a cinematic genre in this way, as being composed of an outer form consisting of a certain number of visual conventions that are, in a sense, arbitrary (in the same way that a tragedy has five acts) then certain problems are on the way to being solved. First, we are not bound to make any very close connexions between the Western genre and historical reality. Of course there *are* connexions. But too many discussions of these problems fall down over this point because it is usually assumed that the relationship must be a direct one; that since in fact there was a West, Westerns must be essentially concerned with it.[6]

Yet Buscombe's discussion following indicates that he is in danger of falling victim of the same problem. Using "history" in its narrowest sense of "historical fact," Buscombe criticizes Kitses for stating that a basic convention of the genre is that films in Western guise are about America's past. Yet in Buscombe's discussion of such history he seems to be employing a meaning much akin to that of Kitses—and much akin to that legendary or even mythic meaning discussed earlier in this study. Thus, when Buscombe says that "history, to which Kitses devotes most of his attention, is a relatively unimportant part of many Westerns," he is speaking of a history which he himself uses as the context of the visual criteria noted above.

But once this ambiguous use of the term "history" is understood, it provides no problem in his discussion of the conventions of the genre. A genre film, says Buscombe, depends on a combination of novelty and familiarity. The conventions of the genre are known and recognized by the audience, and such recognition is in itself a pleasure. Popular art, in fact, has always depended on this.... [7]

The parallels to Cawelti's position on formula are obvious. Obvious, too, is the importance of audience expectation as a basic and significant element in identifying the force of genre in a work.

Richard Collins begins the third article, "Genre: A Reply to Ed Buscombe," with the observation that Buscombe does, indeed, move toward the prescriptive in his listing of the formal iconographic elements basic to the Western genre. Collins, on the other hand, agrees with this emphasis on the importance of the visual image to the notion of genre. He does suggest, however, that the categories of clothes, tools of the trade, and physical objects (Collins calls them "locations") are dependent upon the film being set in that historical past that Buscombe is reluctant to acknowledge as essential to the genre. Collins' point is well taken; it is surely difficult to separate the images characteristic of a Western from a particular kind of locale and era, no matter how historically imprecise that place or time may be.

With regard to structure and theme, however, Collins reiterates the already-noted element of stock situations or basic genre formulas.

> During the long history of the genre, directors have selected a repertoire of situations, antinomies and motifs from the mass of material available in the history of the American frontier.... It is in the formulation of a repertoire of key situations that recur again and again in films, and to a lesser extent in Western fiction, that the distinct nature of the genre is located. [8]

Thus, the repertoire of certain situations must also arise out of history (again, in the broad mythic or legendary sense) rather than being an arbitrary choice on the part of the artist. This, however, is as much of a concession as Collins will allow to the notion of genre.

> I would then maintain that if genre exists as a distinct quantity it is in terms of a repertoire of stock situations, selected from the events of the American frontier, that are themselves unspecific, ambiguous and intrinsically without meaning. That neither a structure of archetypal patterns and myths nor of history is sufficiently precise to constitute a genre, nor do recurrent locations, clothes and props do more than signal a temporal and geographical context for a film. [9]

Collins' rejection of these elements as characteristics of genre signify his rejection of genre study as a workable approach to critical analysis of a body of films. Genre criticism is deficient, says Collins, in comparison with the methodology of the auteur theory, and although such a conclusion seems predestined throughout his article, Collins does provide in his discussion of specific films valuable insights into the inventiveness of individual film artists. He is particularly adept at illustrating these "key situations" as crises of the hero's personal past, rather than a national or historical past. Collins' article illustrates the value of controversy in shaping the tools of criticism in the Western genre.

Andrew Tudor examines the notion of "Genre: Theory and Mispractice in Film Criticism" as a fourth contribution to the *Screen* magazine discussion. After preliminary remarks on the auteur-genre controversy, Tudor poses the problem of the "empiricist dilemma" in genre criticism:

> To take a *genre* such as "Western," analyze it, and list its principal characteristics, is to beg the question that we must first isolate the body of films which are "Westerns." But they can only be isolated on the basis of the "principal characteristics" which we can only discover *from the films themselves* after they have been isolated. That is, we are caught in a circle which first requires us to isolate our films, for which purposes we must have a criterion, but the criterion is, in turn, meant to emerge from the empirically established common characteristics of the films.[10]

Tudor sees two solutions: one, to classify films based on a priori criteria depending upon the critic's purpose; the other, to rely upon "common cultural consensus as to what constitutes a "Western" and then go on to analyze it in detail.

In choosing the second as the more frequently used in criticism, Tudor observes that the consensus is evident chiefly in the agreement on certain established "Western" conventions—visual, situational, and thematic. These conventions, he goes on to say, are so taken for granted in our American culture that all of us feel we can readily recognize a Western, even though we must allow that we can less readily define one—"we must also be willing to admit that the edges are rather blurred." As a further step, not only do the films exhibit certain characteristic conventions, but these conventions are also in some way dependent upon characteristics of our culture. The result is that "*Genre* notions . . . are not critics' classifications made for special purposes, but sets of cultural conventions. *Genre* is what we collectively believe it to be." Moreover, it is not "a way in which the critic methodically classifies films, but the much looser way in which an audience classifies its films."[11] The classification thus becomes informal consensus rather than rigid prescription.

Tudor qualifies what he means by "culture" and "audience" when he indicates that identical genre expectations are not universal. Over a period of time and from place to place (e.g., the United States, Europe, the Orient) the conventions of the Western are not exactly the same, although all are patterned after the American model. However, it would be difficult to accept Tudor's view that the conventions themselves *change*. It would seem that the focus, emphasis, or selection of conventions change, but not the conventions per se. Much of the material written on the "new" Western focuses on such alterations in form and content, reflecting the passage of chronological as well as cultural time in the experience of Americans.

Finally, Tudor's separation of myth from genre is consistent with his view that genre is a culture-bound concept, while myth is "a general term referring to ideas, stories, beliefs, or whatever, which operate *in the same way in all* societies."[12] This definition is consonant with the position taken in this study, and reflects in paraphrase Cawelti's distinction between myth and formula.

Tudor summarizes his contribution to the discussion of genre in his concluding remarks. These represent still another useful approach to genre study—that of sociology and psychology:

> In sum, then, I have argued that *genre* is a term best used in the analysis of the relation between groups of films, the cultures in which they are made, and the cultures in which they are exhibited. That is, it is a term which can be usefully employed in relation to a body of knowledge and theory concerning sociological and psychological aspects of film. It is crucial to understanding the ways in which people respond to films, the relations between films and the societies and cultures in which they exist, and to the various factors involved in the film-making process.[13]

The views of Ryall, Buscombe, Collins, and Tudor, although not presented here in their entirety, still embody many of the basic arguments surrounding the problem of genre. And although the *Screen* discussion is not by any means the only available material on genre, it has been examined here because the authors have attacked the question of genre in a particularly useful fashion. Their material faces the problem head on and in its essence, whereas others have approached genre chiefly in order to sort out its various components and then move on to a consideration of films, film makers, or some sociological, historical, or literary value.[14] The four views selected, therefore, illustrate basic problems in dealing with the concept of genre and its place in a study of the Western hero. It seems useful at this point to clarify the relation of these genre concerns to this study.

First, it is obvious that the question of genre can be neither discounted nor ignored. The fact that discussions like the auteur-genre controversy receive wide hearing and provoke continual response indicates that there is matter for investigation and the possibility of discovery. Such potential should not go untapped. Yet the notion of genre is not confined to the often rarefied air of criticism or to the small and elite coterie of aestheticians. Generic terms are used with both frequency and ease by the audience—the great public—when everyday descriptions are needed, particularly descriptions of popular narrative art forms (e.g., "western," "thriller").[15] Any doubts about the widespread consensus of genre sortings can be dispelled by a glance at the arrangement of titles on bookstore shelves, the identifying categories of a day's listing of television programming in the newspaper, or the shorthand identification (useful, though not always totally accurate) of films in reviewers' columns or trade journals (e.g., "the new Peckinpah Western," "a delightful musical").

Second, although the categories are in general use, it is much more difficult to define precisely what is meant by a specific genre. In theory, definitions usually start out as tools, empirical and tentative, to be used for further exploration. In practice, however, a definition frequently becomes an end rather than a means, prescriptive and limiting, enclosing a small segment of the reality within its parameters and growing narrower as investigation continues. Thus the analytic process can often become involuted and confining rather than expansive and enriching. Certainly definitions should be attempted, but always with the qualification that they be capable of expanding and changing to accommodate rather than exclude the newly developing varieties of phenomena to be examined.

The third concern about genre—after it has been acknowledged as an entity and at least tentatively defined—is the question of its function. Can it be useful as a critical tool? If so, to what extent and in what way? And if it is used, does that use exclude other approaches to criticism, such as the auteur theory?

The first concern states a fact; the second and third pose difficulties. But these difficulties, far from dismissing a consideration of genre from the study of the Western hero, are instead quite basic to that study. Examining the nature and function of genre can provide ways of analyzing works categorized in a specific genre. And since these categories represent a popular consensus (however ambiguous that consensus may be), the study of genre can open up alternative approaches to assessing the larger and more diversified sociological relationships between the work, the artist, and the audience.

A Definition of a Western

At this point, a definition of the Western genre is necessary. If it is a useful one, containing the possibilities for expansion noted above, it will embrace a broad enough spectrum of works to provide access to the more important concerns of this study. Definitions are basic, but are not among those more important concerns.

A Western, as treated in this study, is a visual and verbal story form depicting a repertoire of situations in a frontier setting and involving the particular types of characters consensually associated with those situations and that setting. An expansion of this definition will help to clarify the terms.

1. *A* Western, not *the* Western, is the qualifier of the term. The implication is that there is no touchstone, model, or prototype that embodies the essence of "Westernness." There are individual Westerns that illustrate specific aspects of the total image; there are some that seem particularly rich in every aspect.

Setting up an ideal, however, can be an escape from the labor and precision required of descriptive study. In some instances such an attitude will result in critics' simply writing off any work that they judge does not sufficiently measure up to the ideal. A touchstone approach also tends to confuse the two distinct critical elements of description and evaluation, whereas each element better serves the process when description precedes and is kept separate from evaluation. If value judgments are to be of any use at all, they must come only after concise description, careful analysis, and as thorough an understanding as is reasonably possible.

2. *Visual and verbal elements* work together in mass media Westerns. These, of course, are the formal qualities of the work, not simply imposed upon the content or coexisting with it but inseparable from it. This union (as opposed to superimposition) is one of the strongest characteristics of a specific genre— each element contributing to and dependent upon the other elements in a tightly woven network. Therefore, it is difficult to speak of content without touching on form, or of form without referring to content. A separation of the two elements of form, however, is in some ways a more manageable task. Still, iconography and language perform the same functions in the genre. They are both a means of telling the story, of communicating mood as well as plot; furthermore, both employ a structure, grammar, syntax, and imagery to do so.

Among the characteristics of the visual and verbal elements of the Western, three will recur in the examination of films and television programming in this study.

First, the balance between the two elements is an important factor in examining the impact of the work upon its audience. This balance or proportion obviously influences the overall shape of the work as well. Actor James Stewart illustrated this result from his own experience:

> There's a thing around the trade that the western script weighs less than any other kind of movie script. In the old days when we had the radio shows, the big de luxe [sic] theatre of the air, they always did radio adaptations of movies. They had gotten a western picture that I'd done and I remember going to the first rehearsal and they said, 'It's just impossible for us to do this because no one says anything.' And of course in radio this is the only thing they have. So they had to have all sorts of writers come in and give us all things to say which made it an entirely different thing.[16]

In addition to influencing the form of the work and the audience's response to it, the arrangement of verbal and visual elements indicates to a certain extent the concerns and world view of the creator as well.

A second aspect of iconographic and linguistic elements is their ability to illuminate the conventions of the Western genre. But although the look and speech of an American Western are generally recognizable in any culture that has been exposed to its conventions, imagery lends itself more readily to cross-cultural communication than does language. Word and sound suffer much in translation; image does not. For example, when an American hears a character being addressed as "Monsieur Hoss" or listens to the tonality of *Bonanza* in German or Japanese the effect is jarring at least—at worst, it approaches the bizarre.

A third aspect is the twofold function of the visual and the verbal in the genre: one, to tell the story or develop some narrative aspect of the action; another, to illustrate certain aspects of the characters or situations which are more forcefully depicted through symbolic speech or image. Gary Cooper's "Yup!" tells more about this taciturn but self-possessed loner than an entire sequence of expository dialogue by two other characters. Two tiny dots of mounted pursuer and pursued racing across an endless expanse of desert, rock, and sky can economically and vividly set up the situation of relentless chase culminating in an exciting climax.

Further examples of the function of iconography and language will appear in the discussion of specific works, but in brief summary, the skillful use of image and speech enhances, reinforces, expands, explains, and clarifies the persons, events, and setting of the Western genre.

3. *Story form* is specified in the definition in order to clarify the relationship of a specific plot or action to the larger concept of the Western as myth. Besides reiterating the definition of myth noted earlier in this study—a symbolic articulation of a human experience—it is necessary to distinguish between two uses of that meaning in the Western. The first is specific to the American cultural milieu; the second is universal.

One view acknowledges that the Western depicts certain symbolic elements of American life—the self-made man, the Edenic dream, the clever Yankee, the ultimate success of the work ethic, the triumph of physical prowess and personal energy, independence and freedom of movement. Another view accepts these myths but further insists that they are merely American versions of older tales common to all nations and cultures—the death and resurrection of the hero-god, the journey, the quest, the demon trickster, the duel to the death between good and evil.[17]

The second view seems the more logical of the two for several reasons. First, the extensive similarities among the basic myths of both Eastern and Western cultures present a strong case for the consideration of an archetypal approach to myth.[18] Despite the unique aspects of the American experience, the American psyche shares in a common humanity. This nation's symbolic heritage—that of a child of European philosophy, religious belief, and literature—reflects the myths characteristic of Western thought from the Greeks through medieval adaptations and into present forms. Third, it is reasonable to expect that the unique physical, social, and political conditions of the American nation would alter the traditional myths to suit its own purposes and milieu. Thus, the

Western depicts the old stories in new ways and provides for the continuing function of myth in its literary as well as social context.[19] The stories told are ever ancient, ever new; they are told less for the purpose of encouraging invention than to reinforce convention. In this aspect of reinforcement, the Western story bears both its chief weakness and its greatest strength.

4. *A stock repertoire of situations* illustrates the weakness; for the most part, if you see one Western, you see them all. Yet at the same time, as Cawelti notes, this formula and the reinforcement it provides by way of ritual, game, and collective dream may be one of the strongest appeals of the genre.[20] Furthermore, when one is dealing with myth there is only a limited number of basic themes to draw upon. These are then embellished, twisted, reversed, convoluted, and sometimes parodied in order to produce variations upon the theme. Most creators of popular Westerns are engaged in such activity.

In the literary field, for example, Frank Gruber said he "started writing Westerns—for money—a long time ago and [never saw] any reason for quitting." He contended that there are seven basic Western plots: the cavalry and Indians story ("they're due for a comeback"); the Union Pacific or pony express theme ("fighting the elements of nature . . . these are usually big budget pictures"); the homesteaders or squatters story ("has been a little overdone"); the dedicated lawman type ("always good . . . like my own show *Wells Fargo*"); the outlaw story ("humanizing or glorifying some outlaw"); the revenge theme ("probably stems from the old *Riders of the Purple Sage*"); and the empire story ("the builder of a ranch or a way of life threatened with decline because of an outside threat or maybe a weak second generation").[21] Gruber's listing may be somewhat arbitrary and more than somewhat dogmatic; but his categories are basically acceptable for identifying the thematic concerns that have recurred throughout the history of the genre.

Contained within these basic plots and reinforcing the myth are the several microcosmic situations which form the content (frequently ritualistic) of the Western. These are, to name a few, the initial face-off between the hero and the villain and the hero and the heroine, the fistfight, the pursuit, the walkdown, the final shootout. These peak situations—all involving urgency or suspense or plenty of excitement—are combined with the less eventful elements of the love story, the helpless town or weakling official, and the comic characters and situations of traditional nineteenth-century melodrama. These segments of action fit into the larger story themes to form a repertoire of events which are recombined in a varied but essentially recognizable formula.

5. A Western takes place in a *frontier setting* of chronological time, geographical place, or psychological point of view. Most often the frontier is related to all three elements.

The Western has its roots in American history—that history earlier referred to in its broadest sense of encompassing myth and legend as well as fact. It is most frequently set in the past, during that span of years from about 1830, when the first frontier was located at the margins of the original colonies, and extending perhaps to as late as 1915, when (even though the frontier had been formally declared closed about twenty-five years earlier) the final conflicts between freedom and encroaching civilization were fought by renegades in the Texas and Mexican territories. Theoretically, such a broad chronological spectrum would readily lend itself to great diversity in depicting Western themes. In reality, however, most Westerns have been set within a very limited time span of the frontier era, usually in the years between 1865 and 1890. Few Westerns deal with the opening of the Ohio valley or the early Indian wars of the Great Lakes area, Florida, Georgia, or Tennessee. Moreover, Civil War themes are usually not categorized as Westerns, although many Western heroes are identified as having participated in that conflict before the story begins.

Westerns more frequently depict the era of the great cattle drives, when the now legendary Texas ranches were in the process of developing a few head of Mexican strays into the massive herds that trail drivers headed north each year to the railheads in Kansas and Nebraska. These were the days when cowtowns like Abilene, Dodge City, and Ogallala sprang up to accommodate the thirst and appropriate the newly earned wages of the men who had endured weeks on the trail by anticipating the rip-roaring "spree" to come. Thus, the cowboy became the central character of the Western; the badman, the marshal, the saloon-girl, and the schoolmarm were the supporting cast; and the prospector, the town coward or drunk, and the homesteaders and cattle barons rounded out the story.

Like the historical time, the geographical setting of the Western is less likely to be the trans-Allegheny frontier. More frequently the locale will be the rugged mountain areas of Colorado, Wyoming, Montana, Utah, or California; the desert regions of Nevada, Arizona, or New Mexico; or the arid flatlands of Texas, Oklahoma, Kansas, or the Dakotas.[22] And as the man of the West became the central character, the infant town—and its antinomy, the Western wilderness—became the geographical focus of the story.

But before attention can be turned to the cast of characters in that setting, something must be said of the contemporary Western, which takes place at a moment when the frontier of both time and place are but a memory. This is the setting for films like *Hud* and *The Misfits* and of television series like *Empire* and *Cade's County*. Later discussion will indicate the relationship of these works to the Western genre—if, indeed, a relationship exists. If it does, the frontier is located in the characters' frustrated nostalgia or in a world view that is basically anachronistic and out of touch with contemporary life. These stories frequently refer to the past as a comment upon the present or as a portent of the future. Treating of lost hopes and unfulfilled dreams, they are usually less successful than period pieces because their creators rarely achieve the degree of delicacy and sensitivity necessary to build and sustain such difficult themes.

The frontier setting, therefore, provides the milieu in which a specific group of individuals act out a certain set of conventions consistent with that setting. The interplay among these elements (frontier setting, frontier conventions, frontier characters) is a vital aspect of the genre.[23]

6. *Particular types of characters* in the Western have already been noted. Cawelti divides these characters into three general categories: townspeople, savages, and the hero. The townspeople are then subgrouped into pioneers or decent folk, escapees from civilization, and banker-villains. Cawelti gives special note to women as symbols of civilization, whether they be the virginal type (schoolmarm) or the earth-mother figure (the dance-hall girl). The savages are designated as either Indians or outlaws, both reflecting the antinomies of innocence and barbarism. The third category—the hero—Cawelti places at the center of the scheme, and rightly so.[24] It is the hero's relationship to the other characters that provides the initial motivation, the constant progression, and the ultimate climax of the Western story. The Western hero—American Ulysses, questing knight, noble Leatherstocking—is the central focus of the Western myth. And it is the hero as an individual historical person or a collective legendary persona who has dominated the popular literature of the Western genre from the pages of dime novels to the color television screen.

7. This cast of characters—the townspeople, the women, the Indians and outlaws, the hero—*is consensually associated with those situations and that setting* characterized as "frontier." Noted earlier, the concept of cultural consensus is basic to the definition of the Western and is highly useful in assessing the role of the genre in popular culture studies. The iconography and language, the mythic dimension and the stock situations, the characters and setting are all readily recognizable if they are consistent in their relationship with each other within the requirements of the genre. No one mistakes a Western for a spy thriller, although both are adventure stories and both contain the elements of character, setting, action, myth, and verbal and visual form. If the story is set on the American frontier, if the action is consistent with that setting, and if individuals are involved who look, speak, and live out a particular life style characterized as "frontier," these specific colorations will harmonize into an integral world view. The world is the mythic West and the story is a Western.

The integrity and harmony of its parts qualifies a particular work for inclusion in the genre. What characteristics are essential, or which may be omitted without excluding the work and impairing the "rightness" of the combination must be left to cultural consensus to determine. But since the American Western has been created and developed in a volatile cultural milieu, the emphasis and focus of that consensus are dependent upon the shifting base of cultural change. Historically, various elements have always been stressed, or suppressed, or recombined, or even satirized in order to conform to audience expectations of a particular time. Perhaps the only constant factor characteristic of the Western—or any other genre for that matter—is the harmony and consistency that unites the elements selected.

The definition above is intended as a continuation of many beginnings by others, and is in no way a final word. It is exploratory in nature rather than definitive—a tool rather than a model. By this means, description can proceed in the direction of formulating judgments; categorizing can move through understanding toward evaluation. It is a good place to end a definition.

Genre Study in Media Criticism

With a working definition of the Western genre as a basis for further discussion, it is now possible to turn to the question of the function of genre as a critical tool. Mass media studies have been faulted for simply borrowing the tools of literary criticism rather than creating instruments unique to media needs. Although the accusation is a bit provincial in tone and overblown in importance, the basic assertion is true. The genre approach to criticism does indeed lend itself quite readily to a study of popular culture and to an examination of that culture's dissemination through the technology of film and television. Thus it is a basic premise of this study that the notion of genre is a valid and highly useful tool in the examination of mass media popular culture products. Its usefulness lies chiefly in the possibilities it provides for investigation of popular culture as both art and product—as aesthetic creation and mass media communication.

In an examination of popular culture as art, genre furnishes the critic with a way of looking at the tripartite structure of the creative act: the artist, the work, and the audience. In popular culture terminology, the artist might be an Ash Upson, a Ned Buntline, a Frank Gruber, a John Ford, or a David Dortort— each creating a cultural product for a popular audience. The work might be *The Authentic Life of Billy the Kid, The Scouts of the Plains, Peace Marshal, My Darling Clementine,* or *Bonanza.* The audience is the most difficult to pinpoint, but it may be said safely that the audience is heterogeneous, international, and dedicated.

Certain of these names or titles may seem out of place in a list of artists and artistic works, but they are all examples of creators and creations in the popular form of the Western. And since the degree of artistry varies (and this is unquestionably a matter of judgment), the creators will be examined as workers in mass media and will be evaluated in the context of whether or not theirs are excellent, good, or merely mediocre products. This approach will preclude distracting, certainly pointless, and possibly endless argument about "mass" versus "elite" culture and/or art. Such discussion is better reserved for those who feel that there must be a duel to the death between the two, and that the survival of one necessitates the extermination of the other. This is not the position taken in this study. Rather, each artist and his work will be examined within the framework provided by Ray B. Browne in his essay, "Notes Toward a Definition:"

One serious scholar defines a total culture as "The body of intellectual and imaginative work which each generation receives" as its tradition. Basing our conclusion on this one, a viable definition for Popular Culture is all those elements of life which are not narrowly intellectual or creatively elitist and which are generally though not necessarily disseminated through the mass media. Popular Culture consists of the spoken and printed word, sounds, pictures, objects and artifacts. "Popular Culture" thus embraces all levels of our society and culture other than the Elite—the "popular," "mass" and "folk." It includes most of the bewildering aspects of life which hammer us daily.[25]

Admittedly, the framework is a broad one, but it is so of necessity and in order to avoid the debilitating effects of restrictive definitions noted earlier. Furthermore, it is a workable definition for application to Western films and television, since it touches upon elements present in the genre and already discussed—i.e., dissemination through the mass media; spoken word, sounds, and pictures; participation in the popular, mass, and folk tradition.

It is therefore possible that the Western genre can produce popular culture forms which are truly art within that tradition; it can often provide works qualifying as artistic creations in the elite tradition as well. In other words, just as an Aristotle could appreciate the genius of a popular artist, so can an André Bazin, an Andrew Sarris, or even a John Simon—on occasion. Without necessarily placing them at the same eminence as the Greek theorist, these contemporary critics can analyze with pleasure the artistry of a man working in a highly popular genre tradition and understating his case with the oft-quoted throwaway comment: "My name is John Ford. I make Westerns." Ford, and other popular artists who have used the Western as their mode of creation, have taken the elements of Browne's definition and informed them with their own competence and skill. Expanding popular convention through artistic invention, such creators have enriched the genre in both its mass and elite forms. In turn, the limitations and discipline of working within the Western formula, as Kitses suggests, have sharpened and enriched their own personal artistic styles.[26]

At the same time that genre study provides a way to examine the Western as art, it also presents that form as another aspect of mass media communication. From this perspective, the three basic elements of the communication act are the speaker, the message, and the audience. The speaker may be a writer, an auteur, a mythmaker. The message may be in the form of a dime novel, a biography, a film, or a television series. The audience is again an amorphous entity, crossing the boundaries of age, class, sex, and language. In viewing the Western as mass media communication, those aspects noted earlier must be reiterated and their implications taken into account.

A product of complex technology, mass media communication is a multisensual experience, a group effort, and purveyor of both reality and myth. The iconographic and linguistic aspects of a Western readily lend themselves to the multisensual presentation of the media. The almost authorless (or, at least, auteurless) condition of Westerns in their early history in film and present state on television illustrates the characteristic ensemble approach of the mass media to communication. The Western—combining as it does both history and myth—is but another example of the fact-fiction paradox haunting the mass media critic and, to a lesser extent, the audience and the creator as well.[27]

The Western genre is a useful tool to investigate the complex phenomenon of mass media communication. But rather than becoming a predictable formula in that setting, the Western instead points up the complexity of its own nature and that of the media. It is a formidable task to approach both genre and mass media with the hope of attaining some measure of understanding of either the form or the disseminator of that form. Nonetheless, the usefulness of genre study lies in its ability first, to look at the Western as both popular culture and elite art; second, to view its peculiar characteristics as illustrations of the complexity of mass media communication. In other words, genre can explore a specific work as well as examine its relation to its creator, its audience, and its sociocultural milieu.

Finally, a word about the auteur-genre controversy. Critics who adopt the unreasonable dogmatism of an either-or approach not only burden themselves with a damaging restrictiveness but are detrimental to the cause of healthy criticism as well. The present study employs the approaches of both genre and auteur criticism—using one with the other to explicate meaning and enrich the artistic experience.

In summary, then, a Western is defined through the setting, action, characters, and verbal and visual aspects of its content and form. In addition, the Western genre can be a useful tool in examining the work, the artist, and the audience through a variety of roles in the mass media: as entertainment and art, as product and communication.[11]

The Western Hero and the Mythmakers

From the perspective noted above, the Western is considerably more complex than its humble beginnings or present reputation would allow. And the beginnings, at least, were humble indeed.

Leatherstocking Transformed:
Daniel Boone to Richard Boone

If the roots of the Western are in frontier history, the roots of its heroes are in the history of frontier men. From Leatherstocking to Hec Ramsey (who, incidentally, is closer to Leatherstocking than most of his fellow-heroes in between) the myth has developed from the adventures of real persons through embellishments of those adventures to fact-fiction legends to outright myth.[28]

In *Virgin Land,* Henry Nash Smith discusses the myth in the context of the agrarian interpretation of history—that   is, the paradox of the American wilderness as Garden. Examining this myth, Smith places the Western hero squarely in the center of his argument as the symbol of the antinomies of wilderness and civilization.

Expanding the basic myth, the contradictory elements are charted in *Horizons West* into a provocative web of opposites, highlighting the complexity of themes that the Western genre depicts:

THE WILDERNESS	CIVILIZATION
The Individual	The Community
Nature	Culture
The West	The East[29]

These, with slight variations, are reiterated by others in their exploration of the Western form. But the analysis of Western themes rarely remains in such abstraction. Instead, the analytic movement is consistently from theme to the individual who personifies that theme. For example, John Williams, in exploring the impact of archetypal forms, moves easily and naturally from the Western myth to the Western hero:

> I believe that the most usable and authentic myth available to us may be discovered in the adventure of the American West. Viewed in a certain way, the American frontiersman— whether he was hunter, guide, scout, explorer or adventurer—becomes an archetypal figure, and begins to extend beyond his location in history. He is a nineteenth-century man moving into the twentieth century; he is European man moving into a new continent; he is man moving into the unknown, into potentiality, and by that move profoundly changing his own nature.[30]

Smith, however, documents that change as it developed in American popular literature from about 1830 to the turn of the century, tracing the metamorphosis of the historical Daniel Boone into the mythic hero of the West. It is a good place to begin an examination of the several character types who, with variations, appear again and again as the heroes of mass media Westerns.

It is difficult, however, to trace the evolution of the hero without noting those who contributed to his legend. Therefore, the following discussion will: (1) identify the basic character types and those who mythologized them, together with a summary of the chief characteristics of the Western hero; and (2) point out the specific categories of pre-mass media mythmakers, together with notes on how a legend is created and sustained.

The Prototype. Daniel Boone, a Kentucky woodsman, explorer, hunter, and farmer, was first mythologized by John Filson in an adventure story written in 1784 titled: *The Discovery, Settlement, and Present State of Kentucky.* Filson's approach—embellished with classical allegory in a biography by Boone's nephew Daniel Bryan in 1813—depicted the hero as founding father and benevolent sustainer of the small knots of civilization which were just beginning to invade the trans-Appalachian wilderness. But, says Smith, hand in hand with the image of Boone as empire-builder and philanthropist there was emerging another hero, based upon the popular notion of Rousseau's "natural man" fleeing into the wilderness to escape the encroachments of civilization on the move. And although in reality Boone's westward movement was necessitated by his inability to get and hold land,

> The impulse that produced Western tall tales transformed him into the type of all frontiersmen who required unlimited elbow room. "As civilization advanced," wrote a reporter in the New York *American* in 1823, "so he, from time to time, retreated"—from Kentucky to Tennessee, from Tennessee to Missouri. But Missouri itself was filling up: Boone was said to have complained, "I had not been two years at the licks before a d—d Yankee came, and settled down within a hundred miles of me!!"[31]

Toward the end of his life Boone denied this basic myth upon which the popular tales of him had been based,[32] but it was too late; the myth had taken hold. So deeply were the reality and myth entwined that the historian Cecil B. Hartley, in attempting to describe a period in Boone's life in the wilderness, turned to fiction in order to describe fact rather than the other way around. Hartley says: "A reader of Mr. Cooper's *Last of the Mohicans* may comprehend, in some measure, the arts by which he [Boone] was preserved."[33]

Hartley's reference is a logical one, for James Fenimore Cooper's tales did take up the familiar element of the Boone myth: the "central issue of the old forest freedom versus the new needs of a community which must establish the sovereignty of law over the individual."[34] This conflict between the individual and the group—one of the strongest motifs of the Western—appeared early in American literature and reflected the older and more universal theme of the human dream of freedom and self-determination.

There were other similarities between Boone and the Leatherstocking character. Like Boone himself, Cooper's creation was a man of some years, of rough and uncultured speech and manners; a man dressed in the skins of animals, moccasin-shod, and armed with a long rifle. And like Boone, Leatherstocking needed considerable tidying up to conform to the conventions of gentility necessary to the literary hero of the 1830s. The consumers of popular culture required the hero to mirror the values of culture, education, and civilized ways they held in esteem. But at the same time, the myth of the uncivilized frontier was firing the American imagination. The paradox was built into the historical situation, and Cooper resolved it after twenty-five years with a compromise:

Since the basic image of Leatherstocking was too old for the purposes of romance, the novelist doubled the character to produce a young hunter sharing the old man's habits, tastes, skills, and, to some extent, his virtues.

In some of the stories, Smith continues, the young hunter-companion of Leatherstocking was at last revealed to be a gentleman in disguise. The result: "the hero retained all his genteel prerogatives by hereditary right, and at the same time claimed the imaginative values clustering about Leatherstocking by wearing a mask, a persona fashioned in the image of the old hunter." In other tales, the young companion is of vague origins, but with gentler ways than Leatherstocking. Furthermore, he does not share with his older counterpart the feelings of hostility toward civilization.[35] Thus one more step was taken toward the younger, more romantic figure of the man of the West. It was a move dictated by the need to create a man of heroic mold who would still conform to the cultural consensus of the time prescribing what sort of man that hero must be.

But while some writers were creating heroes in the genteel mode, more popular—and, for the most part, anonymous—story-tellers were developing a comic counterpart to the staid and melancholy Boone. His name was Davy Crockett—"half horse, half alligator, a little touched with snapping turtle, who could wade the Mississippi, leap the Ohio, ride upon a streak of lightning, who could whip his weight in wildcats and eat any man opposed to Andrew Jackson."[36] The mythmakers had a heyday with Davy, who became the blustering, brawling, larger-than-life hero in whom young America delighted. He rode a tame bear called "Death Hug" and gained such notoriety with both man and beast that when he went hunting some animals "would die when he just grinned at them and others, looking down from a tree and seeing him reach for his gun would holler, 'Is that you, Davy?' Then when he'd say, 'Yes,' they'd sing out, 'All right, don't shoot! I'm a-comin' down.'"[37] Crockett's comic fame was at its height in the 1830s, and his place in the more serious Valhalla of American folk heroes was secured at his death at the Alamo. Crockett is noted here as a transitional figure, rather than as a type of Western hero; he represents the movement from the mild woodsman image toward the rough mountain man persona. Moreover, although both Boone and Crockett played a part in the development of the Western hero, the mass media have paid little attention to sustaining and developing their myth.[38]

From about 1830 to 1850, the mythmakers—travelers and chroniclers who ventured across the Alleghenies for their material—developed two themes: the general theme of the wilderness versus civilization, and the more personal notion of the desire on the part of the overcivilized to escape back to nature and the original harmony enjoyed by innocent savages.

The hero's move toward assimilation into savage life is manifested by some midnineteenth-century writers in the growing moral ambiguity of the character as he moves Westward. Scalping of Indians by white trappers (to the horror of the genteel hero) was often noted, and Smith says of the Westerner at this point: "His costume, his speech, his outlook on life, often enough his Indian squaw, gave him a decidedly savage aspect."[39] He becomes, as well, more isolated and self-sufficient; he is a man of freedom—sometimes verging on anarchy. He is now the mountain man.

The mountain man. Kit Carson, the historical model for the mountain man, owed the beginnings of his legend to Jessie Benton Fremont's creative editing of her husband's journals in the early 1840s. Carson was John Charles Fremont's guide and companion in their many adventures.[40] Although Carson's exploits interested the Eastern audience, it was once again evident that the mythmakers needed to change his image to conform to the notion of gentility still valued by that audience. As Smith wryly notes, "Barbaric life in the wilderness held grave dangers for the ethical purity considered obligatory in national heroes."[41]

The rough guide was therefore transformed by his biographers into a nobleman—but the character showed little resemblance to the reality. Carson himself admitted that one of his biographers—DeWitt C. Peters in 1858—"laid it on a leetle too thick."[42] The dime novelists—those purveyors of perpetual peril—laid it on a bit thicker with titles like *Kit Carson's Pledge; or, The Prince of the Gold Hunters. A Powerful Novel of Gallant Kit Carson.* Published by Street and Smith, this novel was by Charles Averill who, writing as early as 1846, began mythologizing Carson while the scout was still alive. A title indicative of the more romantic side of the Carson persona was *Kit Carson's Bride; or, The White Flower of the Apaches. A Tale of Indian Adventure.* This story by George L. Aiken for Munro's Ten Cent Novels had some remote basis in truth, for Carson had at least two wives—an Arapahoe woman, Grass Singing, and a Spanish woman living at Taos, Maria Josefa.[43]

Thus the biographies provided a gentlemanly hero, while the dime novels depicted Carson as a more primitive—at times, savage—adventurer. Neither was the historical man. But whether the basis was the real or the mythic Kit Carson, he became the object of veneration for at least two young Westerners growing up at the time (and who very possibly read many of his dime novel adventures): William F. Cody and James Butler Hickok.

In his study of the Western hero in history and myth, Kent Steckmesser examines both the real and the legendary Kit Carson and them summarizes his portrait of the mountain man:

> For Kit Carson, then, less of a gap exists between history and the legend than is the case with other Western characters, particularly the outlaws and gunfighters. He did perform some notable exploits, although he had no great historical significance. He was virtuous, although

somewhat less so than the legend claims. He spoke of his exploits with becoming modesty, and he was respected by most of his contemporaries. Thus he could become a model for his group, and he did. The prominence of the mountain man as a type in the literature and legend of the West is linked with the popular representations of Kit Carson.[44]

But in the larger context of the Western myth, Smith indicates that the mountain man had been both secularized and magnified with his crossing of the plains:

He no longer looks to God through nature, for nature is no longer benign: its symbols are the wolves and the prairie fire. The scene has been shifted from the deep fertile forests east of the Mississippi to the barren plains. The landscape within which the Western hero operates has become...a "dreary waste." It throws the hero back in upon himself and accentuates his terrible and sublime isolation.[45]

From about 1860 to 1890, the Beadle dime novels played the leading role in forming as well as changing the image of Cooper's original Leatherstocking character. But with the move westward, Leatherstocking takes to his horse and, instead of pursuing Indians to rescue the heroine, he transfers his enmity to road agents and other outlaws. He is still associated with the Indian and Indian mores.

However, according to Smith, it is the younger hunter produced by doubling the Leatherstocking character who became father to heroes like Deadwood Dick and Buffalo Bill—the two-gun literary heroes of the 1890s. And in a delightful comment, Smith notes the introduction of yet another idea in the metamorphosis of the venerable eastern woodsman into the young western cowboy:

The touch of this delicate member [the hand of the gentle heroine] on the horny palm of the hunter is a moment charged with meaning in the development of the Western hero. It shows [the author] confronting the possibility that an upperclass heroine might love a man of the Wild West, as Cooper could never quite bring himself to do.[46]

This moment marks the beginning of a whole new set of interesting plot possibilities for the Beadle dime novel empire.

Near 1880 the young Leatherstocking character was allowed to win the heroine. In one Beadle tale, as a matter of fact, it was the heroine who needed two years in a ladies' seminary in St. Louis before she had acquired the necessary polish to be worthy of the hero (she had been reared by Indians and was deemed in need of many refinements). At this same time in Beadle history, Deadwood Dick made his appearance.

Dick's creator was Edward L. Wheeler, a man who did not let himself be hindered in his mythmaking by the fact that he "had never been west of West Philadelphia."[47] The character of Dick represented a considerable step in the metamorphosis of the Leatherstocking persona—now at last, a hero had appeared who was much closer to what we recognize as the Wild West cowboy:

> By 1877, when Wheeler began his Deadwood Dick series, the Wild Western hero had been transformed from a Leatherstocking with an infallible sense of right and wrong and feelings which "appeared to possess the freshness and nature of the forest" into a man who had once been a bandit, and who even after his reformation could not easily be distinguished from the criminals opposing him. Cut loose first from the code of gentility that had commanded Cooper's unswerving loyalty, and then from the communion with God through nature that had made Leatherstocking a saint of the forest, the Western hero had become a self-reliant two-gun man who behaved in almost exactly the same fashion whether he were outlaw or peace officer.[48]

But in order to avoid alienating his hero from the popular audience, Wheeler incorporated into the Deadwood Dick stories—frequently with illogical and eclectic abandon—the usual elements of suspense, action, and romantic love— the latter in the formidable person of Calamity Jane.[49]

In addition, the more savage aspects of the hero's personality were balanced by his skill, grace, cleverness, and self-sufficiency. This roster of Horatio Alger virtues reflected the tone of most dime novelists of the day; the lad of humble beginnings and little education was appealing material for the myth of the self-made man. Heroes like Dick "confirmed Americans in the traditional belief that obstacles were to be overcome by the courageous, virile, and determined stand of the individual as an individual."[50] Such a heterogeneous—almost schizophrenic—character reflected the sensationalism that Smith notes as increasing in the dime novels of the later 1870s. Wheeler, together with other popular mythmakers like him, was not about to risk his audience, his pay, and his ego by not being all things to all fans at all times.

The less civilized aspects of the hero—his wildness bordering on savagery and his often marginal position as a reformed outlaw—were particularly thrilling to the popular audience. The possibility of being both good and bad at the same time was a fascinating prospect even in pre-Freudian times; it met the eternal need for a vicarious taste of forbidden fruit. Aside from audience response, however, the hero at this time continued to grow even more complex and morally ambiguous as he moved deeper into the Western wilderness. From these origins, this "man with a past" has endured as a basic hero type into the films and television of today. The character of Deadwood Dick is a transitional figure reflecting the move toward savagery and preparing for the hero as the man with a gun.

Before the gunman is examined, however, there are two other historically based character types that deserve attention. One is the soldier, who frequently appears in the company of the mountain man. The other is the cowboy, who has come to epitomize the hero of the Western.

The Soldier. The introduction of the cavalryman as a type of hero brings the Indian into focus as well. Historically, the soldier was an employee of the federal government. Symbolically, he was the sole defense of each tiny outpost of civilization against the "hostiles" who fought in vain against the steady march of that civilization until it reached the western ocean.

Just as locale in the Western is frequently limited to a particular time and place, the Indians depicted are usually the Plains Indians: the Cheyenne, the Sioux, the Kiowa, the Apache, the Comanche and others. To the Indian, the land was not a geographical, economic, or political empire but a holy thing—mystical in meaning and integral to the sense of racial survival. And in spite of what other motivations initiated and perpetuated the warfare from the early colonial massacres to the final submission of Geronimo, the Indian fought with a ferocity of purpose driven by a desperate need to preserve sacred things. These nations, pushed farther and farther West by the white man's extermination of their chief means of subsistence—the buffalo—were consistently portrayed as losers in the battles waged by the cavalry against the "redskin." The soldier whose name is commonly associated with Indian warfare is that of General George Armstrong Custer.

Custer's own contribution to the beginnings of his legend were in the form of a series of articles for *Galaxy,* later published as *My Life on the Plains; or, Personal Experiences with Indians.* The title is descriptive of his efforts in the book; Custer gives detailed attention to his attitudes towards and dealings with the Indian, whom he terms "a *savage* in every sense of the word; not worse, perhaps, than his white brother would be if similarly born and bred, but one whose cruel and ferocious nature far exceeds that of any wild beast of the desert."[51] Such testimony from an eyewitness not only whets the interest of the audience but fires the imagination of the dime novelist story-teller as well. According to one of his biographers, Custer had learned the proper prose style, but

> He was better with the sword than with the pen. His literary style adhered to the Victorian convention whereby adjectives and nouns were wedded for life. For Custer, "rifle" never appeared in public without its consort, "trusty." "Comrades" forever was linked to "gallant." "Steed" and "noble" were eternally joined. His writing had vigor but scant skill. He hewed to his task, letting infinitives split where they might.[52]

These last two sentences approximate a description of the dime novelist at work. In fact, with the exception of Buffalo Bill no military man has received more attention from the mythmakers as an Indian fighter than General George Armstrong Custer.[53] At the present time, perhaps no frontier man has undergone such extreme scrutiny by revisionists in the areas of history, sociology, and the arts as has that same General Custer.[54] Under that chilling gaze, the Custer image has become one of the more fragile of the American

Western legends; the hopeless panache of the final battle has become more admirable than the fatal glory-seeking of its foolish hero. Foolishness, however, would be considered praise in comparison with an assessment of Custer by one of his fellow officers. During a Yellowstone expedition in the summer of 1873, Custer's commanding officer wrote to his wife:

> I have had no trouble with Custer and will try to avoid having any, but I have seen enough of him to convince me that he is a coldblooded, untruthful and unprincipled man. He is universally despised by all the officers of his regiment, excepting his relatives and one or two sycophants.[55]

This, of course, is a quite different picture from the Custer of the dime novels or of his own and his wife's memoirs. Among his records of "personal experiences with Indians" Custer devotes considerable space to his version of the Washita massacre in 1868—one of his most glorious moments as a soldier. It was left to others to chronicle and apotheosize the other more famous massacre which ended in his death. *My Life on the Plains* was entered at the Library of Congress in 1874 with a publishing date of 1876—the year in which the American centennial exposition celebration was momentarily stunned by the news of the incredible defeat at the Little Bighorn.

But Custer finally achieved by his death the degree of glory that, in life, he felt eluded him. The death was considered glorious because it occurred in battle against the enemies of the nation. Under such favorable circumstances many men who were ambiguous in life have been apotheosized as heroes in death. Other men of the West became legends in their lifetimes or after; it is quite possible that George Armstrong Custer became a legend chiefly *because* he died. Indeed, the mystery of legend surrounds the death itself; although his corpse was found among the slain, no soldier survived to tell who had killed the man the Sioux called "Long Hair." This too, becomes material for myth; the legend of the giant-killer is often as compelling as that of the giant himself.[56]

His glory tenuous, his image tarnished by his own foolishness, Custer is for today's skeptical audience an instance of a frontier soldier rather than the essence of the soldier-hero. In fact, the Custer character in the Western frequently represents the flawed officer whose megalomania the hero—as underling or civilian scout—must challenge in order to save the situation from total disaster. There have been several attempts to portray the Custer type in mass media; in an age of hero debunkers such ventures have usually met with small success. Rather, the far more sympathetic and successful portrait of the soldier-hero has been achieved by John Ford's cavalryman in *Fort Apache* (1948), *She Wore a Yellow Ribbon* (1949), and *Rio Grande* (1950). The hero of Ford's cavalry trilogy—portrayed in each instance by John Wayne—is based more on a collective and fictional type than on an historical person. This collective persona is shared by the frontier soldier with another Western hero— the cowboy.

The Cowboy. Frantz and Choate in their study of the myth and reality of the American cowboy refer to this frontier man as both pathfinder and empire builder.[57] This role he shares with Boone, Crockett, Carson, and Custer but, unlike these men, the cowboy as a person has no historical name. Specific individuals like Charlie Siringo, Gene Rhodes, and Andy Adams are considered cowboys, but none of them has come to be representative of the type in either fact or fiction. The cowboy seems to be as anonymous and numerous on the Western scene as the faceless cattle from which he earned both his living and his name.

Around 1887 there is notice in the dime novels of "cowboys" operating in Leatherstocking's traditional rescue style and wearing his buckskin leggings—with the addition of sombrero and other Mexican trappings of dress and equipment. Buck Taylor, "King of the Cowboys," was the first of this specific type. Prentiss Ingraham created him in a Beadle novel that was advertised as "A Story of the Wild and Thrilling Life of William L. Taylor," who was at that time a star appearing with Cody's Wild West Show.[58] Ingraham's success signaled the birth of the fictional cowboy hero. This fictional creation is, in fact, the only cowboy we know today. And since the cowboy is pure myth, Fishwick notes in his study that "fiction writers are more important sources than historians and participants who recorded the mere facts of cowboy life."[59] Here again, the legend is the reality.

Outside the dime novel world, however the term "cowboy" was generally used pejoratively in the 1880s, applying to those hired men on horseback whose small-time border wars earned for them a reputation that would have horrified their hero ancestors from Leatherstocking on. Although their origin was Texas, these men became famous—and infamous—in the plains cowtowns as trailers on the great cattle drives during the last decades of the nineteenth century. Deadwood Dick's reputation for doubtful morality was perpetuated in these men of the Wild West, who led lives of hard work and—reputedly—hard play.

The good citizens of the cowtowns reacted to the coming of the cowboy with a mixture of moral indignation and canny pragmatism. While condemning the intruders for disturbing their peace, they were also well aware that the cowpokes were buttering their bread: the trail drivers replenished the town slush funds through paying petty fines for gambling, wearing guns, or disorderly conduct; more important, they kept the town alive by their role in the increasingly prosperous cattle business.

In order to live with their ambiguities and salve their still Victorian consciences, the inhabitants of the cowtowns began to distinguish between the good guys and the bad guys. This attitude was reflected in one of the first mythmaking media of the frontier—the town newspaper. The *Texas Livestock Journal,* on July 5, 1884, moralized thus:

There are cow punchers and cow punchers, and as gentlemen we are ready to compare the "men" and "boys" of the Panhandle with any set of men in any business anywhere. We are led to this remark because we have lately had opportunities for comparing our boys with those from other ranges....

The old, sure enough cowboy, worthy the name of gentleman, is the sort we are used to here, and the invasion of weaklings with assumed coarseness shows the contrast vividly. Cheap boys cannot fool this community.

On March 20, 1886, the *Laramie Weekly Sentinel* scolded:

There is a style of cowboy very rare, let it be said to the credit of the guild, who think it smart to "shoot up" a town, though of late several of these Smart Alecks have had their cowardly carcasses punctured with cold lead, and this amusement is not so popular with them as of yore.... Some time they will make one of these plays [terrorizing train passengers] in the presence of a sure-enough cowboy, one of the sort that attends to his own business, takes off his hat to ladies even in a smoking car, and if he wants a row, hunts up some one in the same humor, and then these bad men from away up high on Bitter Creek will receive a deposit of more lead where it will do the most good, and a jury of decent citizens will say, "Amen."

According to dispatches, an 1883 train robbery was the work of seven "cowboys" and the *Trinidad Daily Advertiser* on November 30 wrote in a defensive mood:

Now these robbers were masked, and, so far as we have been able to learn, it is not known who they were. The term "cowboy" is getting too common. It is used on occasions when it is not at all applicable. We do not believe "seven cowboys" wrecked the train. It may have been done by men who claimed to be cowboys, but there must be some evidence of the fact before we take any stock in it.

Finally, the *Cheyenne Daily Leader* on October 3, 1882, finished by damning what it set out to praise:

As you mingle with these cowboys, you find in them a strange mixture of good nature and recklessness. You are as safe with them on the plains as with any class of men, so long as you do not impose upon them. They will even deny themselves for your comfort, and imperil their lives for your safety....

Morally, as a class, they are foulmouthed, blasphemous, drunken, lecherous, utterly corrupt. Usually harmless on the plains when sober, they are dreaded in towns, for then liquor has the ascendency over them.... This dark picture of the cowboys ought to be lightened by the statement that there is occasionally a white sheep among the black. True and devoted Christians are found in such company—men who will kneel down regularly and offer their prayers in the midst of their bawdy and cursing associates. They are like Lot in Sodom.[60]

This bit of vacillating on the part of the *Leader* summarizes the ambivalence of the townfolk toward the cowboy: he was lovable and fearful, virtuous and wicked, gentle and wild. He was an inescapable element in the life of the town—an integral part of its economic and cultural milieu. Therefore, the paradoxes and ambiguities of his character had to be endured as best they could. Such a situation was ripe for the creation of myth in order to explain the origin, development, and life style of this man on horseback who rode into the life of the town, stayed long enough to make an impression, and then disappeared again. It is not surprising, therefore, that the cowboy legend is about a nameless man, is much more glamorous than the historical facts, and has become far more real to Americans than any of those facts could be. This growing myth was duly noted by an Englishman in the American cattle business as early as 1887:

> The cowboy has at the present time become a personage; nay, more, he is rapidly becoming a mythical one. Distance is doing for him what lapse of time did for the heroes of antiquity. His admirers are investing him with all manner of romantic qualities; they descant upon his manifold virtues and his pardonable weaknesses as if he were a demigod, and I have no doubt that before long there will be ample material for any philosophic inquirer who may wish to enlighten the world as to the cause and meaning of the cowboy myth.[61]

Although their contribution to philosophic enlightenment is questionable, the dime novelists did their share to embellish the developing myth. And, as Baumann notes, the myth developed in an incredibly short time. Americans seemed able to create their legends as rapidly as they settled their frontiers.

In analyzing the cowboy legend, then, it is necessary to deal "not so much with specific individuals as with a recognizable type; not with a mere historical reality, but with a fictional ideal."[62] And by the turn of the century the ideal had become more believable than the reality. Moreover, the truest believers were often the cowboys themselves. Carey McWilliams, remembering his youth on his father's Colorado ranch, tells of the hired hands—the cowboys—spending hours in the bunkhouse reading Beadle pulps and attempting to imitate the cowboy heroes depicted therein.[63] Still other authors make frequent reference to the tall tales told at cowboy reunions, where fellowship and the passing of years rendered humdrum fact into fascinating fiction. And nobody, says Western writer Larry McMurtry, watches television Westerns more avidly than cowboys.[64] Thus an anonymous, representative man became the epitome of the Western hero—even to the real but anonymous Western men themselves.

In his popular persona, the cowboy frequently appeared in purest form: a strong, taciturn loner who roamed the West with no apparent purpose, with no visible means of support, and with no desire to engage in adventure or take up any particular cause. Yet adventure seemed to dog him—relentlessly thrusting him into dangerous situations caused by the town, the bad man, or a woman. In the popular literature of the day, the hapless hero most often had to contend with all three dangers in the same tale. Riding across countless movie screens in theatres throughout the land, this traditional cowboy image has been portrayed by actors ranging from William S. Hart in the 1920s to Randolph Scott in the 1950s.

The cowboy as aloof itinerant, however, was balanced by another character type of the Western man. This was the person the cowboy frequently became before the story was ended—the outlaw, the gunfighter, or the lawman.[65]

The Man with a Gun. Two historical circumstances paved the way for the rise of the man with a gun. The first situation was an outcome of the Civil War; the second was a result of eastern lawmaking. Both were symptomatic of the painful growth process taking place in the nation.

During the Civil War, men and boys were being trained in the use of weapons at the same time that the weapons themselves were developing in sophistication. After Appomattox, the men from the disbanded armies attempted to pick up the pieces of their homes and lives but discovered that it was a next to impossible task. Many had fought in the regular armies during the war years; others had had experience as young members of the guerrilla bands participating in the Missouri-Kansas border skirmishes prior to the war.[66] Those who had become accustomed to a violent way of life were unable to readapt to peace and a settled existence. Moreover, they had now become masters of a new talent—often called an art—that could not find a market in a peaceful and law-abiding milieu. That talent was handling a gun. Such men— frequently Southerners—drifted westward like their fathers who had emigrated a generation before, hoping for a fresh start. Jobless, the war veteran soon discovered that there was a market for his unique skill in a territory whose social controls could not keep pace with its exploding population.

The West was lawless, says Walter Prescott Webb, for two reasons:

> first, because of the social conditions that obtained there during the period under consideration; secondly, because the law that was applied there was not made for the conditions that existed and was unsuitable for those conditions. It did not fit the needs of the country, and could not be obeyed.[67]

Furthermore, there was the nature of the land itself. Legislation drafted by Easterners was adapted or simply copied from English law—serviceable for the still-English coastal society. Farther west, the accumulation of centuries of European jurisprudence proved worthless before a simple but formidable barrier—geography. The methods for disposition of land and the settlement of water rights as promulgated by English law seemed ludicrous in a country of rock upheavals two miles high and deserts where less than twenty inches of rain fell each year. Moreover, the formality of law was simply not worth bothering with when the nearest judge, prosecuting attorney, or jury were six days away from the scene of the crime and on-the-spot justice was left to a paper-appointed marshal and a few deputies who themselves frequently operated on both sides of the law. Thus, not only did the frontier peoples need protection from hostile Indians and wild animals; they just as urgently were compelled to defend themselves against each other.

If the Eastern lawmakers did not understand the situation, the Westerners did and they acted accordingly. Law—at least the Eastern variety—was frequently ignored in the cowtowns, the mining camps, and even in the burgeoning cities like San Francisco. In its place the Westerners created their own kind of law, often based on a show of strength by a man with a gun. This man might appear on the scene and sell his services as a federally appointed lawman, as a privately hired gunfighter, or—as an outlaw—he might go into business for himself. It was not unusual for a man at one time or another during his life to appear in all three roles. The man with a gun was, indeed, an extension of the half-civilized, half-savage mountain man of historical fact and the wild and woolly man-with-a-past of dime novel fiction.

Terminology differs in describing these Westerners. Aficionados of gun lore do not always agree on the distinctions among the men who were called "gunfighters," "gunmen," "pistolmen," "pistoleers," or "shootists." Eugene Cunningham, in his study of the art, indicates that in the heyday of "gun power" the term "gunman" took on a generic meaning:

> When you said of a man that he was a gunman, you meant not only a pistolman—a man bearing one or more pistols. You meant to designate (and were understood to designate) a man specially skilled in the use of a pistol—and much more than normally ready to demonstrate that ability in blazing, homicidal gunplay. The word gunman had flexed to neatly take into account, not only the weapon, but the character, of the man you were discussing.[68]

And although this was not always the case, Cunningham adds, when frontier journalists used the term it was usually synonomous with "killer."

The gunman as killer was frequently called a "badman" or "outlaw" as well. And given the character of Western culture and the independence of Western society, it is not at all surprising that this type of man became a Western hero as well. One such hero was a young man whose name was probably William Bonney but who became a legend as Billy the Kid.

The Kid is a classic example of the making of a mythic hero out of the raw material of an outlaw. Not only does Bonney fit smoothly into the mold outlined by Raglan, Frye, and Campbell in their studies of the hero,[69] the development of the Kid's legend follows step by step the process of popular mythmaking as well.

There are several requirements that must be met, says folklorist Mody Boatright, before a badman can become an American hero. First, he must belong to the Anglo-American majority and come from a respectable but poor family. Second, he must have had an unfortunate childhood, through poverty, injustice, or the like. Third, he must have committed his first crime under extreme provocation. Fourth, in his badman career he fights the enemies of the people: Yankees, corporations, railroads, the rich. (Pinkerton men cannot be heroes, nor can feudists, since the hero must be above clannish fights and must serve the public as its benefactor rather than as a representative of establishment interests.) Fifth, during his career as outlaw, he performs acts of kindness and generosity, often at the same time that he is robbing or escaping. Sixth, he must atone for his crimes, but he cannot do this by becoming an informer. He can atone by death, however, but it must be martyrdom, and often he lives on since in reality someone else has been buried in his stead.[70]

The life and death of William Bonney meet Boatright's requirements. The Kid's origins are obscure; even his real name is uncertain.[71] His falling into evil ways was attributed by the legend-makers to an injustice done to his mother when he was but a boy. The Kid's outlaw existence was condoned—as was the checkered career of the good-bad cowboy—by transforming him into a Western Robin Hood. He became a defender of the poor and downtrodden and a fighter against the corruption of land barons, railroad empire-builders, and other ruthless men backed by Eastern money. His invincible gun, his magical escapes, and his mysterious death all contribute to his stature as an outlaw hero of the first order. So fascinating the character, so colorful the legend, that in 1952 an informal bibliography compiled on Billy the Kid consisted of 437 items and described not only newspaper accounts and books, but also phonograph recordings, a radio broadcast, comic books, films, and a ballet.[72] Billy the Kid, whoever he was, has left a body of legend that has obliterated whatever the facts of his life may have been. And while the factual threads are hopelessly frayed and twisted, the legend woven from them is colorful and varied indeed. As Lyons notes in *The Wild, Wild West*, it is true that Billy the Kid did not die. He will continue to appear in popular entertainment media "whenever appropriate, a figure freshly refurbished so as to embody the hero who appropriately symbolizes the need of the hour: brutal killer, avenging angel, mama's boy, slayer of capitalist dragons, bewildered cat's paw, or gay, gallant carefree cowpoke."[73] The reality may be obscure, but the myth provides a far clearer picture of what his audience in his own time and in ours wishes to believe.

There were others of William Bonney's kind, but no single outlaw has equalled his reputation. In many cases, gunmen banded together and earned their livelihood by robbing banks, trains, and stagecoaches. Such daring gangs have been depicted in films from Porter's *The Great Train Robbery* (1903) to Kaufman's *The Great Northfield Minnesota Raid* (1972); their crimes have provided the motivation for heroic retaliation in countless television shows from Hopalong Cassidy films to the most current Western series.

Gangs like Butch Cassidy's Wild Bunch and the James and Younger brothers turned plain folk into an adoring audience who followed with breathless interest the newspaper accounts of robberies, followed by posse hunts, followed by hairbreadth escapes, followed by more robberies. Interspersed among the facts were tidbits of fancy that seemed to be taken for granted in the journalism of the day—imaginative details that the reporter could not possibly have known second-hand or even detected as an eyewitness. But these embellishments added to the story's interest, sold newspapers, and helped to create a following for the outlaws who came to be heroes of the same Robin Hood stamp as Billy the Kid. Although law enforcement exacted retribution of a much more stringent kind when the Wild Bunch and the James-Younger gang were riding, the sympathetic sentiment for these outlaws was similar to that described in DeVoto's tongue-in-cheek account of outlawry in the early days of the Nevada territory:

> To steal from the Wells-Fargo Company was held venial or even praiseworthy. The social consciousness of Washoe observed that Wells-Fargo levied a tribute on the people which differed only technically from robbery, and felt that stage hold-ups were a redistribution of spoils actually in the public interest. Wherefore a caste of specialists in the art sprang up in the Territory and flourished without more than a perfunctory opposition and quite without social penalty.[74]

Just as the Robin Hood syndrome worked for the literary audience of the Victorian era, it works for the mass media audience of today. Films like *The Left-Handed Gun* (1958), *The Wild Bunch* (1969), and *Butch Cassidy and the Sundance Kid* (1969) rework from a psychological viewpoint the same sympathy that existed for the good-bad outlaw one hundred years ago. Boatright attempts to account for the myth taking this particular form and to what extent it is national or universal:

> At any rate it is a pattern imposed by the popular mind—that is, the mind of the American middle class—upon a prototypical historical character in order to make his career emotionally intelligible in terms of American culture. This mind sees no problem in a character almost wholly evil; it accepts the villain. It sees no problem, either, in a character in the main good. But a character who commits offenses against life and property, two things sacred in our culture, and who yet manifests traits of goodness, seems to require explanation. This simplified explanation is the myth of the western bad man.[75]

Boatright's conclusion is consistent with the function of myth: an attempt on the part of the human mind to explain in symbolic form what is inexplicable through logic or intellectual reasoning. The myth of the badman resolves the paradox and the conflict while at the same time permitting the audience to enjoy the story.

But not all outlaws were heroes. Many were simply considered bad and dangerous men, scavengers who deserved no more than to be shot down like the animals they were. This type of outlaw, who killed with little or no provocation, was the most feared by the frontier population, since he could be challenged only by one equal to him in daring and skill. Of the genus "gunman," the species "gunfighter" was most capable of meeting that challenge.

Perhaps the most famous of the old gunfighters was John Wesley Hardin, a Texan who had killed a deputy sheriff on his (Hardin's) twenty-first birthday and was captured by Rangers three years later in a spectacular gun battle in Florida.[76] Hardin served a prison term, married, became a drifter, drinker, and brawler in later years, and was finally murdered. But like Custer, Hardin is an example of—rather than the model of—the gunfighter hero. This historical type of frontier man as described by Joseph Rosa

> was not a difficult man to spot. Treading the thin line between life and death made him a more than cautious individual. He avoided dark alleyways and the direct glare of street lamps. Indoors he kept a wall at his back. He was a drifter; where he came from few people cared, and where he was going only the devil knew. He was the product of a violent era that encompassed the struggle for Texas, the California gold rush, and the Kansas-Missouri border wars. It might be said that he was conceived when Samuel Colt patented his first revolver in England in 1835.[77]

In this description the ambiguity of the historical character is a reflection of his ancestral roots in the half-savage, half-civilized mountain man. As adapted to fiction, the character type can be—and consistently has been—both hero and villain, savior and menace, god and devil.

The portrayal of the gunfighter in popular and elite literature as well as mass media forms gives evidence of at least two strong characteristics: first, he is a dramatic means of splitting the persona of the hero into Jekyll-Hyde dimensions (as Cooper split Leatherstocking to make him acceptable to a genteel audience); and second, he is perhaps the most allegorical and directly mythological figure of the Western hero types.

The Jekyll-Hyde gunfighters provide possibilities for richer characterization by using two heroes instead of one; moreover, the device permits the audience's vicarious participation in the less than noble activities of the evil half. In mass media, one of the classic characterizations of the evil persona is Jack Palance's malevolent gunman in *Shane* (1953); another, more animalistic portrayal of the same type was that of Aldo Ray in *Welcome to Hard Times* (1967). The godlike gunfighter has been depicted by Yul Brynner in *Invitation to a Gunfighter* (1964); the pared-down, directly mythological version of the savior-figure was Alan Ladd in *Shane,* even to the golden coloring of the hero in sharp contrast to Palance's skeletal figure garbed in unrelieved black. More realistic and psychological aspects of the gunfighter have been portrayed by Gregory Peck in *The Gunfighter* (1950), which attempted in fiction to probe the complexities of a type of man historically analyzed as one

> bolstering a weak ego with a display of physical strength. His desperate desire to be top dog was manifest in the gunfight. Living on the edge of self-destruction for so long, he wore on his face a fixed expression of pain and misery. Because of his way of life the gunfighter was the most pitied, and sometimes the most despised, Old West character. This man, who held the power of life and death in his hands and used guns to solve his problems, was a mixture of fears. Condemned by his reputation to continue a life of danger, the gunfighter was in reality a

composite of many characteristics, the overriding one being that he was a killer. Environment made him; circumstance guided him.[78]

In television Westerns, the gunfighter character is usually an evil persona created as a foil for the hero rather than being a hero himself. This reluctance on the part of television creators to develop a gunfighter hero indicates another area of concession to audience expectations.[79]

The second characteristic of the gunfighter myth in story form—the allegorical dimension—is succinctly illustrated by a theologian who tells of a discussion with a friend speculating about the appeal of the Western on a deeper level than that of mere escape:

> "If just once," said he, "I could stand in the dust of the frontier main street, facing an indubitably bad man who really deserved extermination, and with smoking six-gun actually exterminate him—shoot once and see him drop. Just once to face real and unqualified evil; plug it and see it drop...."
>
> None of this complex business of separating the sin from the sinner, of tempering justice with mercy, of remembering our own complicity in evil. To blow, just once, an actual and visible hole in the wall of evil, instead of beating the air with vain exhortation and the nicely calculated less and more of moral discrimination and doleful casuistry.[80]

Here is a deep-rooted desire to reduce the situation to black-and-white choices and then act with a simplicity and sureness that today's world can no longer afford or possess. The gunfighter myth is the battle between good and evil in its most elemental form; the walkdown is the ritual integral to that spiritual confrontation.

Bernard DeVoto attributes the origin of the walkdown to Wister, who climaxed his 1902 novel *The Virginian* with that classic Western form of duel to the death between the hero and Trampas, the villain.[81] Lyons, however, indicates that a walkdown between James B. Hickok and Dave Tutt was recorded in *Harper's Magazine* in 1867.[82] These actual gunfights, however, rarely occurred at high noon, nor did they follow a particular pattern of action. It seemed that women, gambling, or revenge were frequent causes of a shootout, but not necessarily in that order.[83]

But whatever the historical facts are, the fictional ritual of the walkdown is closely associated with the heroic image of the gunman—be he outlaw, gunfighter, or lawman. The deserted street, the uneasy silence, the two figures approaching the confrontation, the almost simultaneous draw and shot, the fall—all these elements in visual or verbal accounts are as carefully choreographed and rigidly constructed as any solemn ritual. And until the Western began to depart from its traditional format, the outcome, too, was always the same: the "good" man won.

It has been noted earlier that the historical relationship between the man with a gun and the law of the West has always been ambiguous; so, too, the lines between outlaw, gunfighter, and lawman were fine ones and often crossed. Historically, it was difficult to tell the good guys from the bad guys; consistent with the casual attitude toward law in the West, those who transgressed and enforced it were frequently the same.

As the guardian of order, the figure of the town marshal has become the subject of his own particular myths. The "lone man" image, however, is merely that—an image. Historically, the marshal's duties were varied. Backed by a force of deputies who actually did the tracking down of criminals, the marshal is frequently given much of the credit in Western stories. This team effort in law enforcement by no means indicates that the marshal was ineffectual or a mere figurehead. A brief look at career highlights of Bat Masterson, Wyatt Earp, and Wild Bill Hickok offers convincing proof that these were men to be reckoned with—gunmen and lawmen at the same time.

William Barclay Masterson, as he preferred to be called, was at one time a Kansas sheriff, at other times a gunfighter, faro banker, and burlesque troupe manager, and finally ended up as an Eastern sportswriter and teller of tales about his gunslinging cronies of earlier days.[84] His natty dress, bowler hat, and walking stick—incongruous attire for a man with his reputation—marked him also as a lady's man, which he was. But his fastidiousness extended to the more crucial tools of his trade, as witnessed in a letter he wrote from Dodge City on paper imprinted "Opera House Saloon" and dated July 24, 1885. It was addressed to the Colt Company in Hartford, Connecticut:

> Gents
>   Please send Me one of your nickle plated short 45. calibre revolvers. It is for my own use and for that reason I would like to have a little Extra pains taken with it. I am willing to pay Extra for Extra work. Make it very Easy on the trigger and have the front Sight a little higher and thicker than the ordinary pistol of this Kind....
>
> > Truly Yours
> > WB Masterson[85]

Although the mythmakers assessed Masterson's skill with a Colt to be much greater than it probably was, he was a colorful character and thus good material for legend. And while legend-makers took up his cause, not the least of these spinners of tales was Masterson himself. In 1907 he wrote a series of articles on the West for the magazine *Human Life,* and probably embellished his own myth as much as that of the many outlaws, gunmen, and peace officers he wrote about during that time.[86]

Wyatt Earp, who once worked with Masterson, has been mythologized, demythologized, and remythologized in the span of years since he—together with his brothers Virgil and Morgan and their friend Doc Holliday—made history at the OK Corral. That event of October 26, 1881, has been the subject of historical probing and popular mythmaking dating from Stuart Lake's biography of 1931 to John Ford's mythic film treatment of *My Darling Clementine* in 1946 and John Sturges' *Gunfight at the OK Corral* in 1957 to *Hour of the Gun* in 1967. The character of Earp has been portrayed in numerous films, has sustained a television series, *The Life and Legend of Wyatt Earp,* and has appeared in vignette form in other film and television Westerns. The facts may never be completely known about the fight; Rosa claims that political ambitions, personal feuds, and a possible involvement in stage coach robbery actually precipitated the events at Tombstone in which three men died and two were seriously wounded.[87]

The facts, however, are no more important today than they were during the hearing held in Tombstone following the shootout. Even at that time, Earp's image was that of a dangerous man. Today it is that of a courageous peace officer doing his duty, even though the most cursory glance at the records of the event would force the reader to consider a less respectable portrait of the marshal of Tombstone.[88] Nonetheless, the legend has almost totally obscured the facts and historians are still sorting through the conflicting testimony of both eyewitnesses and principals concerning the events of that day in 1881. Meanwhile, the city of Tombstone annually recreates the shootout for tourists—the event has become a traditional ritual celebration of what is now known as the classic gun battle of the mythic West.

While the mythmakers cultivated a "law and order" image for Earp, they unabashedly created a wild and woolly image for James Butler Hickok—"Wild Bill." Brought to Abilene in 1871, Hickok was hired as marshal to help control gambling dens and brothels, and during his tenure of eight months he enforced the law principally through his established reputation as a gunfighter. Although Hickok's skill commanded a cowed respect from the citizens of Abilene, he was also highly criticized for his individualistic style of law enforcement. During the months of the 1871 cattle season Abilene had the usual problems from the Texas cowboys pouring into town. One day in October when Hickok rushed out of the Alamo saloon at the sound of a shot, he confronted Phil Coe, described by a contemporary as "a red-mouthed, bawling thug." As Frantz and Choate describe what followed, Coe,

> pistol in hand in violation of the local ordinance, replied that he had shot at a dog, though no dog was in sight. Without hesitation, from eight feet away Wild Bill promptly shot Coe fatally, growling slightly because his usually impeccable aim was a bit low in the abdomen....
>
> A deputy, Mike Williams, hearing the shots, rushed to the scene. Hickok, not recognizing him, shot again, and Williams was dead. Five minutes later there wasn't a Texas cowboy in town. The Texans, as well as the town citizens, except for maybe a few of Wild Bill's mistresses scattered about the environs, felt the marshal was a mad dog, but as it was near the end of the season, it seemed the easier way to permit Hickok to serve out his contract. He was not rehired, as it was generally argued that his marksmanship was far superior to his character.[89]

Frantz and Choate record the incident in a style that approaches mythmaking, but the basic facts are corroborated by other accounts. In addition, Wild Bill's skill and craftsmanship are more specifically detailed by Charles Gross, who claimed that Hickok once told him:

> "Charlie, I hope you never have to shoot any man, but if you do shoot him in the guts near the navel; you may not make a fatal shot, but he will get a shock that will paralyze his brain and arm so much that the fight is all over."[90]

The truth of Gross' claim—or Hickok's, for that matter—is not at issue, but the calm, analytic pragmatism of the advice should not pass unnoticed.

The usual discrepancy in numbers is evident in the records of how many men Hickok killed, but the facts of his own death are clear. In August, 1876, while in Deadwood on a prospecting trip, Wild Bill made a mistake that no gunfighter had a right to make: he neglected to sit with his back to the wall. Gunned down from behind by Jack McCall, Hickok died holding—according to legend—the "dead man's hand" of aces and eights.

The Hickok mythology has developed in many forms; "Wild Bill" himself aided the creation of the legend by his appearance in Cody's Wild West Show in the 1870s. The dime novelists told and retold Hickok's adventures and the similarities between Wild Bill and Deadwood Dick are numerous in the Wheeler stories. William S. Hart, who had learned from his father and other contemporaries of Hickok about the gunfighter's life, made a sentimentalized version of his story in 1923, while DeMille romanticized Hickok in *The Plainsman,* starring Gary Cooper in 1936. A television series with Guy Madison appeared in 1954.

Fictional adaptations of the Masterson-Earp-Hickok persona are common as well. The Western hero as frontier marshal has appeared in countless forms in both film and on television; the most famous being Dodge City's Matt Dillon of *Gunsmoke*—a man possessing the skill of the gunman, the moral rectitude of the Victorian hero, and the approachability of the common man.

Outlaws, gunfighters, lawmen—all historical representatives of these three categories of the man with a gun have been romanticized by the mythmakers on the same basis: that of making good guys out of questionable guys and heroic action out of violent deeds. The purpose in each instance is the same in popular American mythology: to present a hero that is acceptable to the audience toward whom the myth is directed. For the most part, the mythmakers have suffered for their story-telling—enduring scorn from historians, condemnation from moralizers, and castigation from debunkers. Peter Lyons, in the role of both debunker and moralist, is particularly virulent in his summary of such men as Hickok, Jesse James, Wyatt Earp, Masterson, and Billy the Kid:

> As outlaws they were first adored because, it was argued, they robbed only the railroad monopolist and the banker, the men most heartily hated west of the Mississippi. As law

officers they were first adored because, it was argued, they enforced the peace in perilous circumstances, against overwhelming odds. Both propositions are cockeyed. Outlaw or law officer, it made little difference, they were one brutal brotherhood. The so-called law officers more often caused than quelled crime. Hendry Brown, an outlaw in New Mexico, could ride to Kansas and pin on a sheriff's star; Jim Younger, an outlaw in Missouri, could ride to Texas and pin on a deputy sheriff's star; even Billy the Kid rode for a time as a member of a sheriff's posse and had his side won the Lincoln County War, might well have come down to us in folklore as a force for law and order. The whole boodle of them careened through lives of unredeemed violence and vulgarity, to fetch up—where else—in the Valhalla of the comics, the movies, and television.[91]

Television, it seems, has brought the evolution of the hero full circle in the journey from history to myth. The 1972 fall season opened with only one new Western series, but one portraying an old myth. The leading character of NBC's *Hec Ramsey,* played by Richard Boone, is a hero possessing the ambivalent morality and consummate canniness of the frontier peace officer, the charm of the cowboy image, the bravado of Carson and Crockett, and the venerable stature of Leatherstocking. Boone and his series avoided the fatal shots of the critics and the venture went into a second season, although sandwiched among detective heroes, policeman heroes, and computerized heroes.[92]

At any rate, from the 1830s and Cooper's literary adaptation of Daniel Boone and extending to the present mass media versions of that evolved persona, the Man of the West has become an established figure in the gallery of American heroes. However far removed he might be from historical authenticity is unimportant, for he is no longer a particular Western man but rather *the* Man of the West—the result of myth being applied to history.

The Western Hero: A Composite Portrait

Following the main trunk and excluding many of the lesser branches, the preceding review of the Westerner's family tree has traced the geneaology of this American popular hero as he crosses and recrosses the line between fact and folklore, history and legend. But before the discussion turns to those who have created and sustained the popular image of this figure it is necessary to summarize briefly the chief characteristics of the Western hero as he has been depicted in popular media and described above.

In sketching a composite portrait, two observations should be made: first, the characteristics will reflect the same mixture of fact and legend, truth and exaggeration, human and godlike qualities exhibited by classical heroes; second, the qualities will range along a continuum rather than remain in a fixed locus, since a popular hero is also a public figure and will reflect the constant flux of popular values.

Tradition paints the Western hero as, first and possibly foremost, a loner. He is a man who may at times come in contact with persons and situations that involve him for a time, but he can never become "domesticated" or "civilized" in full sense of the word. Like Huck Finn, he has been there before. He is a man in the middle—poised between savagery and civilization, the desert and the Garden—who in some Western myths can sustain that position and in others must give up one or the other existence in order to survive. The Westerner's independence is a manifestation of his desire to preserve his integrity—his identity as Warshow calls it—in the face of encroaching civilization and the restrictions that accompany it. The Westerner's concern for his identity is also reflective of his roots in the Mediterranean cultural notion of honor as integrity and the medieval European idea of the questing knight's single-mindedness. The Western hero's American identity is further refined, according to some analysts, by the contribution of the peculiarly American emphasis on the traits of prowess (valued by the Yankee) and cleverness (valued by the Southerner).[93] Again, the clearest portrayal of the loner quality is the wandering gunfighter Shane in both Schaefer's novel and Stevens' film.

Closely aligned with the hero's aloneness (and utilizing his prowess and cleverness) is his resulting ability to be in command of both persons and events. There is, in the classical Westerner, a clarity of purpose and decisive manner that render him unerring in judgment and therefore able to act with a sureness and speed that are denied those around him. However, the self-direction and clarity of the Westerner fluctuate with the cultural stance of a given time. Whereas the early and middle film hero viewed life in simple—often simplistic—terms, the later film and television Westerner finds decision making much more complex and, at times, virtually impossible.

But whether the hero is portrayed in the classical or existential mode or any mode in between, he is usually a skillful man both physically and mentally. He handles tools well, whether they are equipment or weapons. He is at home with nature—the desolate terrain of mountains and deserts, the raging fury of treacherous streams, the awesome storms of rain, snow, dust, and wind. His relationship with animals is almost that of a kindred spirit; he understands the untamed and befriends the tamed. The Westerner's horse is both historically and fictionally the most valuable animal in the Western myth. The hero is equally skillful in handling events that come his way—events usually unwanted and unsought. He slips into deadly encounters with an almost fatalist nonchalance—doing "what he must do" and then departing from the scene almost as unobtrusively as he appeared. The classical Westerner's attitude towards persons is a reluctant relationship; he seems uneasy in society—even primitive frontier society—and eager to return to the more congenial elements of nature and solitude. His skill at handling persons, however, is no less evident whether they are villains, officials, pillars of the society, or women of any kind. This aspect of the Westerner, of course, is reflective of the ancient hero's almost magical ability to command nature, animals, and persons to do his will. It is most frequently portrayed in the early Westerns and becomes less evident as existentialist thought erodes one's hope of being able to control either oneself or one's world. Ultimately, many contemporary Western heroes are complete failures in their human relationships.

The element of fatalism in the Western hero points toward an aura of melancholy which, in more complex portrayals of the myth, may border on tragedy. There is something mysterious and sad about this man; there are hints of a tragic past and forebodings of an ominous future. He seems merely to be resting momentarily in the present, poised between what has happened to make him what he is and what will happen because of what he is. This near-tragic quality is evident in the classical Westerner as a melancholy, a nostalgia, or a romanticism. In the later, more existential hero it becomes a pessimistic, sardonic attitude toward life. The tragic aspects of the Westerner reflect again the qualities of the ancient hero who, destined by fate to follow a certain path, must do battle, suffer, sacrifice, and through his wounding or death bring new life to the community.

The Western hero, then, is generally a loner. He is, however, a man in command of things, persons, and events, handling them skillfully but with a certain aloofness that preserves his integrity. He is a man of mysterious and frequently melancholy past; his future is tenuous and foreboding. He is almost always a man with one foot in the wilderness and the other in civilization, moving through life belonging to neither world.

These characteristics of the legendary Westerner are, of course, generalizations that are modified, stressed, or suppressed in accord with the values of the culture in which a particular version of the myth is being promulgated. The hero, even though his image towers over that of common folk, must always conform. He is a product of history, myth, and social conditions and he will consistently reflect all three.

Marshall Fishwick, in his study of the myth and reality of American heroes, states that heroes are not born. Rather, they are products of their own times, created by others who give to the hero a second, mythic life and image. While the hero's province is both history and folklore, Fishwick says, the key to the hero's existence is function.[94] Fishwick's comment is a reflection on the origin of that hero in some form in history; it is also an affirmation that folklore, legend, and myth are basic elements in the hero's creation. Finally, his statement reinforces the functional aspect of the hero as a social force for his time and his audience as well as a legendary embellishment of history. If the hero is truly a product of his time created for his time, then his characteristics will vary along a continuum while his function for his audience will remain basically the same. He represents and reflects certain needs and values of his audience that can often by better expressed and worked out in symbolic or story form than through logical or rhetorical discourse. Human beings have always been makers and users of symbols. The image of the Western hero and the legends of his deeds are simply another way to live out aspects of that symbolic life. The role of the Western hero as humanity's symbolic surrogate is, indeed, a far more complex and vital one than that to which he is usually assigned—an escapist image in popular entertainment.

In order to better understand the Western hero's function it is necessary to understand those who helped to develop it. These are the mythmakers who extracted the Western hero from the relative obscurity of factual history and imbued him with legendary fame.

East Coast Chronicler to West Coast Creator: "Print the Legend"

In John Ford's nostalgic tribute to the vanishing Westerner depicted in *The Man Who Shot Liberty Valance,* there is a sequence in which a man who had been mistakenly acknowledged as a hero for some years finally attempts to set the record straight. After the facts of the true story have been told to assembled reporters, their genuine respect for the "hero" does not permit them to destroy the long-believed myth. One reporter, tearing up his notes, declares, "This is the West, Sir. When the legend becomes fact, print the legend." Indeed, the hero— once make-believe—had long since earned his own spurs.

The printers of legend concerning the Western hero have been many and varied, beginning with the early diarists and chroniclers of exploration to the creators of the most current television series. The forerunners of the film and television creators, however, can be grouped roughly into five categories which, though overlapping at times, indicate slightly different approaches to the Western myth. The transformation from history to legend has been accomplished, in roughly chronological order, by the following groups of creators— some of whom were acutely conscious of their mythmaking, others of whom at least partially believed they were recording history: the Eastern travelers and chroniclers who wrote of the West and its people; the journalists, biographers, and autobiographers who recorded events and the activities of those who made the events happen; the dime novelists who made little or no attempt to keep fable separate from fact; the popular and "serious" novelists who contributed much to both the conventions and inventions of the Western myth; and finally the artists and photographers who provided a visual dimension to the printed legend. Although certain mythmakers have already been noted in connection with their hero subjects, a sampling of creators from each category will provide an understanding of how myths come about and what their function is for the audience.

The Early Chroniclers. History, although it may attempt a high degree of objectivity, is more realistically the relating of facts from a particular perspective. In reading history, the student is made aware of only those events which the writers choose to record, and only that perspective from which they are able to record events—their own. Through selectivity, therefore, historians are themselves somewhat mythmakers, however reluctant they may be to assume that role.

The earliest chronicles of the frontier were, of course, chiefly the work of Spanish, French, and English explorers who penetrated the wilderness of the American continent from Mexico, Canada, and the Eastern seaboard. Balboa, De Soto, Coronado, and other conquistadores have provided narratives of the journeys together with descriptions of the land and peoples they found along their way. Both Spanish and French priests have recorded in the form of missionary reports some of the most valuable information available on the Southwest, the far West, and the Canadian frontiers. French explorers and trappers have joined their contribution to that of missionaries to fill in the gaps of early American history. The Anglo-Saxon contribution, however, is perhaps the most direct in the mythmaking tradition treated here. Some of the richest early material is found in the journals of the Lewis and Clark expedition, Josiah Gregg's chronicles of the Santa Fe Trail, and George Ruxton's account of the Rocky Mountain area.[95]

There were others writing of the West but, unlike the explorers, trappers, and guides, they were Easterners who had never seen the territory and who began early to detail glowing accounts of the strange and wondrous lands that lay beyond the frontier. Some even wrote travelers' guides of routes they had never seen describing landmarks, watering places, and areas affording either safe or hazardous passage.[96]

Besides the early writings of Crèvecoeur and De Tocqueville, there were other Europeans who traveled to America and wrote of their adventures and the Westerners they met. Many of these men were involved in the cattle interests of the Southwest and Great Plains areas, and their business took them to the still untamed towns that sprang up as instant—and often short-lived—centers of commerce during the second half of the nineteenth century. The records set down by these men of their travels, frequently published in British and European journals, contain hints of the mythmaking process at work. Attempting an objective look, the European nonetheless tended to view the American as a curious and colorful creature—a perspective that encouraged a certain amount of embellishment of the facts.[97]

It is only a small step from these primary source records to personal accounts that also were intended to be factual but in reality shifted toward an even more fabulous treatment of their subjects. This second group of writers moving in the direction of legend-makers were the journalists and biographers. They were, however, writing for a far different readership from the educated Easterner or European. Literacy—widespread in America as it had never been in Europe—was quickly creating an audience receptive to a more popular form of narrative and an approach to the image of the Westerner that did not shrink from unabashed hyperbole.

The Journalists and Biographers. Daniel Boorstin, in his study of the American experience, labels the writing of the frontier era a "declamatory literature." It was dramatic, Boorstin continues, and intended for speaker and listener rather than for writer and reader.[98] It had a sound, a swagger, an aural and visible style rather than being intellectual or cerebral. Frontier literature was earthy, sensual, robust. The relationship of this written style to the oral tradition of the tall tales of American folklore is obvious; but since the reading audience and the listening audience were no longer limited to the elite, drama did not desert the narrative when it reached the printed page.

The printed pages most widely read were the newspapers, whose journalists recounted degrees of fact and fiction to please every reader's taste from staid citizen to hungry sensation-seeker. The newspaper accounts cited throughout this study are used, not for the purpose of obtaining factual accounts, but to present the flavor of the mythmaking process at work in a supposedly factual medium. In defense of journalistic digressions, however, newspapers did provide for frontier folk much of the entertainment that was available in addition to facts; citizens felt entitled to a bit of colorful editorializing mixed with the news. Thus, headlines like "Three Men Hurled Into Eternity in the Duration of a Moment" could appear in the Tombstone *Epitaph* following the OK shootout, and Jesse James, confident of an enthusiastic press, could say to the engineer of a train he had just robbed: "When you see the reporters, tell 'em you was talking to Jesse James!" After which statement, the story goes, the gang fired a few shots into the air, swung into their saddles, and raced off with a wild halloo for the benefit of bystanders.[99]

Moreover, an editor performing at the top of his bent in the Santa Fe *Weekly Democrat*, need feel no qualms in satisfying his readers through this account of Billy the Kid's death:

> No sooner had the floor caught his descending form which had a pistol in one hand and a knife in the other, than there was a strong odor of brimstone in the air, and a dark figure with wings of a dragon, claws of a tiger, eyes like balls of fire, and horns like a bison, hovered over the corpse for a moment, and with a fiendish laugh said, "Ha, ha! This is my meat!" and then sailed off through the window. He did not leave his card, but he is a gentleman well known to us by reputation, and thereby hangs a "tail."[100]

This example, illustrating journalistic entertainment in the extreme, also displays the unabashed tall-tale teller at work, confident of the appreciation of his audience—to say nothing of their willing suspension of disbelief.

Eyewitnessing of events and encounters with outlaws provided frontier newspapers with copy that spilled over into serialized articles in magazines and eventually found its way into book form. The authors of such material ranged from itinerant reporters to intrepid missionaries; many of these writers were capable of making the most of an experience.

For example, the *Fortnightly Review* provided Britons with stories of the American Westerner, while *Harper's Magazine, Scribner's, The Police Gazette,* and others were sources of fact mixed with fancy for Eastern gentlemen. John Hammond, writing a series of articles for *Scribner's Magazine* entitled "Strong Men of the Wild West," tells of his experiences as a mining expert during the Coeur d'Alene strike in 1891, the "salting" of the Nevada mines in 1879, and the Yukon strikes and rushes. Interspersed throughout the narrative are dark references to Wyatt Earp, Black Bart, and "Kid" Curry, climaxed in Anglophile Hammond's final plea for the United States to develop in its citizens the respect for law and order that he maintains the British have.[101]

The missionary effort produced, among others, a record by a Sister of Charity describing her journey along the trail to Santa Fe. Sister Blandina Segale's account of her first fearful meeting with a wild Westerner finishes with the Sister extracting from the chastened cowboy a promise to mend his ways and write more frequently to his aging mother.[102]

The cowboys themselves who wrote of their experiences were men born on the frontier like Charlie Siringo and Andy Adams, as well as Easterner-turned-Westerner Gene Rhodes. These accounts, many written in a simple but clear style, probably come closest to depicting the life of a cowboy.

Besides the journalists, missionaries, and cowboys, there were other writers who sought out the gunmen of the Old West in order to record their adventures from their own lips. Most of these were Easterners; unease at the outbreak of peace in 1865 could very well have caused them to migrate West, following the paths of the gunfighters and for much the same reasons.

Such a one was Ash Upson—editor, politician, notary public, surveyor, postmaster, and gossip. Like most journalist-biographers of the Westerner, Upson was an Easterner who moved west. He came to Colorado after the Civil War and moved later to New Mexico, where he encountered Pat Garrett. Upson collaborated with Garrett in writing a life of the Kid, contributing an adulatory introduction to what was supposed to be the lawman's account of his one-time friend William Bonney. However, in a letter to a relative after the book was published in 1882, Upson confided:

The book, "Life of Billy the Kid," will be a success. It has been bungled in the publication. The Santa Fe publishers took five months to do a month's job, and then made a poor one. Pat F. Garrett, Sheriff of the County, who killed the "Kid" and whose name appears as author of the work (though I wrote every word of it as it would make it sell), insisted on taking it to Santa Fe, and was swindled badly in his contract. I live with Garrett, and have, since last August. His contract said they were to settle on the book every sixty days. One week from today the first 60 expires. It is 220 miles to Santa Fe (no R.R.). The publisher does not know how to put the book on the market.[103]

Besides the early confirmation this passage gives to the suspicions of many writers concerning the ineptitude of publishers, Upson's letter further illustrates the confidence of the mythmaker about what his talents can sell. As for Upson's statement on authorship, the truth of the matter remains far more elusive than the legend.

Upson also managed to create a few legends about himself. One day while listening to a court case in Lincoln, he became impatient with the two lawyers arguing about the proper instructions to give the jury on the law in question. Upson claimed that he could expedite the case and when the judge agreed, Upson did so, producing the following statement:

> In making your decision, gentlemen, please bear in mind that the deceased was reaching for his hip pocket when the defendant blazed away at him. The Territorial statutes, you understand, gentlemen, allow one man, when he sees another make this motion, to produce his gun and commence the bombardment. To be sure, it has proved in this case that the deceased was reaching for his handkerchief, but that, gentlemen, does not make any difference; the law does not recognize any such movements. The very fact that he was carrying a handkerchief while in New Mexico, shows that he was an unfit member for our territorial society. Please carefully weigh all these important facts before bringing in your verdict.[106]

This instruction itself is an example of a tall-tale teller at work, but the swagger of the statement is probably closer to the spirit of Lincoln County in the 1880s than a more staid observation—if indeed, there were any—could indicate.

One of the more colorful mythmakers, Upson was not by any means the only one to record the career of the Westerner. In fact, in their later years the Westerners themselves often sought out someone who could tell their story—a story by that time frequently colored by the passing of years and contradictory to other tales told by other old men about the same experience. Most of the old-timers found their biographers and dreamed their memories for what usually amounted to little profit but considerable self-vindication.[105] The reminiscences of these Westerners are rich in nostalgia and display a penchant for tall-tale exaggeration and personal need to justify their lives—perhaps mostly to themselves—as they approached old age and death. Such accounts have swelled the body of legend about all these men, at the same time making the fact almost impossible to ascertain. Certainty of fact, however, was not as important to an eager audience as was the recounting of adventures and the creating of heroes who fit into what was considered to be the American mold.

Frank Dobie has said, "What happened doesn't matter. What people like to believe does."[106] Thus there came into being, in midcentury, an enterprise that produced legend-makers who grew and thrived upon that premise.

The Dime Novelists. The premise was a promise as well, and the Eastern publishing houses could deliver. In the spirit of P.T. Barnum, the enterprises of Beadle and of Street and Smith grew from modest beginnings into empires of pulp. By secret candlelight or behind barns schoolboys reveled in the adventures of their paper heroes. The adults—like many adults today—viewed the pulps with overt scorn but covert delight. The dime novel emperors, it seems, knew their audience better than the audience knew itself.

The original aim of these publishers was, according to Charles M. Harvey's assessment of the phenomenon in 1907, "to give, in cheap and wholesome form, a picture of American wild life." In its early days the dime novel and the half-dime novel tradition was that of relating frontier adventures, but Orville Victor reminisces that in its decline the dime novel turned of necessity to other themes:

> As editor I sought the best work of the best writers in that particular field of fiction.... All was up to an excellent standard of literary merit. The detective and love story came later, when rank competition on the ten-cent trade made it seem necessary to introduce these elements. Almost without exception the original dime novels were good. Their moral was high. All were clean and instructive.[107]

Victor's apologia could have been formulated today as believably as it was at the turn of the century. The story is the same: the pressures of competition forcing an inferior product into being despite the originator's resistance to such compromise. Marketing competition destroyed the original, "pure" dimes as product. As aspiring literature—according to one literary theorist—the deterioration of the dimes was due to increasing emphasis on action and external activity rather than action combined with moral and rational judgment.[108] Deprived of this balance, the dimes became purveyors of a simplistic view of good and evil. But whether product or literature, the dime novel owes its transformation to competitive forces and adaptive changes that might as readily describe corresponding forms in the mass media of today. The impetus for increasing pressure on both marketing and content was the necessity of courting and retaining the consumer of such popular forms: the audience. The pulps "portrayed a level of character, of morality, courage, honor, and action, that found a response in the popular mind. They offered Americans an image of America and themselves that met widely-felt needs."[109]

The Beadle and the Street and Smith writers were many and wrote under multiple pseudonyms. At some time or another, almost all employees of the dime novel enterprises wrote Western stories, whether or not they wrote from experience. The creator of the Frank Merriwell stories, William G. Patten, admitted crossing one corner of Wyoming on a passenger train, yet was rechristened by Beadle editor Orville J. Victor for the purpose of lending a more authentic air to the authorship of Western dimes. Patten thus found himself writing frontier adventures under the pen name of William West Wilder—Wyoming Will.[110]

Patten, however, was not primarily a writer of Western dime novels. Among the many names that appeared beneath Western titles—names often more colorful than the content of the tale—three stand out as enthusiastic creators and ardent perpetuators of the myths of the West and its heroes. They are Col. Prentiss Ingraham, Edward C. Wheeler, and Ned Buntline.

Ingraham's Buck Taylor and Wheeler's Deadwood Dick have been noted earlier as popular fiction images of the Western hero. Neither Ingraham nor Wheeler, however, was master of the "total myth" as was Ned Buntline in his creation of Buffalo Bill.

Daniel Boone was resentful of his portrayal by popular biographers as an "anarchic fugitive from civilization;" Kit Carson slyly admitted to the exaggeration of his exploits; but William F. Cody is probably the only instance of the real personage having little existence outside his press-agent-created, popular persona. And although Cody was as historical a person as Boone or Carson, he was less real as a person—in fact, Wheeler's wildly improbable Deadwood Dick in all his flamboyance seems more real than does William F. Cody. The story of Buffalo Bill is mythmaking at its pinnacle, and Cody was one of the first to believe not the myth itself, but that the myth was possible.

He started out as a buffalo hunter for the Kansas Pacific Railroad and when construction work stopped he became a civilian scout for General Sheridan. It was at that time that he was "discovered" by an entrepreneur named E.Z.C. Judson who wrote under the pseudonym of Ned Buntline.

Buntline was, according to Marshall Fishwick, "in an age of screwballs, an amazing character" and Buntline's own life was far more incredible than any fictional character he invented in the course of writing about four hundred novels. During what might be conservatively termed a full life, Buntline: fought seven duels in one day while a midshipman; participated in a Seminole Indian war; captured two murderers single-handed and unarmed; survived lynching (when the rope broke) as the result of an accusation of adultery; acquired a wife in Westchester County, another in New York City, and later a third in the Adirondacks; was a leader in the Astor Place riot of 1849 and in the Know-Nothing Party a few years later; enlisted in the army at the outbreak of the Civil War but was dismissed after a furlough and a month's confinement after which he headed West.[111] Sandwiched between these escapades Buntline was turning out words by the hundreds of thousands in the form of novels and articles for his magazine, *Ned Buntline's Own*.

In Omaha in 1869 Buntline was looking for more material when he was told of a young scout at Fort McPherson to the west. Not one to miss seizing opportunity by the throat, Buntline sought out the young Cody and the rest—literally—is legend.

Part of the legend is that Buntline was the first to give Cody his nickname, wrote a novel about him called *Buffalo Bill: The King of the Border Men,* in

1869, and added visual dimension to the legend in 1876 by a four-hour theatre production titled *The Scouts of the Plains* (starring Cody himself, as well as Buntline, "Texas Jack" Omohundro, and several "Indians" recruited from the Chicago streets that afternoon).

The team of Buntline and Cody united in their common cause of creating a hero; it worked well for both men. Buntline was always in search of new adventures, and the making of Buffalo Bill was but one of many seemingly effortless projects of Buntline's amazing career.

Along with other popularizers of the Western hero like Frederick Faust writing as "Max Brand," and Zane Grey, the Ohio dentist, Buntline was one of the most prolific writers of Westerns for a mass audience. His method of production is itself material for a tall tale, as told by a fellow Beadle writer, William G. Patten, in reminiscences of dime novel days. Buntline, according to Patten, was usually still writing later installments of the same story while the first chapters were already in print. One day during the time when one of his novels was in series, Buntline disappeared and a substitute writer was assigned at the last possible moment to finish the next installment while the presses were held. The writer did so, and the presses rolled. A few days later the missing Buntline reappeared, read the ghost-written installment, and groaned: "He has killed my hero!" In midseries, such a catastrophe seemed irreparable but through long experience, Buntline was equal to such inconveniences. Patten relates that Buntline "ran his hero through the ensuing installments as a ghost, and let him haunt the villain to his doom."[112] Thus did the intrepid Buntline, like the Beadle heroes themselves, triumph over all obstacles to achieve success.

Cody, on the other hand, achieved a different kind of fame but one equally suited to the talents he brought to the Cody-Buntline mythmaking team. Cody was not by any means a pawn in the hands of unscrupulous literary hacks; he knew a good thing when he saw it. Rather than admitting like Kit Carson that his biographer might have poured it on "a leetle too thick," Cody unashamedly embellished his own legend. "Buffalo Bill" began by claiming to have killed 4,280 buffaloes in eight months as a scout, and moved on to become the hero of a stream of Buntline novels as well as the star of Buntline's theatrical production. In old age, Cody moralized about his heyday: "I stood between savagery and civilization most all my early days"—a statement almost verbatim from a Beadle production describing his adventures.[113]

Perhaps the expanded medium of the stage attracted Cody; perhaps he saw in it new and conquerable worlds that the less complex modality of the printed page could never afford his ego or his ambition. In any case, in 1882 Cody organized in North Platte, Nebraska, a corps of riders and performers and took the troupe into Omaha for the first Wild West show. Freed from the limitations of the stage proscenium as well as from the covers of a dime novel, the arena of Cody's show became a three-dimensional unfolding of the Western heroic legend with a scope that was hitherto undreamed of by an audience eager for the excitement, color, and drama of the Western saga. That this was not the real West mattered little to the enthralled onlookers; it was the West they wished to see, and Buffalo Bill became the epitome of the Westerner—especially to Europeans who never had known and never would know the reality.

But the legend became more and more difficult to sustain with the passing of time. Popular audiences are inconstant lovers; novelty is still a basic ingredient of mass appeal. Cody was aware of this; indeed, he had built his image upon it and would attempt to sustain it in the same way. By 1910 his show had been enlarged into the "Buffalo Bill Wild West—Pawnee Bill Far East Great Combination" and the program, as Douglas Branch remembers it, included:

A Grand Review.
The World's Rough Riders, introduced and led by Buffalo Bill.
U.S. Artillery and Cavalry Drill.
The Buffalo and the Famous Huntsman in pursuit of his native game.
The Prairie, under a scorching sun—"Oh, what a good drink! Pass it around."
Mexican Joe illustrating the use of a lasso.
Perfection of High-School Equestrianism.
Mr. Rhoda Royal's Famed Blue Ribbon Thoroughbreds.
Rossi's Musical Elephants.
Riding Wild Bucking Horses and Mules, introducing the only lady bucking horse rider in the world.
Buffalo Bill shooting glass balls.
Football on Horseback, between Indians and Cowboys.
The Final Salute! Buffalo Bill Bids You Good-by.[114]

The combination of the Western scenes with High-School Equestrians, Musical Elephants, and Football on Horseback between Indians and Cowboys indicates the desperate, something-for-everyone approach that had by then overtaken the show.

The scatter-shot appeal to rake in ever-larger audiences was reflective of a dying image that Cody tried to sustain in person as well as in his show. E.C. Abbott ("Teddy Blue") recalls an incident in a North Platte saloon when Cody entered and removed his hat, whereupon his long hair that was kept rolled up fell down onto his shoulders. He proceeded to roll it back under his hat when the bartender said: "Say, Bill, why the hell don't you cut the damn stuff off?" Cody replied, "If I did, I'd starve to death."[115] At that moment of his life, and despite the glitter and the golden hair, no one was more aware of harsh reality than Cody himself.

Marshall Fishwick summarizes the career of this mythmaker who was himself a myth:

> The sham that was his act was mirrored in the irony that was his life. . . . Galloping forward on his white horse, he looked as free as the air; but he was putty in the hands of others. Despite his large income, Cody finally petitioned the Federal government for the $10-monthly Congressional medal-holder's dole. In his twilight years he had to appear daily to avoid bankruptcy, and go through every performance with the fear of death in the arena. Here was poverty in opulence, chagrin in victory, despair in hollow triumph.[116]

Fishwick's assessment itself leans toward the dramatic, but could scarcely be faulted for doing so since his subject is possibly one of the most colorful, flamboyant, and theatrical images of a West that never existed outside the sawdust arena. And in spite of his reputation for cheap theatricality, Cody was only reflecting the wish of his audience to see greatness in the flesh—to glimpse the ancient hero reincarnate. Perhaps only an anonymous Western ballad can say it succinctly and with the proper ironic twist:

> Caesar and Cicero shall bow
> And ancient warriors famous
> Before the myrtle-wreathed brow
> Of Buffalo Williamus.

Although Cody stands out in the Western heroic tradition, it is difficult to place him in any category. He is generally considered a departure—almost an aberration—from the hero types noted earlier, yet in many minds he is inextricably associated with the American West.[117] Not a dime novelist, he is noted here because of his alliance with Ned Buntline, since both were collaborators in the creation of the Cody myth. Buffalo Bill is the product of an age of audiences that demanded heroes to show them the no longer existing frontiersman as it seemed he should always be—a dashing strong man astride a prancing horse, centered in a brilliant circle of light and gallantly waving his sombrero to applauding audiences who willed to believe.

If Buffalo Bill represented the glamor of the myth, Ned Buntline was a purveyor of the myth as product. Instant adventure, excitement and thrills for a dime—Buntline produced them in abundance and for profit. Together with Cody, E.Z.C. Judson deserves to share the circle of light, since this mythmaker is himself as much a legend as any he chose to create.

The Cody-Buntline phenomenon provides the beginnings of the visual aspect in this review of mythmakers, but before introducing the visual artists some attention must be given to those other popular and "serious" writers whose work built on that of the early chroniclers, journalists, biographers, and dime novelists. The evolution is consistently toward a richer and more widely disseminated image of the Western hero.

The Novelists. It has been noted earlier that the image of the Westerner as delineated by fiction writers can virtually be as real as the historical persons themselves. Not all novelists, however, have built their stories about the lives and legends of historical characters like Billy the Kid, Wyatt Earp, or George Armstrong Custer. Many have brought fictional life to new characters through their art—or attempt at art, depending upon which literary critics one reads—of story-telling. Distinguished names like Emerson Hough, A.B. Guthrie, Willa Cather, Walter Van Tilburn Clark, and Bernard DeVoto have been fully analyzed elsewhere, yet each of them has contributed to the evolving figure of the popular Western hero.

An attempt to list the principal novelists writing in a more popular vein, however, would produce results bordering on chaos. Not only are the pulp Western writers far more numerous than the "serious" novelists, but many also wrote under several pseudonyms—for example, Frederick Faust signed most of his Westerns with "Max Brand" and used as many as nineteen other names in writing various types of fiction. Faust will be briefly noted here, together with Owen Wister, Zane Grey, and Frank Gruber as examples of popular novelists providing a particular perspective on the Western hero.

Owen Wister, the frail youth who went West in 1885 to regain his health as did his idol Teddy Roosevelt, is credited with creating the most famous of all Westerners—the Virginian. Never before had such a character captured the American imagination. Here was a true Man of the West—gentle yet strong, possessing both the cowhand's sense of fun and the hero's seriousness of purpose, and exemplifying the image of the Westerner as the man in the middle but at home with both the savagery of the West and the gentility of the East. No matter that he was, as many critics complained, a "cowboy without cows"[118] (the Virginian seemed always at leisure, as Warshow characterizes the true Westerner). No matter that Wister failed, as did Cooper, to resolve the disparity between the genteel hero image and the Leatherstocking persona (the Virginian was amazingly adept at living in both worlds; moreover, he possessed a distinct advantage with his audience in coming from a good family of Virginia). Unconsciously or not, Wister created the sort of hero that was desired—even expected—by his audience, and this 1902 tale has since become one of the most popular books of its kind.

Two years after the appearance of *The Virginian* an Ohio dentist gave up his practice and went into writing as a full-time profession. Unhappy as a dentist (the only aspect of the job he liked was pulling teeth), Zane Grey aspired to write. If being a writer were determined by quantity of output, Grey unquestionably achieved his dream. While Wister's claim to fame rests chiefly on *The Virginian,* Grey wrote fifty-six popular novels about the West, almost all of which hve been made into films (many remade several times); in addition, his name was appended to a successful television anthology series on the West in the late 1950s produced by Dick Powell. Grey's output of Westerns was only a portion of his total writing but his name is frequently linked with the Western story. Building upon the image of the Virginian, Grey developed a series of heroes who solidified more and more firmly into a formulaic mold. Although some Grey heroes could be genteel—even stuffy—others were men of action and command, men to be feared, hated and loved (all these emotions being displayed with great passion). According to Russel Nye, whereas Wister introduced love into the Western, Grey "introduced sex, good and bad."[119] But action is really the key word in a Zane Grey Western. Character tends to be preset rather than developed; the dash and drama of the adventure is all. Again, depending upon what critics one reads and believes, Zane Grey is either a hack, an artist, or somewhere in between.[120] While his talent is not at issue here, Grey's considerable contribution to the development of the popular image of the Westerner cannot be denied.

In 1917, five years after the phenomenal success of Grey's *Riders of the Purple Sage,* a lean and hungry young writer whose poetry was not selling was told by a publisher that he was looking for another Zane Grey. Ten days later the poet submitted a novel titled *The Untamed*; the editor sent for him, told him that his own name—Frederick Faust—sounded too literary, and gave him a name that was short, easy to remember, and had a "Western flavor to it." The name was Max Brand.[121] Although born in Seattle and having grown up in California, Faust wrote most of his Western stories during the twelve years that he lived in Italy. Russel Nye calls Faust the Western novel's version of Erle Stanley Gardner, referring to Faust's tremendous output of 530 books (the equivalent of a book every ten days for years), thirty film scripts, and material used later for a television series. One of his publishers announced after Faust's death in 1944 that there was enough manuscript on hand to market for the next century.[122] If Grey called for action from his heroes, Brand called for more. With book jackets describing rip-snorting action and romantic adventure, the West of this "King of the Pulps" appeals to the active rather than passive instincts of the audience, reflects a growing interest in tales of violence and violation, and provides an image of the hero that is as far removed from the gentle woodsman of the Leatherstocking Tales as the story itself is removed from the traditional Western formula. Real or not, the West of Max Brand has been steadily and successfully sold as real to millions of readers since Frederick Faust stopped writing poetry in 1917.

The writer who probably wrote more about his writing than Wister, Grey, and Faust combined is Frank Gruber. Gruber, whose seven basic Western plots have been noted earlier, turned out suspense novels, detective stories, Westerns, a biography of Zane Grey, and an autobiography, *The Pulp Jungle,* which reads in the simplified, "Wow!" style of pulp story-telling. From his first Western in 1934 until his death in 1969 Gruber wrote at least four dozen novels, about half of which were made into films, and worked on the creation of *Shotgun Slade, Wells Fargo,* and *The Texan* for television. As a mythmaker of the electronic age, he provides an interesting example of a contemporary creator who profited from the heritage of the late nineteenth- and early twentieth-century popular writers. Not only are his stories a perpetuation of the myth, but his own attitude toward the West reflected the eternal problem of the popular writer: the conflict between art and product. In Gruber, the problem was delicately balanced by his sometimes romantic, sometimes pragmatic, always assured approach to his work—this being the characteristic stance of the true mythmaker. For example, at a meeting of the Long Beach Writers' Conference in 1961, Gruber stated:

> "I'm not a Westerner myself, and I don't like horses. This is strictly a business with me. . . . [I] have no love for it. I don't like ranch life or cowboys. Maybe [the Western is] popular because it's unique to this country." [123]

But in a previous article on the Western he had claimed:

> I traveled extensively in the West: I went to the home of Jesse James and met some of the James family; in New Mexico I talked to Charles and Frank Coe, who had actually ridden with Billy the Kid; I met partisans as well as detractors of famous outlaws; I talked to a few surviving old-time peace officers.
> I acquired a love for the old West. . . . " [124]

At the same time that writers were drawing images with pen, paper, and typewriter, visual story-tellers were at work developing another dimension for the myth. Soon, technology would unite the visual and the verbal to produce the legend in the sight-sound-movement dimension as well as on the printed page. But during the latter part of the nineteenth century the visual artists were preparing the way.

The Artists. Like the verbal mythmakers, the visual story-tellers were most often Easterners. Some of them never or rarely visited the West, others traveled there for the purpose of portraying the land and the people, still others ultimately came to make their home there. John James Audubon, an ornithologist and painter with a background in French art drew the birds and animals of the West; Catlin chose to dedicate his talent to capturing the remarkable character lines in the faces of the original dwellers of the land, the Indians. Others, like Frederick Remington, were more likely to choose the conquerors rather than the conquered for their subject; men like Charlie Russell, Joe DeYong, Ross Santee, and Will James depicted the ease, grace, and beauty of animals and men in motion and repose. [125]

Although artists depicting the West and its people continued to provide colorful blends of romanticism and realism through the medium of pen, pencil, or brush, a new and amazing art form was being born that claimed to bring unvarnished reality to an eagerly waiting audience of both elite and common folk. "The camera does not lie," was the axiom and that authoritative voice was backed by the photography of Matthew Brady. These brilliant and poignant studies of the Civil War illustrated that the artist with a camera is not only able to capture an image but to invest it with resonance.

Packing bulky equipment over rough terrain, the frontier photographers set out to imprint on their glass plates memorable events and memorable people—particularly the heroes about whom so many stories were already being circulated. Thus did men of action like Hickok, Earp, Masterson, and Holliday patiently submit themselves to the necessary moments of stillness required by the primitive camera's sensitive but slow eye. The stiffness of such frontier portraiture is no doubt due in part to the requirement of some moments of immobility on the part of the subject, but the results are nonetheless impressive of the solemnity of the occasion. For example, one portrait—and there are certainly many others that could illustrate the same thing—from the Forrest Collection of the Arizona Pioneers' Historical Society depicts Commodore Perry Owens, former Texas trail driver and, at the time that the photograph was taken in 1886, sheriff of Apache County in the Tonto Basin in Arizona. He was a formidable man in fact, having been hired by the town of Holbrook to clean out rustlers (which he did); his photographic likeness is reflective of that reality. In characteristic nineteenth-century photographic manner, the lawman is almost directly facing the camera—eyes looking into the lens, mouth closed tightly beneath a full moustache. His body, however, is forced into a slight turn because his right foot rests upon an ornate seat partially draped with a buffalo hide. The sheriff's right elbow rests casually on his knee, his hand loosely grasping the barrel of his rifle placed firmly upon a pair of antlers on the floor beside him. His left hand is on his hip, just above the double row of loaded cartridges in his belt, and his Colt is in reverse holster on his left side. He is wearing leather chaps, a homespun shirt, a broad-brimmed sombrero, and a kerchief at the neck. His hair reaches halfway down his back and is arranged visibly and loosely over his shoulders. The studio background canvas is a classical scene of marble columns moving back in perspective toward a cupola; an Indian blanket is partially visible draped loosely in the lower left corner of the photographic frame.

The likeness of this Arizona sheriff is unconscious but eloquent testimony of the mixture of savagery and civilization characteristic of the West; it is also an illustration of the attempt to merge the classical tradition with the trappings of a new form of heroic myth being created. The portrait of this long-dead lawman epitomizes the paradox, vitality, and fascination of the Western myth. It is a remarkable photograph, arranged and executed by a visual mythmaker whether he intended it thus or no. It is the Western hero surrounded with—almost luxuriating in—the regal trappings befitting his station as the ever-ancient ever-new, self-determined man.

Concluding this review of mythmakers by noting those who contributed to the visual aspect of legend-making serves a dual purpose: first, the treatment of both verbal and visual aspects acts as a transition to the more complex mass media perpetuators of the myth; second—and more important—the picture of the Western hero is placed again in the center of the frame.

Imagery is a powerful mythmaker in its own right. Perhaps that is why we remember the look of a Western or a Westerner more readily than we recall the story: the weather-beaten, time-lined face of the hero; the wild and beautiful land he rides, the drab huddle of false-front buildings he knows are the beginnings of the end of his beloved wilderness. But whatever we see or recall having seen, we find ourselves placing the Man of the West squarely in the center of the action. From chronicle to dime novel to photography to television the Western hero has grown—in spite of his less than elegant image—to myth-size. Indeed, might not the mythic character of this hero contribute in large part to holding the strong and sustained interest of print, film, and television audiences through countless "bad" Westerns without destroying the form itself? The Western, it seems, we have always with us; the Western hero may be the reason why.

The Western Hero: A Study in Functional Creativity

In his analysis of popular heroes, Orrin Klapp reviews three aspects of the hero: origin, cult, and the factors involved in creation. Klapp further indicates that heroes tend to emerge in four general ways: first, by spontaneous popular recognition; second, by formal selection (through society's sign of reward or canonization); third, by the growth of popular legend; and fourth, by the poetical creations of dramatists, story-tellers, and writers. Once heroes have emerge, Klapp continues, their audience gives them a certain type of worship. They are honored with special status. They are commemorated by legends, memorials, and relics. Often, they are the object of special celebration by organized cults. A hero may be defined, says Klapp, as a "person, real or imaginary, who evokes the appropriate attitudes and behavior." Thus, in the social milieu, the hero is

> essentially more than a person; he is an ideal image, a legend, a symbol. The study of growing hero legends shows us that the fame of a hero is a collective product, being largely a number of popular imputations and interpretations. Once formed, as has been often said, the legend of a hero "lives a life of its own." The creation of a hero from a historical person is therefore visualized as the attachment of certain roles and traits to him through drama, news, publicity, rumor, and other media, so as to show him in a collective interpretation.[126]

Klapp then suggests that the study of the rise of popular heroes can aid in evaluating certain factors in their creation: the situations of interest, crisis, and drama from which heroes emerge; their heroic and antiheroic roles; their "color"; their personal traits; stories and rumors about them; their publicity; and the organization of popular reaction toward them.

Klapp's study is focused upon his interest in the making and unmaking of a popular hero; thus his synthesis of the basic elements in the hero's origin, cult, and factors in creation apply specifically to the Western hero and that hero's creators and perpetuators.

The Origin. Of the four ways in which heroes generally arise, the first two indicated by Klapp are less true of the Western hero. Rarely has society given a formal stamp of approval to the Westerner's heroic credentials—with the possible exceptions of Davy Crockett by virtue of his death at the Alamo and Custer by his futile attempt at the Little Bighorn. If the Westerner has received formal recognition for his heroic deeds, the records do not show it. On the contrary, far more often the newspaper accounts, memoirs, and quasihistorical narratives relate the adventuresome deeds of the Western hero with a mixture of admiration for his prowess and healthy but grudging respect for him as a slightly dangerous man. Here again the ambiguity of both the image of the Man of the West and the attitude of his admirers is made plain: then, as now, the audience tends to choose as its hero the man of mixed morality. The forbidden fruit has always been the most tantalizing. And although this attraction originates in spontaneous recognition for deeds of bravery and prowess, the basic characteristic of the legend-making process necessitates that the story be told and retold with embellishments at each step. The recognition is spontaneous but it rests more on the image of the hero than on the actual person himself.

On the other hand, virtually all the types of Western heroes noted earlier developed through a combination of the third and fourth characteristics—the growth of popular legend and the poetical creations of writers. Indeed, most popular legends and poetical creations were one and the same thing. This is not always true of other folk heroes. There is a distinct difference between the deliberate formulation of the heroic image of the Westerner by the various mythmakers noted earlier and the chiefly oral tradition of other American folk heroes whose stories are told and retold and then finally gathered into written form by the folklorist or literary historian. The oral tradition in the making of the Western hero has, of course, been noted earlier in this study, but the emphasis has more often been on the written recording of the hero's legend—with the legend frequently being rushed into print during the lifetime of the hero himself. Thus the Western hero's origin—though based on reality—is dependent upon the mythmakers, whether they be embellishers of popular legend or creators of pure fiction. Most often mythmakers indulge in a bit of both.

The Cult. Klapp's comments on the cult of the hero are affirmed in the worshipful stance developed by a popular audience more than one hundred years ago. Klapp notes honor through status, commemoration through legend, memorials and relics, and celebration through organized cult. Although there are signs that the Westerner's popularity is waning, at his zenith this hero has indeed been venerated in these ways. In particular, the film and television Westerner has been endowed with special status in the person of the "stars" who have portrayed him, many of whom, in fact, owe their initial career opportunities to media exposure as a Western hero.

In addition, the collective and anonymous Man of the West has been given a place of honor in the American hall of fame of the common folk; he represents those qualities of pioneer spirit, initiative, skill, and daring that we Americans have always wanted to believe are uniquely our own. Therefore, the hero cult is strengthened through commemoration of this faceless man through legend, through memorials, and through the preservation of relics. Any frontier museum can readily give evidence of all three in its display of yellowed papers, noble statuary, and artifacts of all kinds. The more media-oriented and myth-created legends, memorials, and relics, however, are found in the constant renewal of the Westerner's story through films and television series, the restoration and recreation of the media hero's habitat (the Ponderosa ranch near Virginia City, Nevada), his costumes (the John Wayne Theatre in Anaheim, California), and his personality (the countless appearances of actors in their media personae at rodeos, benefits, and shows of all kinds). Mention of artifacts must also include those synthetic relics developed by the economic ally of the mythmaker—the merchandiser. One wonders upon how many heads have rested the Disney Crockett's coonskin cap, how many small hands have gripped the Hoppy or Autry or Rogers six-gun.

Finally, hero worship is further reinforced in special celebrations of the Westerner through organized activities. The rodeo, originally an offshoot of the routine but skillful work performed by the cowhand, is an example of the development of the cult through organization. Societies of trail drivers—now almost extinct—are gathering places not only for the old-timers who participate but are means of stimulating further legend-making that in turn burnishes the elegiac glow surrounding the dying Man of the West. And of course, the existence of fan clubs gives witness to the strong influence of organized cult in sustaining the hero's image.

Cults need to be cultivated; they will not survive if left alone. Thus, the briefest review of Western hero worship reveals not only the mythmaker at work, but the entrepreneur as well.

The Factors in Creation. Klapp indicates that heroes tend to arise in situations of interest crisis, and drama. The historical review of frontier history and the specific history of hero types noted earlier in this study attest to the drama inherent in the opening of the West and the perpetual crisis existence of those who opened it. The development of the mythmaker's art also noted earlier was dependent upon audience fascination with the exciting events of frontier living and the characters who made the excitement. American Western history and the Western genre are fertile ground for the breeding of both factual and legendary heroes.

The hero's role in Klapp's analysis is interesting in comparison to the character types of the Western hero noted earlier. Like the classical hero, the popular hero can assume several roles; Klapp lists the following: the conquering hero, the Cinderella, the clever hero, the delivering and avenging hero, the benefactor, and the martyr. The self-effacing yet victorious Virginian, the wily Carson and Crockett, the Robin Hood outlaw-avenger, the benevolent Boone, the martyred gunfighter or soldier—all these types portray the roles designated for heroes to the manner born. Whether classical and elite or American and popular, the hero plays out basically the same scope and variety of role.

The antiheroic aspect of the role in Klapp's analysis, however, is defined as the process of destroying a hero who has already been established. Klapp does not discuss the antihero as depicted in the media today. In this study, however, the antiheroic role is considered to be yet another modification of the hero evoked by certain sociological and psychological conditions.[127]

Klapp's factor of "color" refers to actions or traits evoking popular response. "Color" has three main functions: first, to excite attention, interest, imagination, and interpretation; second, to set the person apart as unique; and third, to render the hero unforgettable. As functional characteristics of mythmaking, these elements could very well have emerged directly out of a story conference creating a new Western television series. The heroic qualities noted earlier that distinguish the Western hero do, indeed, evoke an audience response that makes the Western interesting, unique, and memorable.

Klapp's remaining factors in the creation of a hero—personal traits, stories and rumors, publicity, and organization of popular reaction—are all closely connected with the art of Westerner mythmaking. Klapp asserts that the audience is usually ignorant of its heroes' personal traits, since the audience knows them only in their public roles. Therefore, the audience must rely upon biographies, anecdotes, and other accounts that are the tools of the mythmaker's trade. These are more often than not developed into stories and rumors far more colorful than the facts of the case. Publicity, says Klapp, cannot of itself create a hero; "in the age of mass communication, however, heroes can be more arbitrarily manufactured and more quickly and widely diffused, once a formula for making heroes is found."[128] The organizing or popular reaction to the hero, as in the case of personalities who portray the Westerner, is again the job of the mythmaker in the guise of press agent and promoter.

The many factors at work in the creation of a hero point toward conclusions about heroic image that are applicable to the Westerner and integral to this study. First, the Western hero has been made more often than he has been born. Second, he has been made to respond to simple, fundamental, and popular needs and desires. Third, his cult has developed through mass dissemination of a public image that began in oral folk tradition, rapidly moved into print, and finally exploded into visual and aural technology. The result is the development of an American folk tradition and style through the artistry of the creators, a lasting impact upon the American audience, and a niche in the pantheon of American immortals for the hero himself.

"The Western hero's career," says Steckmesser, "has thus become an American epic by virtue of the form and content of the legends rather than because of the historical importance of his activities."[129] The emphasis here is on the legendary or fabulous quality of the hero's story rather than the historical value of the individual or event. This focus is basically correct, since the sweep of the epic form requires a broadening and deepening of specific fact into the universal "truth" or reality of some moment in history. This, indeed, is the beauty of myth: it can present the ideal as the real; it can offer a story of events that might have been possible so that people can envision what may yet be possible; and finally, it can present the image of a once and future king upon whom one can fix memories, dreams, and hopes. If such deeds might have been done at one times, then they might possibly be done again.

This, then, is the genre of the American Western: rooted in a classical mythic tradition, spilling over into a specific period of American history, displaying a particular type of hero grafted from European to American stock and nurtured, pruned, and further grafted by the cultivators of the legend. The American Western genre has produced an overwhelming number of variations upon the theme of the heroic story—American style. The coming of mass media communications has added still other dimensions to this complex but fascinating hero of American popular culture. The media story-tellers of the twentieth century have tools at their disposal for fabricating legends that reach beyond the wildest dreams of the early chroniclers, story-tellers, and dime novelists—as far beyond as the dream of the garden in the desert was to those who finally succeeded in wrestling with the land to make it bring forth fruit. The media mythmakers are still grappling with their electronic myth-machine. In spite of dazzling advances in technology, the struggle today remains an attempt to explore a still unknown, scarcely penetrated land.

3

Cinema: The Myth as Epic

The History: How the West Was Done

The technological roots of the mass media Western are far deeper than the origins of the literary form of the genre. While James Fenimore Cooper was spinning tales about Leatherstocking, a few curious souls—among them Nicéphore Niepce and Louis Daguerre—were experimenting with the sensitivity of certain chemicals reacting with light when exposed upon a metal plate. By the middle of the nineteenth century, when the pseudonymous dime novelists were grinding out their verbal images of the Western story, another handful of the curious were recording the visual image of the same tale from the battlefields of the Civil War to the last battleground of the badmen in Tombstone, Arizona.

The photographer of the old West very much resembled the forty-niner in both appearance and purpose. Accompanied by horse or mule laden with the tools of his trade, he left the well-traveled roads and struck out into the hills and valleys searching the unlikely spots for a kind of treasure that was invisible to the untrained eye. When he struck pay dirt, he captured it in his black box and set up his portable darkroom to process the find. Today, even a cursory study of these early examples of photography indicates that the pioneer Western photographers discovered wealth in the American hills. The photograph could speak as eloquently as—some said better than—the painting. And once a still image could be captured upon glass or paper, the next step was to dream of how to make the image move. If that could be achieved, the imitation of life—many thought—would be complete.

The details of the dream becoming reality are of less importance than the fact that the moving image was achieved. What at first was an invention of curious experimenters developed into a product and built an industry—all the while struggling to become an art.

To attempt to capsulize over seventy years of Western film history is to select—at the risk of distorting, minimizing, or omitting—aspects of that history which are essential to some analysts and extraneous to others. The following perspective attempts to balance several factors. Outstanding artistic contributions to the genre stand side by side with films that are undoubtedly less artistic but more typical of a particular period or industry policy. Furthermore, some films which have received little critical praise have been noted because they are significant as landmarks in the evolution of the genre. Other works have been included as touchstones from which later film makers have derived basic attitudes toward the Western myth and characteristic modes of handling it. Certain artists and works have been included which reflect the change in audience expectations and demands from one period to another. These expectations and demands are, in turn, another reflection of larger changes in the culture. Finally, artists have been noted who have been able to transcend the limitations of the genre yet remain true to it—film makers who have enlarged our understanding and deepened our insight into the human condition. They have used the myth to bring us to the reality.

The history of the Western film parallels the history of the film industry itself. Both were born of dubious parentage in the nickelodeons of the turn of the century. Both survived a precarious infancy, a scapegrace youth, and naive but enthusiastic adolescence to emerge into a sophisticated and somewhat bewildered maturity. The story of the film industry is told in detail elsewhere; the highlights are here only insofar as they reflect the evolution of the Western film and its central character, the hero.

The Beginnings

In 1890, the United States government census report declared that the frontier was closed. In 1893, Frederick Jackson Turner presented his interpretation of the fact together with his thesis on its significance for the past of America and for its future. During that same decade a new frontier was opened that would attempt to explicate the meaning of Turner's philosophical analysis; that frontier was the American cinema. From that time, the art of the film would combine both history and fantasy in depicting the myth of the American West.

As the nineteenth century ground to a close, slightly embarrassed but overwhelmingly curious Americans were peering into machines to view in rapid succession a series of still photographs that appeared to move. Patrons were mesmerized by the movements of a simple action or incident and then—all too soon—the image lapsed into stillness again. The machine was the Mutoscope, and the first brief glimpses of the Western legend that passed before the eyes of the viewer were scenes of buffalo herds or cattle roundups; others, of a less documentary nature, were reconstructions of scalpings or stagecoach holdups. William F. Cody appeared in these vignettes, and the first depiction of that most familiar of Western settings—the saloon—appeared in a "flicker" called *Cripple Creek Bar-room* directed by W.K.L. Dickson for the Edison Company in 1898.[1]

In 1901, Butch Cassidy, Kid Curry, Bill Carver, and Deaf Charlie Hanks held up a Union Pacific train in Wyoming; and in an instance of art imitating nature, two years later Gilbert M. Anderson, Frank Hanaway, and George Barnes held up a borrowed Delaware and Lackawanna train in New Jersey for Edwin S. Porter's camera grinding out the sequences in *The Great Train Robbery*. The now-famous closeup in which George Barnes fired pointblank at the startled audience (which dramatic moment, according to the Edison publication instructions, could be placed either at the beginning or the end of the film) was also that audience's first memorable introduction to a Westerner in a moving picture. If, however, the audience thought they were also being introduced to the first Western hero, they were mistaken. Instead, they would have to look—and look quickly—within the filmed story itself at an unpretentious member of the robber band during their getaway in the woods. The badman who encountered some difficulty while attempting to mount his horse was to become the first Western hero of the cinema.

This unfortunate outlaw—whose unheroic lack of equestrian skill was only too evident in the days before retakes sharpened the hero's image—was Gilbert M. Anderson. Like most film pioneers, Anderson worked in production as well as in acting. Together with George K. Spoor, Anderson formed the Essanay Company in Chicago and then moved to the west coast to form a branch of the studio there. *The Great Train Robbery* had been a smashing success, and Anderson wanted to discover why so many subsequent Western stories had failed to capitalize upon the possibilities of the genre. Concluding that there had been no central character upon which to focus the attention of the audience, he decided to create a cowboy hero to fill the need.[2] Casting about for a star to create proved a formidable task, and Anderson in desperation finally was forced to play the part himself. Now an actor as well as a producer-director, Anderson was still not a cowboy; he therefore employed a double to work in his films and thus introduced the role of the stuntman to the Western.[3]

Anderson, now known as "Broncho Billy," launched himself as a cowboy star with *Bronco Billy and the Baby* (1908), a small film depicting the Western hero in a role that he was to play consistently, if intermittently, up to the present—that of the good badman, the hero of ambiguous and mixed morality. Neglecting the amenities of screen adaptation rights, Anderson encountered initial difficulties with the author of the story and the originator of the character of Broncho Billy, Peter B. Kyne. But Kyne liked the film and the legal difficulties were settled while new Broncho Billy one-reelers were added to the initial success: for example, *Broncho Billy's Redemption* (1910), *Broncho Billy's Christmas Dinner* (1911), and *Broncho Billy's Oath* (1913), all produced by Essanay.

Around 1915, with Bill Hart and Tom Mix gaining in popularity, Anderson relinquished his Broncho Billy weekly role and moved into features and production. Anderson's total career output was about 500 films, all based chiefly on the hero image perpetuated by the dime novel Western. He retired in 1923, but returned to participate in an NBC television special on the Western in 1958 and appeared in *The Bounty Hunters* in 1965.

This first cowboy actor not only introduced the concept of the Western good badman as hero, but Anderson's own physical qualities set another style that has remained a strong characteristic of the Western media hero. Neither young nor handsome, his bulky frame and rugged features seemed to belong to a man of the West; these qualities combined with his characterization of an appealing shyness with the ladies. Anderson's boyish grin and awkward twisting of the hat became at one point standard equipment of the cowboy hero image.

At the time Anderson was creating the first typical cowboy hero, other films were being produced that attempted to depict historical Westerners and their adventures. In 1911 an unknown actor played in a film called *Jesse James;* the next year Francis Ford acted in *Custer's Last Fight* for Thomas H. Ince; and in 1917 Frank Lloyd produced *Davy Crockett* starring Dustin Farnum. It is interesting that the earliest of these films portrayed the then most recent of the heroes, albeit a badman, Jesse James; in fact, Jesse's brother Frank was still alive in 1911.[4] James, Custer, and Crockett were only the beginning of a long list of media characterizations of historical Westerners extending from those early days through seven decades of films and spilling over into television. It is difficult to know how closely the stories of these early films followed the facts of the heroes' lives, but it is certain that the legends that had been developed up to that time through news accounts, biographies, and the ever-increasing numbers of dime novels were adapted to the retelling of the tale in visual terms. Not one to lose out on such a venture was that intrepid entrepreneur, William F. Cody. He formed the W.F. Cody Historical Pictures Company and obtained permission from the Secretaries of War and of the Interior to use regular army cavalry and agency Indians to film the "true story" of the last of the Indian wars. Like most of Cody's business enterprises, the venture was not a financial success.[5]

Two other creators in the new medium, however, did use the Western to display their talents and build successful careers. They were D.W. Griffith and Thomas H. Ince. Although neither worked solely in the Western genre, both did produce some Western films of note, while the actors and actresses who appeared before their cameras became some of the early stars of the medium. Griffith's genius for putting together a story built upon the primitive narrative methods of Porter and produced examples of the genre like *The Last Drop of Water* (1911), *Fighting Blood* (1911), and *The Battle at Elderbush Gulch* (1913). Ince, on the other hand, was a talented production manager who was the first to make use of the economy measure of employing stock footage for elaborate action scenes. Ince frequently depicted the Indian's conflict with cowboys and cavalry, with titles like *The Indian Massacre, The Invaders,* and *The Battle of the Redmen,* all produced in 1912. Ince's treatment of the Indian affirms one critic's belief that James Fenimore Cooper was a greater influence upon the Griffith and Ince films at this time than was Zane Grey. There were in evidence at that time both direct and indirect adaptations of many Cooper stories.[6]

Film historians George Fenin and William Everson capsulize the contributions of Ince and Griffith to the art of the Western genre film by summarizing the difference between the two men:

> Ince was a showman, a routine director, and a mediocre editor. He did not know how to build excitement as Griffith did. Ince's stories were strong, full of drama and complications; Griffith's were really little more than situations.[7]

Although Griffith's particular genius needs no further expansion here, Ince must be noted once more for a major contribution of introducing to the audience an actor who became *the* legendary film Westerner.

In 1908, Gilbert M. Anderson was searching for a way to revive the success of the Western story as depicted in *The Great Train Robbery.* When the genre was again slipping from popularity in 1914, a forty-four year old actor who had done the stage classics *Ben Hur* and *Romeo and Juliet,* and—interestingly enough—played the heroes in *The Squaw Man* and *The Virginian,* once again saved the Western from a fate worse than death for a popular genre. The fate was a decline in audience response; the rescuer was a born and bred Westerner named William S. Hart.

It may or may not be fact that Hart wanted to become a Western film actor in order to present the true picture of a West crudely distorted by insensitive movie-makers. Such motivation does, however, create a legend worthy of a man who wanted to become a Westerner both on and off screen. Hart remained true to that ideal as he saw it, developing a film persona of the good badman that has not been equalled, although it had been copied. Integrity shone through the initial villainy or lawlessness in the badman's devotion to a faithful horse or a beloved sister; ultimately the basic nobility triumphed in his reformation through the love of the heroine or a small child. With little variation, Hart repeated this pattern during his comparatively short career as a Western star.

His first picture for Ince—an old friend who gave Hart the chance he sought to become a film actor—was *The Bargain* (1914), an astonishing success. For the next five years during a growing hostility between Ince and Hart, the actor not only starred in but directed a series of successful short films and features that established him on an equal star footing with his contemporaries: Charlie Chaplin, Mary Pickford, and Douglas Fairbanks. His "star" status with the audience and the behind-the-scenes manipulation of Ince prevented Hart from receiving at that time the recognition as a director that he deserves. Like "Broncho Billy" Anderson, Hart was both the creator and the created of the particular image of the Westerner that he left for future mythmakers to embellish. As a director, Hart limited himself chiefly to Westerns, but William K. Everson ranks him in the company of Cecil B. DeMille, Maurice Tourneur, Herbert Brenon, and Charles Chaplin, adding that Hart films were the first "adult" Westerns in the truest sense of the term:

> His films were raw, unglamorous, and gutsy, the costumes and livery trappings accurate, the ramshackle Western towns and their inhabitants like unretouched Matthew Brady photographs, the sense of dry heat ever-present (panchromatic film stock, developed in the twenties, softened and glamorized the landscapes in later Westerns), and the clouds of dust everywhere. (This naturalistic quality vanished later when directors took to wetting down the ground so that the riding scenes would be cleaner and crisper.)[8]

But despite these qualities in his favor, Hart's films became formulaic and stereotyped for the popular audience of this day. From the vigor of *The Aryan* and *Hell's Hinges* (both made in 1916) through lesser works of films like *The Toll Gate* (1920), *Three Word Bond* (1921), and *Wild Bill Hickok* (1923)—in which Hart, in an opening title, apologized to the audience for resembling Bill Hart more than Bill Hickok—the increasing sentimentality of the films gave a Hart Western an out-of-date look to the ever-increasing film audiences. Besides, Hart was growing old but still insisting upon playing the boyish hero romancing a girl sometimes twenty to thirty years younger than he. The businessmen involved in his productions—notably Adolph Zukor and Jesse Lasky—were all too aware of the inevitable results of a popular artist rejecting changing audience tastes. Hart, however, would not or could not conform and his films and his hero became even more rigidly cast into the unpopular mold. His final film for United Artists, *Tumbleweeds* (1925)—although Fenin and Everson rank it in the epic mold of Cruse's *The Covered Wagon* and Ford's *The Iron Horse*—marked the end of a career which had been moving downward since 1919. Moreover, the audience had now become interested in a new hero who offered youth, showmanship, and plenty of action. His name was Tom Mix.

Within a year of the opening of twenty million acres of land in the Cherokee Strip of Oklahoma, Tom Mix was born in Pennsylvania of Irish and Cherokee-Scotch parentage. His action-packed film career was a mythic extension of the exciting adventures he claimed during his prescreen days. Within his first thirty years Mix maintained he had seen action in the Spanish-American War and the Boxer Rebellion; had been a cowpuncher, a rodeo rider, and a lawman; and by the time that he offered the use of his ranch and stock to William Selig for the filming of a documentary on life in the West, had created as full and exciting a life as other men twice his age.

But the career that would make him a legend was just beginning with his association with Selig, who offered him a job keeping stock in control during the shooting of the studio's Western; there was also a chance to do some stunt doubling and an occasional small acting role. The roles grew, and from 1911 to 1917 Mix made about one hundred short Westerns for the Selig studio. In 1917 he went to work for Fox and by the mid 1920s Mix was making seventeen thousand dollars a week starring in profitable films that enabled the Fox studio to risk making unprofitable but "prestige" films like Murnau's *Sunrise.* The Mix Westerns could pay the tab.

The heroic persona that Tom Mix developed was in sharp contrast to Hart's austere, square-jawed, steely-eyed good badman. Whereas the Hart films emphasized character and straightforward sentimentality, those of Mix displayed fast-moving action and light-hearted sentiment. Hart's West was, as Richard Griffith terms it, "drab and sinister"—a West of realism. Tom Mix's mythic frontier land was theatrical, adventuresome, glamorous, and sometimes gimmicky. The heroes in each case fit their surroundings. The Mix hero was conscious, as was the actor himself, of cultivating an appeal to the young audience; therefore, along with drinking, swearing, or romancing of the heroine in a Mix film, together with violence or killing, Tom Mix conquered his villains by fancy roping or stuntwork; and within the framework of such implausible activity, the Mix hero came into being. He was a man who,

> possessed all of the virtues and none of the vices, helped usher in the code of clean-living, non-drinking, and somewhat colorless sagebrush heroes, a code that remained in force until the early fifties, when Bill Elliott, playing the tough Westerner characterized by Hart, began to restore the balance to a more realistic level.[9]

Mix himself outlined the type of Westerner he played, foreshadowing in some respects the sort of hero that Randolph Scott was to portray so successfully in the Boetticher film of the 1950s:

> "I ride into a place owning my own horse, saddle and bridle. It isn't my quarrel, but I get into trouble doing the right thing for somebody else. When it's all ironed out, I never get any money reward. I may be made foreman of the ranch and I get the girl, but there is never a fervid love scene."[10]

Some of the better films in which Mix was developing his distinctive hero persona were: *Chip of the Flying U* (1914), *Sky High* (1922), *The Great K & A Robbery* (1926), and *The Rainbow Trail* (1931). But with an eye to attracting a wide audience and in order to capitalize upon the popular appeal of exotic romance, Fox at one point insisted upon clothing the Mix image in the period costume of a British highwayman in *Dick Turpin* (1925), and at another time cowboy Mix found himself in Arabia, Ruritania, or, in the manner of Griffith's *Intolerance,* participating in allegorical interludes in ancient Babylon.[11]

Tom Mix Westerns did, however, display the magnificent riding and stunting talent of the hero, shot against the spectacular natural backgrounds of the Western national parks that Mix insisted upon using for location shooting. His films also marked the debuts of many talents that were to be associated with the development of the Western from those early days into the present. John Ford directed two of the Mix films; Buck Jones was a trick rider in the unit; George O'Brien was an assistant cameraman; and a young football player from the University of Southern California who later changed his name to John Wayne served as a prop boy for some of the Mix films.[12]

With the coming of sound, Mix, now nearing the age of fifty, left films for touring circus performances. Mix was one of the many silent stars whose screen image was more appealing than the sound of his voice. He made his last appearance in a 1935 serial for Mascot called *The Miracle Rider;* he was killed in an automobile accident in Arizona in 1940.

Tom Mix not only introduced to the screen audience a facet of the Western hero different from that of both Anderson and Hart, he also did his share to develop an off-screen image of a flamboyant, glamorous Hollywood hero of the day. His white hat, the impeccable and dandified cowboy costume which he wore as a badge of his cowboy image, his luxurious home and lavish automobile—all these trappings of the Hollywood cowboy were ludicrously inconsistent with the historical person of the Westerner. When Mix adopted them, however, they became essential elements in the legend.[13] Far more glamorous than the austere image to which Hart had clung in spite of the threat of rejection by his audience, the flamboyance of the Mix persona began a trend that developed—with very few exceptions—to its logical and ludicrous conclusion in the 1930s. That decade introduced the singing cowboy, the dancing cowboy, the cowboy dandy—the cowboy, in short, who became a silly parody of all that Bill Hart sought to expunge from the image he felt had already been tarnished in 1914.

Historians Richard Griffith and Arthur Mayer suggest that the American middle class, the "stern guardian of morality and respectability," had by the end of World War I become a substantial portion of the movie audience and "entered the postwar decade with a gleam in its eye."[14] Movie theatres in the twenties became lavish temples of splendor; the filmgoer settled back, luxuriating amid exotic surroundings to view—surely not the common cowboy sweating out a dusty gun battle with a swarthy, unkempt villain.

Instead, a suave, brilliantined Rudolph Valentino was carrying resisting heroines into his tent, Erich Von Stroheim was creating his very personal vision of decadence and exoticism, and Chaplin, Keaton, and Lloyd were zigzagging their way through comedies swiftly developing into art. Thus it is not surprising that Hart's good badman austerity could not survive; indeed, Mix would probably have been forced into his romantic and spectacular version of the cowboy, had he not been inclined by talent and perhaps temperament to choose it himself. At the same time that D.W. Griffith was expanding the screen to epic size, Cecil B. DeMille was introducing the American film audience to the bedroom and the bathtub from ancient Babylon to the modern but equally decadent high society of the 1920s. In these lush epics, character was swallowed up in the spectacle of the whole—the depicting of an era rather than an individual, a history rather than a story.

The cowboy hero, too, found himself swept up in the surge toward spectacle. The first epic version of the Western genre was James Cruze's production of Emerson Hough's *The Covered Wagon* in 1923; John Ford following with *The Iron Horse* in 1924.

Historian Everson maintains that *The Covered Wagon,* though it does not stand up well through the passage of years, is one of the few key Western films that have made a major contribution to the genre's development. Labeling it a "milestone" film, Everson adds that Cruze's achievement is "supremely important in that by being made at all it introduced the epic tradition to the Western, and gave it scale and poetic and documentary values."[15] And while praising Ford's *The Iron Horse* for its excitement and creative values, Everson concludes that this far superior entertainment epic owes its very existence to the popular and widespread appeal of *The Covered Wagon.*

The potential for panorama and scope realized by these two films opened up whole new worlds for the Western. No longer need it be confined to the studio lot or the nearby hills and canyons of Hollywood. Both Cruze and Ford moved their entire production crews into the wilderness to create eloquent pioneer and empire images of the taming of the West. A panorama such as this was indeed worthy of the austere and intense hero that Hart had created; it provided a splendid backdrop for the spectacular skill and adventures of a Tom Mix hero as well. But a small cloud appeared upon the Hollywood horizon during the 1920s that grew formidable enough to obscure the possibilities of the Western epic and shunt aside its development until many years later. The cloud was experimentation with sound.

Before the sound era is discussed, however, it is necessary to acknowledge a few of the other cowboy heroes who were developing variations upon the Mix theme during the years from about 1915 through the 1920s. Buck Jones has already been noted; some of the other stars who appeared at this time were Tim McCoy, Ken Maynard, Jack Hoxie, Hoot Gibson, Bob Steele, William Farnum, and Art Acord. Although these actors were each of them distinct personalities, they all tended to pattern their portrayal of the hero according to the highly successful Mix formula, while none of them achieved the Mix fame. One early cowboy star, however, chose to penetrate the hero image created by Hart. The man was Harry Carey, noted particularly for his work with John Ford, as association of both friendship and business that proved fruitful to both men. Yakima Canutt, who later found his true metier as a superb stuntman, organizer of stuntmen, and second unit director, was also hard at work playing both heroes and villains during the days before the movies learned to talk.

The Coming of Sound

In his essay "The Myth of Total Cinema," André Bazin suggests that the wedding of sight and sound in cinema was a step toward the perfection of the art, rather than an extraneous addition to the "pure" state of the silent film.[16] If one were to draw conclusions upon the evidence of many film products of the early sound years, that conclusion would undoubtedly be in violent disagreement with Bazin. Jazz Singer Jolson's "You ain't heard nothin' yet!" became more threat than promise.

The first sound film experiment itself was a result of a happy fault of the Warner Brothers Studio taking the plunge; in their failing financial condition the studio executives had nothing to lose. When the long shot paid off, careers and fortunes were suddenly and precariously suspended from the sound of a voice. Wild, wacky fascination with sound enamored both industry and audience, so that the noisy, numbing escape of the "all-talking, all-singing, all-dancing" extravaganzas dominated studio output during the initial shock of the Wall Street crash. Such films could not, however, drown out the harsh reality of the depression years of the early 1930s. Without question there were quality films being made through these early sound years, but the stunning phenomenon tended to emphasize sound for its own sake rather than in relation to screen image and story.

Perhaps the very nature of the genre prevented Western films from floundering as deeply or as long in the mires of early sound. While character, plot, and even the movement which gave "movies" their name ground to a halt as everyone stood still and talked, the Westerns were forced to stay outdoors to depict chases, gun battles, and landscape in the sweeping long shots that Ford had made famous. Cumbersome and primitive sound equipment could not be hidden in the great outdoors as it was—however clumsily—on the studio stages. True, there were microphones in rocks and behind cactuses, and some of the cowboy heroes who were far better at fast and spirited action spent interminable minutes talking in barrooms. Still, the Western formula was not confined by sound to the extent that other types of film were. The Western, with its iconography as a basic and strong element of its mystique, simply did not need speech as did the more complex forms of cinematic story-telling. Where Fenin and Everson summarize the role of sound in the development of the Western, their assessment reflects Bazin's theory of completion rather than superimposition:

> Visual action remained more important than dialogue. However, if *speech* was to add little to the Western, *sound* was instead to add a great deal. Sounds of action—stampeding cattle, gunshots, etc.—and the use of traditional Western folk music, particularly in the films directed by John Ford, definitively added another dimension to the genre.[17]

As for the heroes of the genre, sound affected the careers of those who could not withstand its penetration into another aspect of their image; and although there is some disagreement on the subject, most historians attribute the decline of Mix's popularity to his inability to overcome the sound barrier. There were other silent cowboy heroes whose popularity endured during the 1930s. Alan Barbour, in his informal study of the B-Westerns, traces the careers of the cowboy actors who made the transition to become stars of early sound: Buck Jones, Tim McCoy, Hoot Gibson, Tom Tyler, Ken Maynard, and Bob Steele.[18] The B-Westerns—small-scale, low-budget studio products—had already become established as staples of the industry in silent days. During the thirties and midforties, their numbers multiplied unto endless variations upon the Western theme.

Meanwhile other genres were busy producing heroes and villains in a far different mode. Mystery and horror were made popular by *Frankenstein* and *Dracula* (both in 1931), *The Mask of Fu Manchu* (1932), and *The Invisible Man* (1933). The urban badman came into his own with *Little Caesar* (1930) and *The Public Enemy* (1931). Whether through cause-effect or merely by coincidence, new elements began to appear in both feature and serialized Westerns. Scarred and ugly villains, often exotically masked and costumed, wreaked havoc upon the railroad, the town, the rancher, and the rancher's daughter. These bizarre Bs were pat and predictable in plot, with the good guys becoming even better and almost always more bland. The better Bs remained a sturdy staple for years—the myth in its uncomplicated form.

During this time actors who were faces in the crowd or bit players in silent films now began to develop hero images of their own. One of these extras, Gary Cooper, starred in one of the first sound Westerns, *The Virginian,* in 1929. John Wayne appeared—at the request of John Ford to his fellow director Raoul Walsh—in his first major role in *The Big Trail* (1930) but did not become a star as a result. Wayne did, however, appear in a series of Bs for Warners during the thirties.

Other silent screen actors moved into the Western genre with great success. George O'Brien, who portrayed the unfaithful husband in Murnau's *Sunrise* and the hero in Ford's *The Iron Horse,* continued to play both hero and character roles in many Bs of the thirties, Zane Grey adaptations, and other Westerns throughout the next forty years. Warner Baxter, a leading man of the silent screen, starred in one of the first sound Westerns, *In Old Arizona* (1929), as the Cisco Kid—the first to portray O. Henry's colorful creation on the screen.[19]

Another leading man whose career was considered to be at an end by the 1920s was William Boyd. He, too, had begun as an extra, became a star in the 1920s, and appeared in a few Westerns.[20] His legendary persona, however, was the result of a project for Paramount Studios beginning in 1935 and enduring through the next decade and into the era of television. Based on Clarence E. Mulford's character and produced by Harry Sherman, the Hopalong Cassidy Westerns have been one of the most successful series in the history of the genre. The first of the Cassidy Westerns is considered the best, employing a formula that became characteristic of the Hopalong films: a slow build-up climaxing in an exciting chase sequence with background music used for the first time at that point in each film. Almost seventy pictures were made following this stereotyped formula, which was, nonetheless, copied by other producers of Westerns.

The hero image of the Hopalong films did not follow the original Mulford character, but no matter. The Boyd image proved to be immensely popular with both adults and children, and later Mulford novels were reprinted with modifications conforming to the "new" hero image created by Boyd.[21] It might be ventured that here was a case of art imitating art, or possibly, old myth giving way to the new. The new myth, as developed by Sherman and Boyd, is described thus:

> If Boyd followed convention, he did not follow cliche. Boyd's Cassidy was soft-spoken and gentlemanly, not given to brash treatment of the ladies or to exhibitionistic displays of riding and stunting. A mild romance between Cassidy and an old sweetheart was revived on infrequent occasion, and it never was allowed to come to fruition. Romance in the Cassidy Westerns was largely limited to gentle comedy at the expense of Cassidy's perennially lovesick young companion, James Ellison in the earlier films, Russell Hayden later on. There was hardly ever any sentimental "small-boy appeal," and little comedy except that which arose naturally from the story.[22]

The stern code of celibacy that was developing for the cowboy hero is evident in this description of the hero's sidekick. The romantic-comedy relief provided by the sidekick—a character that had existed in the genre from the early days— served the same function for the film hero as did the splitting of the Leatherstocking persona in the Cooper tales. The sidekick extended the possibilities for enriched characterization and complexity of plot without compromising the basic formula of the hero's person—ultimately, the best of both worlds.

The only other Western hero to equal the popularity of William Boyd playing Hopalong Cassidy was Gene Autry playing Gene Autry. Possibly the first instance of a film actor retaining his own name in his screen persona, Autry was also the first to capitalize on the image of a singing cowboy, although he was not the first cowboy to sing.[23] The actor and the cowboy hero merged into a single entity during the course of Autry's screen career. Nat Levine, head of the newly formed Republic Studio, cast the young radio singer and his friend, hillbilly comic Smiley Burnette, in two Ken Maynard films. Autry and Burnette were so successful that they were featured in *Tumbling Tumbleweeds* in 1935 and thereby launched into a career which reached it peak in quality and popularity in the late thirties.[24]

The Autry product, described by Everson as developing within a kind of "horse-operetta" framework, produced pretty cowgirls in short-skirted Western costume, villains operating Broadway-plush nightclubs in the western wilds, and Autry, often cast as a radio or rodeo star, singing his way out of the classic image of the Man of the West. The "frontier" milieu of the Autry films was that of the late 1930s;

> the props included high-powered cars, army tanks, airplanes, and radio stations; and the plots touched on contemporary politics, big business, social problems (the dust bowl), dairy farming as opposed to cattle ranching, problems of soil erosion and crop destruction by weeds. Against this thoroughly modern background, the traditional action ingredients— runaway stagecoaches and bar-room brawls, to say nothing of cowboys toting guns and engaging in full-scale range wars—were incongruous indeed, but here the musical elements came to the rescue.... Admittedly, at times the song and frolic aspect dominated out of all proportion, to the extent that some of the films had almost no action at all. But on the whole the balance was well maintained.... [Autry's production company] knew what was expected, and they delivered it.[25]

The Autry phenomenon, like many others of its preposterous but immensely popular kind, can only be explained in terms of the right combination of creative and interpretive talent striking a response from an audience in the mood to accept it at the time.

Joseph Kane, who directed both Autry and Rogers vehicles, considered the films musicals rather than Westerns. Kane felt that first Autry (as a popular country and western singer) and then Rogers (as an intensely studio-promoted successor) profited from the response of a great segment of the American Southern audience loyal to the "Grand Old Opry" tradition.[26] This possibility of adding a country audience to Western fans could broaden the base of faithful followers of the genre in the film medium. Other factors involved during these years between the slow and painful recovery from the Great Depression and the gathering storm of the Second World War would need careful examination in order to recreate the total picture. The results, however, were manifest in most willing and extremely generous suspension of disbelief allowing the amalgam of absurd anachronisms and something-for-everyone approach that characterized the 1930s singing cowboy version of the Western myth.

Autry's success, of course, raised a host of imitators. One of these, Roy Rogers, was developed by Autry's own studio employer, Republic, as a second-string singing cowboy star. Development of back-up actors and actresses was a common practice of studios at this time and served a purpose that was more to the advantage of the studio than the star. Second-stringers kept the stars in line, since it became obvious that a younger—and possibly more talented—version of the same type was not only available, but working under contract to the same studio.[27]

Rogers had been appearing in bit parts at Republic and singing with "The Sons of the Pioneers" for some years before he was "discovered" with a starring role in 1938 and then developed by the studio into a personality in his own films. Republic did not concentrate its image-building effort upon Rogers, however, until Autry joined the armed forces during World War II, at which time the studio lauched the "King of the Cowboys" image and consequently Rogers' stardom. Rogers was supported in his rising film career by his horse "Trigger," his leading lady—later his wife—Dale Evans, and Gabby Hayes as comedy sidekick. Deliberately designed after the Autry image, Roy Rogers represents an adaptation that is nonetheless closer than Autry to the myth of earlier tradition.

Other aspiring cowboy singers of the late 1930s and early 1940s were: Tex Ritter, Bob Baker, Jack Randall, Smith Ballew, James Newill, Fred Scott, and Dick Foran; and in the 1940s, Jimmy Wakely, Eddie Dean, Monte Hale, and Rex Allen (who also yodeled). Whether through mismanagement, lack of talent, or an unfortunate combination of production circumstances—none achieved the stature enjoyed by both Autry and Rogers during this period.

Many of the steady, popular, and neat little B-Western productions that were consistently turned out during the thirties and early forties relied upon another format than that of the singing cowboy. A good number of "trio" Westerns were introduced, in which the usual lone cowboy or the cowboy-and-sidekick team was expanded into three Westerners as heroes of the films. The most famous of these teams was the Three Mesquiteers, developed by popular writer William Colt MacDonald and first produced in 1935. A year later, Republic bought the rights and made sixteen films in a two-year period with Robert Livingston, Ray Corrigan, and Max Terhune playing the trio in most of the series.[28] The Mesquiteer films ended in 1943 but two other trio series—the Rough Riders and the Trail Blazers—were developed by Monogram during the 1940s.

The Western genre elements of action, suspense, and the melodramatic hero-villain conflict also adapted well to the serial format, which had attained great popularity during the presound years. Several months prior to Universal's *Flash Gordon* serial in 1935, Gene Autry appeared in his first starring role as a cowboy involved in a science-fiction adventure called *The Phantom Empire* and set in a mysterious underground city. Other Western serials of the 1930s starred Ken Maynard in *Mystery Mountain* (1934), Tom Mix in *The Miracle Rider* (1935; his first serial and last film), Harry Carey in *The Vanishing Legion* (1931), Johnny Mack Brown in *The Rustlers of Red Dog* (1935), and William Elliott in *The Great Adventures of Wild Bill Hickok* (1938). One of the most popular of the serials was *The Lone Ranger* produced by Republic in 1938 and based upon the highly successful radio series.[29] The serials reached their peak in the midthirties; Fenin and Everson attribute the demise of the serial to rising production costs and the spectre of television. This new medium would develop in its early years its own unique brand of character continuity—rather than plot continuity—in the form of "series" instead of "serials."[30]

In the epic tradition of *The Covered Wagon* and *The Iron Horse,* the thirties also attempted to depict the saga of the West in broader scope than that provided by the Bs and the Autry or Rogers products. Between 1926 and 1932 the film industry was experimenting with innovations other than that of sound. Three-dimensional films had been attempted and discarded but in 1930, two Westerns—King Vidor's *Billy the Kid* and Raoul Walsh's *The Big Trail*—were shot in 70mm for wide-screen presentation (with the standard 35mm versions being filmed at the same time). Stills from these two films illustrate the possibilities of the wide screen for enhancing genre, but the 70mm process remained only briefly and as a gimmick. A year later Wesley Ruggles' *Cimarron,* with the panorama of its memorable Cherokee Strip land rush, was filmed in the standard 35mm process.

Other Westerns of epic proportions produced in the 1930s were: Edwin Carewe's *The Spoilers* (1930), Edward L. Cahn's *Law and Order* (1932), James Cruze's *Sutter's Gold* (1936, originally to be directed by Sergei Eisenstein), C.B. DeMille's *The Plainsman* (1936, with Gary Cooper as Wild Bill Hickok),[31] Frank Lloyd's *Wells Fargo* (1937, with Joel McCrea), King Vidor's *The Texas Rangers* (1936), James Hogan's *The Texans* (1938, with Randolph Scott), and DeMille's *Union Pacific* (1939). These films, though unequal in quality, provided the seedbed for the growth of an epic tradition in the Western genre that reached a cinematic watershed in 1939—John Ford's *Stagecoach.*

From Ford To Freud: The "Golden Age" of the Western

Although many film critics, particularly the French, have considered *Stagecoach* the epitome of the Western genre and tend to measure all others against it, William Everson's brief comment upon the significance of the film is perhaps closer to the truth and a better point of departure for placing the film in the proper perspective. *Stagecoach,* says Everson, "was not the screen's first adult Western, its first poetic Western, or its first literary Western, but it was the first one in a long while to combine those elements so effectively."[32] Employing a classic—though improbable—cast of characters thrown together by the device of a journey, Ford placed the emphasis upon character rather than star personality, situation rather than action plotting. This approach has certainly been attempted before, but the very "smallness" of the characters and simplicity flung against the vast and wildly beautiful wilderness of Monument Valley create an exquisite and finely wrought film balancing the scope of epic with the intensity of dramatic cinema. The question of whether *Stagecoach* is the best Western ever made (it does, in fact, contain many flaws) is less important, it seems, than the impetus and example it gave to other film makers by indicating the possibilities of what might be done.[33]

What in fact did happen to the genre after *Stagecoach* marked a distinct shift from many of the standard treatments of the thirties in both content and approach. Content focused on restored interest in historical and biographical subjects, providing a rather curious mixture of authenticity and romanticism in the portrayal of myth as history.

Outlaws treated as heroes and portrayed by stars appeared in sympathetic stories of the badman who somehow wasn't as bad as history said he was. Tyrone Power starred in *Jesse James* in 1939, Robert Taylor played *Billy the Kid* in 1941, and the ambiguous Wyatt Earp was apotheosized through Henry Fonda in *My Darling Clementine* in 1946. A serious film starring Gary Cooper, *The Westerner* (1939), produced an excellent characterization of Judge Roy Bean by Walter Brennan, and Randolph Scott starred in *When the Daltons Rode* (1940). The unseen threat of Geronimo had appeared in *Stagecoach;* a few months later Paramount had produced (with the aid of an extensive pastiche of both silent and sound stock footage) the last of the great warriors in his own story and starring Chief Thundercloud as Geronimo. Indian fighter Custer was heroically portrayed by Errol Flynn in *They Died With Their Boots On* (1941) and William F. Cody was romanticized by the popular Joel McCrea in *Buffalo Bill* (1944).

For the most part these films represented a return to a more realistic tradition of authenticity in locale and costuming, yet the portrayal of the historical characters wove both new and old versions of the myth into an exciting, more sympathetic story. The result was a paradoxical amalgam of what seemed to be an authentic picture of the Old West, while factually the Old Westerners moved deeper and deeper into the mist of legend. The results, however, were visually and emotionally exciting and—most important of all for both industry and audience—highly entertaining.[34]

While the content focused upon historical characters, or at least recreated the Western milieu with a greater technical skill and authenticity, the films of the 1940s approached the genre in a variety of ways. Like Polonius' complex categories, the Western was not only biographical-historical, it was often a satirical, erotic, psychological, and social potpourri.

The Marx Brothers heeded Horace Greeley in *Go West* (1940), but with less success than some of their ventures to other lands. Jack Benny, Bob Hope, Dean Martin and Jerry Lewis, Abbott and Costello all parodied the genre as Mack Sennett, Doug Fairbanks, and—in a less athletic manner—Will Rogers had done before them. James Garner would attempt further satire in television's *Maverick* later on in the next decade. In 1939 James Stewart and Marlene Dietrich had teamed in *Destry Rides Again* and Everson, calling the film a "kind of tongue-in-cheek *Blue Angel,*" credits it with introducing sex to the western.

Still another remake of the Billy the Kid legend brought both sex and the censors out of hiding as eroticism found a home on the range. In 1942 *The*

Outlaw was promoted with a "now it can be shown" campaign that launched the career of Jane Russell, confirmed what those who wanted to believed about Howard Hughes, and returned Jack Buetel (as hero Billy) to the obscurity from which he sprang. *The Outlaw* was followed by *Duel in the Sun* (renamed "Lust in the Dust" by wags or the morally indignant or both) in 1946, with Jennifer Jones playing the half-breed heroine and Gregory Peck the no-good hero.

Yellow Sky in 1948 again starred Gregory Peck as a hero, but in the good badman tradition; Anne Baxter provided an excellent and earthy portrayal of the heroine who forces the badman to go good. Other films of the forties explored the complexities of the good badman's dilemma, some with greater depth than others. Ford's *The Three Godfathers* (1949) played upon the theme with characteristic Fordian romanticism. In sharp contrast, John Huston's gritty *Treasure of the Sierra Madre* (1948) might be considered a borderline Western in contemporary setting with excellent performances by Humphrey Bogart, Walter Huston, Tim Holt, and the ubiquitous and deliciously evil Alfonso Bedoya.

Social consciousness was reinforced in the forties through *The Ox-Bow Incident* (1942), William Wellman's unevenly realized adaptation of the Clark novel. Howard Hawks' *Red River* (1948) again dramatized the conflict between individual and individual, and individual and the community or group.[35] Money-hungry adventurers betraying and destroying one another, voices of reason drowned out by the opinion of a fearful majority, strong-minded individuals selecting the course of action for the group—these were the disturbing themes of the Huston, Wellman, and Hawks films of the middle and late forties.

There are some who have always maintained that the artist—consciously or unconsciously—is more sensitive to the currents and shifting moods of the day; others feel that it is more a case of coincidence. In June of 1945, the Western desert near Los Alamos was split with a ball of flame that opened up yet another new frontier; in August of that year the world discovered what could happen to those on the losing end of the argument. The atomic age dawned, and with it a new and perhaps deeper look at the tension between an individual's responsibility to the group and one's responsibility to one's own conscience.

The film of the late forties reflected the conflict. Henry King's *The Gunfighter* appeared in 1950 as a tortured, psychological dilemma—a fatalistic complex of internal motives, external forces, and violent climaxes that were not really solutions but only raised more and bewildering questions.[36]

After countless wartime caricatures of racial and national characteristics of the enemy, a Western produced in 1950 attempted to portray a nonwhite man in a different light. Director Delmar Daves claimed his *Broken Arrow* to be the first sound film that treated the Indian with any reality and sympathy. Though Daves (or someone else involved in the production) did not feel that the audience was ready for a happily-ever-after marriage between an Indian woman and a white man, the director did introduce an Indian-white love relationship as an acceptable possibility rather than as an exotic romance. The woman in question, however, was played by non-Indian Debra Paget, with frequent-Indian Jeff Chandler as Cochise. The white man was the impeccably American James Stewart.

In 1952 Elia Kazan extracted from history a nonwhite hero whom any Anglo strong man would envy. Marlon Brando's intense portrayal of the legendary Mexican patriot in *Viva Zapata* provided the audience with both a mythic theme and an epic sense of history. *High Noon* appeared in the same year, but with a too self-conscious dose of social awareness that linked it very closely in some critics' minds (although it is not all that certain that it should be) with the paranoia raised by the Army-McCarthy hearings. The theme of *High Noon*—repeated in *3:10 to Yuma* (1957) with Van Heflin as the lone man and Glenn Ford as the world-weary badman—was that of the individual deserted by the group yet remaining faithful to his convictions.[37]

But social consciousness notwithstanding, business remained business and preoccupation with the growing popularity of television in the late forties became the chief business of the film industry.

Television as Bad Guy: The New Western and the New Western Hero

The concept "new" has always held a revered position in the American consciousness. If something is new, it is somehow good—indeed, better than what preceded it. Upon this shaky premise the already-researched innovations of three-dimensional, wide-screen, and wraparound image and sound were introduced to the shrinking moviegoing population. Wide screen lent itself to spectacle (one of the first attempts was Henry Koster's *The Robe* in 1953); and what better spectacle could be conceived than the panorama of the Western landscape in larger doses than had been previously experienced by the audience? Bigger, however, did not always mean better; the wide screen did not always enhance the Western. On the contrary, in the hands of less than skilled film makers the vast surface of the wide screen only served to emphasize the director's inability to use the new dimension. However, there were notable exceptions; for example, Bazin comments that Anthony Mann used Cinemascope in *The Man from Laramie* (1955) not as "a new format but as an extension of the space around man."[38] But for several years the exceptions were few. Thus the film makers wrestled with the problem of new technology while the Western hero did battle with his own mixed needs and drives as often as he faced the traditional walkdown.

During the fifties heroes appeared who, like their projected image, were much larger than life-size. Fred Zinneman's *High Noon* provided Gary Cooper with the most famous role of his career and assured him a place in the gallery of Western heroes. A year later Alan Ladd joined him and Jack Palance was enshrined as the ultimate villain thanks to George Stevens' *Shane.* In this film, and in spite of Ladd's small physical size, the image of the hero was apotheosized to full-blown mythic proportions, aided by wide-screen technology and the natural advantages of the spectacular Jackson Hole, Wyoming locations.

Nicholas Ray produced his first Western, *Johnny Guitar,* in 1951—a bizarre film with dark, Freudian undertones in which Joan Crawford and familiar, but understandably uncomfortable Westerners (Sterling Hayden, Ernest Borgnine, Scott Brady, Ward Bond, and John Carradine) jerkily played out the strange story. Miss Peggy Lee presided over the closing moments with song.

The career of John Wayne developed rapidly in important studio products of the fifties. Expert direction and career management helped to create Wayne's own brand of hero persona in John Farrow's *Hondo* (1953), Howard Hawks' *Rio Bravo* (1959), and John Ford's *The Searchers* (1956). Meanwhile Ford himself was reinforcing his own vision of the West in his cavalry trilogy and *Wagonmaster* from 1948 to 1950, with more Westerns to come.

Anthony Mann provided a series of interesting Westerns during the decade of the fifties: *Devil's Doorway* (1950), *Winchester 73* (1950), *The Furies* (1950), *Bend of the River* (1952), *The Naked Spur* (1952), *The Far Country* (1954), *The Man from Laramie* (1955), *The Last Frontier* (1955), *The Tin Star* (1957), *Man of the West* (1958), and *Cimarron* (1960). The better of these films portrayed the subconscious violence latent in the hero and his half-earnest struggle to overcome it. The hero, like other great men, bears within him the seeds of evil and destruction.

In 1957 this darker side of Wyatt Earp and Doc Holliday was displayed in John Sturges' *Gunfight at the OK Corral,* a film which attempted a low-key, documentary approach to material that had already been done and redone in far more romantic style.

During the war and postwar years, the A-Westerns continued to develop old content in new forms, reflecting the growing interest and sophistication of an ever-increasing film audience. When television began to appear increasingly foreboding, films became more elaborate in epic elements and all-star casts, in stunning production values (color, for example, was used more often),[39] and in desperately hyperbolic advertising campaigns.

Meanwhile, back at the B-Western production companies, both the independents and the big studios were attempting to keep up the steady stream of B staples that had existed side by side with the A tradition since the early years. Monogram and Republic in particular were the strongest producers in the B tradition, but even here, and despite a resurgence in the early 1940s, the budget problems became more and more formidable and finally insurmountable. At first corners were cut by combining contract stars in the same film. The production values themselves became shabby; stock footage—always a staple for Westerns and with sources extending back into the silents—was employed more and more often. Running inserts for chase sequences were replaced by pan shots, which were usually less interesting but always less expensive. The serial Westerners fought the Nazis during the war; when the cold war developed, they defended Western uranium deposits against "foreign powers."[40] The most formidable enemy, however, was television, and by the middle fifties both the serials and the Bs had become a chapter in film history.

There were, however, a few bright flashes before the B-Western disappeared. One was the work of Harry Sherman, producer of the Hopalong Cassidy Westerns and an old hand at the genre, who starred Richard Dix in a series of high-calibre, B-class films. During the decade of the fifties there also appeared several B-Westerns that were small, finely wrought, and classical in structure. These were directed by Bud Boetticher, first for Universal and later for the Ranown production company formed by Harry Joe Brown and Randolph Scott, who also starred in the later films.

The 1940s and early 1950s saw stars, directors, and technical advances developing; the genre during the period took on a new look with more complex approaches to traditional material and the further development of controversial themes. Fenin and Everson list sex, neurosis, and racial consciousness as key concepts in Westerns of this period. Lawrence Alloway, in his study of violence in American films from 1946 to 1964, cites postwar attitudes of cynicism joined to an interest in psychoanalysis and existentialism as strong factors in the metamorphosis of the prewar into the postwar action film:

> It is not the dogmatic use of the skepticism, the popular psychoanalysis, or the vernacular existentialism in particular films that is significant; it is their combined diffusion that turned the prewar action film (basically athletic and cheerful) into the more savage, more pessimistic film of violence with its gallery of extreme situations and desperate heroes.[41]

Not only was life more complex and the future less certain for the heroes of the screen, but the giants of the film industry were also fighting—and not always winning—battles to keep their strength intact.

In 1948, the Supreme Court decison in the Paramount case stripped the major corporations of the theatre link in the industry's monopoly. Stars who had been dissatisfied with the studio system became aware of the bargaining power of their own now-established images and did not renew studio contracts. Television antennae were sprouting on rooftops throughout the land.

But while the new medium was keeping the old film audiences away from movie theatres, it was at the same time developing a breed of directors many of whom would eventually move into the film industry to cross-breed video and cinema techniques. One of these directors, Arthur Penn, made his first film, *The*

Left-handed Gun, in 1958, with Paul Newman portraying a tortured, psycho-analytic bundle of drives as Billy the Kid. The Western hero had now become the victim of the modern age—a far different good badman from Anderson's Bronco Billy, Hart's Blaze Tracey, or Wayne's Ringo Kid.

The fifties had seen a showdown between film and that maverick claim-jumper television. When the smoke cleared, the upstart newcomer seemed to have emerged victorious and the film industry limped away to lick its wounds and rethink how it might win back its rightful place. The proposed solution was called the "adult Western:" wide-screen sagas, myth-size heroes, and finally, by the end of the fifties, the rediscovery of Freud and all that follows.

Violence as Good Guy: The Anti-Western and the Antihero

The early sixties saw the death of a man who had participated in the creation of both the history and the myth of the Western hero. In 1962, Al Jennings, one-time outlaw and later small-time actor and advisor for Western films, died—presumably with his boots off—at the venerable age of ninety-eight. Having experienced both the reality and the fantasy of the Western legend, Jennings may have wondered during his last years about the increasing interest in the more gritty, violent, and fatalistic aspects of the legend.

Indeed, the early sixties saw some interesting variations upon the tradition-al themes. Borrowing from Akira Kurosawa's *Seven Samurai* (itself a borrow-ing from the American Western savior-of-the-town theme borrowed from the classical rebirth-through-death theme), John Sturges directed the multi-heroed *The Magnificent Seven* (1960). Marlon Brando was one of the few actors at that time to direct himself in a film, relying upon his old waterfront second-lead Karl Malden to provide a thoroughly dishonorable opponent in a violent revenge tale, *One-Eyed Jacks* (1961). After a long absence from Hollywood and some work in television Sam Peckinpah directed two Westerns with journey themes in 1962—*Ride the High Country* and *The Deadly Companions*—and all but rejected his 1965 study of the tortured megalomania of a cavalry commander in *Major Dundee.*[42]

Meanwhile, the old master John Ford was continually moving toward nostalgia as he proceeded into the decade of the sixties, providing a starring role for a man who could never be a Western hero because he was black—Woody Strode in *Sergeant Rutledge* (1960); a "way west" revenge film that was less successful that *Wagonmaster—Two Rode Together* (1961); an elegy for the dying Westerner and the fading frontier in *The Man Who Shot Liberty Valance* (1962); and an other-side-of-the-coin view of the white man's victory over the Indian in *Cheyenne Autumn* (1964).

LeMay's novel, *The Unforgiven,* provided material for a weaker film version in 1960 of a smoldering problem that would burst into both ideological and real conflagration in the civil rights turmoil of the decade.[43] In 1967, however, Paul Newman portrayed a man of ambiguous origin in Martin Ritt's *Hombre*. This film was a far more powerful, albeit subtle, study of a racial outsider.

In the same year, John Wayne's long cherished dream of recreating the battle of the Alamo became a nightmare of personal disappointment when it was greeted less than enthusiastically by both critics and popular audiences. Three years later a project almost as formidable as the Westward movement itself was produced under the title of *How the West Was Won* (1963). Heavily burdened with directors, stars, publicity campaigns, excessive length, and spectacles of natural and manufactured wonders, the film virtually sank beneath its own weight. A television revival in 1973, with the added disadvantage of diminishment in size, served only to call attention to the film's emptiness.

Veteran Hollywood director John Huston, unknown David Miller,[44] and newcomer from television Martin Ritt each offered films in the early sixties that examined the cowboy hero myth gone sour. In what had to be an uncalculated stroke of casting genius, Huston united aging Clark Gable, troubled Marilyn Monroe, and loner Montgomery Clift as three outsiders who belonged to another time and another way of life. Although *The Misfits* (1961) provided a character study of the standard Western types—the aging cowboy, the castoff dance-hall girl, the unsuccessful rodeo rider—the contemporary setting provided a powerful background and sharp contrast for the rich characterization of the three stars.

While *The Misfits* emphasized traditional character types out of the context of the time, Miller's *Lonely Are the Brave* in 1962 explored the theme of the Western man's lost frontier freedom with sometimes poignant, sometimes heavy-handed symbolism. Producer-star Kirk Douglas' residual image as long-time cowboy hero helped the film, without doubt, over the rough spots.

A year later, the third "contemporary Western," *Hud,* served to further develop the rising career of Paul Newman and earned an Oscar for Patricia Neal in her role of the earthy, tough ranch housekeeper. Melvin Douglas played the first-generation self-made rancher, father to no-good Newman and his hero-worshipping younger brother Brandon DeWilde, who ten years before had worshipped another and eminently more worthy hero in *Shane*. *Hud* is by far the most bitter, most sour of these three negative views of Western myths.

In 1965, Silverstein's *Cat Ballou* parodied the genre with an uneven tone redeemed by the remarkable performance of Lee Marvin in the dual role of menacing silver-nosed badman and drink-sodden has-been gunfighter.[45] Stubby Kaye and Nat King Cole provided comic Brechtian commentary in their performance of the title song throughout the film's series of careening stagecoaches, wild shootouts, and hairbreadth escapes. Two years later, Arthur Penn's *Bonnie and Clyde* would rework much of the same material to infuse new life into a more complex and multileveled characterization of two Depression Era outlaws which confounded critics, enraged public moralists, and further contributed to the steadily growing cult of outlaws as heroic figures.

Indeed, the second half of the sixties saw an increasing move toward the glorification of the loner or outsider hero whose values, methods, and allegiances were more and more often in direct opposition to those of the establishment. The Western was not the only genre affected.

Gone was the private eye of the thirties who could operate throughout the film under the shadow of police suspicion, but who (we knew!) would in the final moments be able to toss off a hard-boiled comeback or wry joke over the whole misunderstanding after he had exposed the killer. Gone, too, were the war heroes of the forties—the GIs or tough captains who were only doing their duty but were proud to be playing on Uncle Sam's team.

Instead, there was a seemingly irreparable rift developing between establishment and hero; he received no support in his endeavors and he asked for none. Constantly betrayed by the establishment, he trusted only himself and began to rely more and more upon his own physical strength, intellectual and instinctual cunning, and ability to—as Marlon Brando put it so aptly in expressing his waterfront philosophy—"get them before they get you."

Thus, during the late sixties the bad guys of each action genre became the good guys, the good guys became the corrupt exploiters of the underdog, and the only recourse—or at any rate, the most popular one—was to retaliate against that exploitation by further acts of violence.

Indeed, the sixties was a decade of violence. Unrest, upheaval, and withdrawal surged across the nation, and the mass media brought it all into the living room just before supper. As the decade drew exhaustingly and not regretfully to a close, the Americans had witnessed their fellow citizens stepping onto the surface of the moon or across police barricades; shooting famous political figures or bombing unknown Southeast Asians; dropping out of a society that they felt had betrayed them or turning on to drugs that they hoped would create new societies; and destroying property and lives on ivy-covered suburban campuses and in decaying inner-city ghettos. With all this came the dull but steadily rising fear that the planet Earth itself was threatened by too many people, too much pollution, too little concern for the conservation of that which nature had provided to insure continued life. The queston of life itself, in fact, seemed to be more and more at stake—the value of life, decisions about who should live, the possibility of continued life, the quality of life of a growing segment of the American population.

It is not at all surprising, then, that the films of the sixties grew more "serious," increasingly reflective of the turbulence of the events of the day, and less escapist and entertaining in both content and treatment. Supported by a variety of genre offerings, superstars, and virtuoso cinematic style and technology, the films of the late sixties still mirrored the murky themes troubling the American consciousness.

Even a sampling of titles illustrates the continuum from mediocrity to artistic excellence. The stability of recurrent themes is evident as well. In 1966: *The Sound of Music, Georgie Girl, Alfie, Dr. Zhivago, 2001: A Space Odyssey, Who's Afraid of Virginia Woolf?, Fahrenheit 451, Khartoum, Thunderball.* In 1967: *The Graduate, Cool Hand Luke, Guess Who's Coming to Dinner, Blow Up, The Sand Pebbles, In Cold Blood, Casino Royale, Elvira Madigan, Bonnie and Clyde, Camelot.* In 1968: *Bullitt, The Green Berets, Madigan, Midnight Cowboy, Planet of the Apes, Rosemary's Baby, The Thomas Crown Affair.* In 1969: *Medium Cool, Alice's Restaurant, Bob and Carol and Ted and Alice, Che!, Coming Apart, Easy Rider, Goodbye, Columbus, I am Curious (Yellow), If...*, *They Shoot Horses, Z.*

A sampling of Westerns during those same years indicates the development of the same themes within the limitations of the genre format. *Nevada Smith* (1966) portrayed Steve McQueen as a loner on horseback instead of on a motorcycle, while Charlton Heston provided a pleasantly low-key performance as a lonely cowpoke in the underrated *Will Penny* (1967). A less harmonious but possibly more interesting group than the Magnificent Seven gathered in *The Professionals* (1966) to generate risk and spectacular action in saving an unhappy wife fleeing from a heartless Anglo husband to her Mexican lover—without doubt a different look at the growing consciousness of nonwhite human dignity as portrayed in the genre.

Welcome to Hard Times (1967) pictured Henry Fonda as a down-and-out Westerner—an almost cruel inversion of his role in *My Darling Clementine* of twenty-one years before. Old and embittered, the Fonda character cannot protect the town, the woman he loved long ago, or even his own dignity from the ravages of sadistic badman Aldo Ray. Almost nightmarish in its constant rejection of the comfort of the traditional genre format, the film ends on a note of quiet dignity and tenuous hope that is a distinct departure from the customary view of the Western as escapist fare and the residual image of Fonda as triumphant hero.

The following year *Firecreek* again starred Fonda—this time as the doomed outlaw opposing lawman James Stewart. Here again, the black and white situation turns to shades of grey in a dilemma that is more life than art. Fonda's outsider is a man who has deliberately chosen a path that can only end in his destruction; he therefore has nothing to lose by playing out the game. Stewart, like most of us, has much to lose if he faces a showdown—his life, his home and family, even Fonda who was his old friend. It is a situation of the haves versus the have-nots propelled by their past choices into unwilling opposition in order to defend those choices. It is also the painful position of America today.

Meanwhile, back at the myth, Howard Hawks was winding up the second and third of his John Wayne action films that also happened to be set in the West: *El Dorado* in 1967 and *Rio Lobo* in 1971 (*Rio Bravo* had set the pace in 1959).

But deep in the badlands of the European frontier, Italian director Sergio Leone was fashioning a Western hero type out of a little-known American actor named Clint Eastwood, featuring him in a series of extremely violent films: *A Fistful of Dollars* (1964),[46] *For a Few Dollars More* (1966), *The Good, the Bad, and the Ugly* (1967), *Once Upon a Time in the West* (1969). Though not technically American films, the Leone Westerns have played a part in the increasing preoccupation of film makers with the darker, more bitterly existential side of the hero's persona. Placed in a climate of inevitable violence, Eastwood moved with unflinching stoicism along a path strewn with blood, bullets, and bodies. The Leone Westerns are derided by some and extolled by others; they have, nonetheless, become the pattern into which the Western antihero has evolved. Although Eastwood's persona has been developed further through American films of both Western and contemporary action genre, by 1973 he had dethroned Duke Wayne as the male star with the top box office draw in the nation.

Wayne, however, won his first Oscar (after forty years of playing cowboy heroes) by playing a parody of himself in Hathaway's cinematic version of Charles Portis' novel *True Grit* (1969). Showing up extremely well against the performance of Glenn Campbell as the Texas Ranger and further expanded by stiff-upper-lip little-girl costar Kim Darby, Wayne shed his toupee, donned an eye patch, and delighted in being called a bald old fat man. It was all worth it knowing that his greatest moment would come when, with a shout to villain Robert Duvall to "fill your hand, you son-of-a-bitch!" he would gallop into the clearing toward a three-man ambush with carbine in one hand, Colt in the other, and reins clenched between his teeth.[47] It was a glorious moment; one worthy of the long-cultivated Wayne persona from Singing Sandy to Rooster Cogburn.

But the glorious moments—*True Grit* style—were the exception in the late sixties and early seventies. For the most part, the glory was more symbolic than real. After an hour or so of innocent horseplay accompanied by light-hearted (and Academy Award-winning) song, *Butch Cassidy and the Sundance Kid* (1969) ended with antiheroes Paul Newman and Robert Redford being gunned down in the dusty streets of a border town by an establishment more vengeful than law-enforcing. The similarities to Bonnie Parker and Clyde Barrow are unmistakable. The next year *The Ballad of Cable Hogue* displayed greater depth and sensitivity in its portrayal of a lovable failure, a fading Westerner in a disappearing frontier who is finally killed in mortal combat not with a dyed-in-the-wool villain but with the inevitable symbol of twentieth-century technology—a garish automobile.

Cable Hogue's director, Sam Peckinpah, had returned after the *Major Dundee* fiasco with a film that became the exemplar of the violent cinema of the sixties—*The Wild Bunch* (1969). A paean of praise to the outlaw with his back against the wall, the film placed ultimate value upon a grudging but steadfast loyalty among the group, as opposed to any viable relationship toward anyone outside that dependent, desperate bunch. While presenting all the elements of the traditional Western—the lawmen, the outlaws, the honorable and the tarnished ladies, the railroad, the town—Peckinpah depicted in final sardonic statement the bitter truth that there are no good guys, that there is loyalty (of a kind) only among thieves, and that what has replaced the dead frontier is anything but a brave new world of civilization. Audiences had had a tantalizing taste of explicit violence in the climax of *Bonnie and Clyde*. But the extended "blood ballet" of *The Wild Bunch* was considered excessive by some critics, lauded as a powerful statement by others, and came on far too strong for almost all but youthful audiences. The young, growing up on the increasingly violent events of the day, seemed more able to appreciate the existential dilemma of The Bunch and their cataclysmic demise.

As the sixties became the seventies the pattern continued: violence, explicit sex, nostalgia, and a few frightening looks into the future. A few old-style heroes appeared and many new-style antiheroes operated in the city, in the suburbs, and on the range. In every genre they fought power structures by whatever means would get the job done. They were loners still, but some new faces and features (for heroes) also appeared. Film makers moved en masse into the psyche of the black hero and the American Indian hero. These were character types eminently suited to the loner, the outsider image that had been built for the hero of the sixties. Besides, such a persona resonated well with the ethnic and racial battle cries of almost every movement of that decade. A sampling of titles in varying genres and degrees of artistry is indicative of the move toward more violent and explicit themes. The titles indicate the backlash as well.

In 1970: *Patton, Ryan's Daughter, The Boys in the Band, M*A*S*H, The Andromeda Strain, Airport, Five Easy Pieces, Myra Breckenridge, Cotton Comes to Harlem, Diary of a Mad Housewife, Joe, Catch-22, Love Story*. The most spectacular of the Western genre to appear in 1970 was Arthur Penn's *Little Big Man*, an iconoclastic look at Western heroes in both history and type, providing Dustin Hoffman with an opportunity for an acting tour de force that depicted the seven ages of man—and beyond.

In 1971: *A Clockwork Orange, Summer of '42, THX 1138, Dirty Harry, Carnal Knowledge, Fiddler on the Roof, The French Connection, Klute, The Last Picture Show, Shaft, Straw Dogs*. The Westerns of 1971 were few and less than vigorous. Peter Fonda produced an unwilling but uncanny resemblance to his father in a slow-moving but mood-producing piece called *The Hired Hand;* Paul Newman starred in another remake of *Sometimes a Great Notion*,[48] and the old master Howard Hawks slipped John Wayne gracefully out of the romantic lead position in *Rio Lobo*. Robert Altman directed a gritty version of the myth demythologized in *McCabe and Mrs. Miller*, with superstars Warren Beattie and Julie Christie providing characterizations of the now-popular outsiders caught in the now-current dilemma of the individual against the brutalizing pressures of a society of less than honorable mores.

In the political year of 1972 both legal and illegal politics took to films in *The Candidate* and *The Godfather*, but the variety of genres was still present in films like *Skyjacked, Slaughterhouse Five, Deliverance, The Emigrants, Silent Running, What's Up Doc?, Frenzy, Cabaret*, and *The Getaway*. There was slight resurgence of Westerns: John Wayne played opposite a group of youngsters in *The Cowboys;*[49] both black and white heroes appeared in *The Legend of Nigger Charley* and *Buck and the Preacher;* Steve McQueen starred as a contemporary cowboy in *Junior Bonner;* Clint Eastwood sustained his Italian-made persona in *Joe Kidd;* and Robert Duvall provided a fine characterization of a megalomaniac Jesse James in *The Great Northfield Minnesota Raid*.

During the first half of 1973 the film mythmakers depicted both historical and typical Western heroes, notably: once more around for *Pat Garrett and Billy the Kid* directed by Sam Peckinpah; a self-proclaimed romanticism of *The Life and Times of Judge Roy Bean* starring Paul Newman; an overambitious but interesting attempt to create the mountain man legend in less than two hours with Robert Redford as *Jeremiah Johnson;* and a reappearance of the Clint Eastwood man-with-no-name in *High Plains Drifter*. Duke Wayne was back in the saddle—or on board—again with Ann-Margret in *The Train Robbers* and in *Cahill, U.S. Marshal*. These films seemed to be making more extensive use of the soft lens, the wide angle shot, the simplicity of set design that seeks to reproduce the feel of past reality seen through the eyes of memory. This fond but misty look is just as often a setup for the sharp contrast of violent action integral to each of the films, yet the emphasis is still upon the individual rather than upon plot or exciting events.

And what of the audience for the Western? Like the films produced in the genre, the Western devotees are diminishing in number; like the films, the audience is more slick, sophisticated, and attuned to the particular preoccupations of the seventies—self-analysis, sex, violence, sociopolitical sensitivity (some would say touchiness). Yet whirling along in this mainstream there seems to be an undercurrent of nostalgia—not the hip or campy version of current fad—but an almost regretful sadness for what once was, a wistful looking back to what can never be again. It is the supercivilized nation ever searching for a new frontier—a people seeking to uproot itself, to loose its bonds and escape to a new land to regain lost innocence and become children again. In this dream filmgoers are no different from (indeed, are reflections of) what they see on the screen. The Western film hero is increasingly obsessed by this nostalgia. His excesses against his loved ones, his enemies, society, and himself are the manifestations of frustration in his failure to achieve his dream.

But to many filmgoers who do not want to be reminded of insoluble dilemmas after working hours, the excesses have become excessive. In the late sixties and into the seventies the audience complained that it had become increasingly difficult to assess how much is too much in the depiction of violence to both person and personality in films. The catch-phrase is "pornography of violence," and filmgoers find themselves alternately angered and appalled by what they see when they pay more than they want to for an evening of relaxation and entertainment. A Feiffer cartoon in *The Village Voice* early in 1972 underscores the dilemma: a somewhat catatonic theatre patron ensconced in a comfortable center aisle seat is staring at the screen and pondering:

> "In the old days you went to the movies to see the bad guys brutalize, terrorize and murder.
> And the good guys catch them and kill them.
> That was entertainment.
> Today you go to the movies to see the good guys brutalize, terrorize and murder.
> And the bad power structure brutalize, terrorize and murder the good guys.
> That's art.
> So the choice is no longer between good guys and bad guys.
> It's between brutalizing entertainment and brutalizing art."

And as the decade of the seventies progresses, filmgoers are still transfixed, perhaps benumbed, by the entertainment and art that the film industry continues to provide its audience.

The dilemma is not only in the story on the screen or in the mind of the viewer; it stems from the very nature of the medium itself, child that it is of both technology and art and related to both the nation's economics and its entertainment.

Like the industry itself, film Westerns began with optimism, energy, and a simplicity of viewpoint that provided a rich feeding-ground for the talent and inventiveness that came tumbling out of the tiny Hollywood studios like so many Keystone cops out of their painted-flat station house. Heroes, heroines, villains, and exciting adventures were created according to the image of those creating. Those creators, in turn, followed the lead of the current mores, causes, politics, and even fashions of the day.

Stereotypic in format, the best of the Westerns have avoided stereotype. Like any enduring form of popular culture, the genre has consistently been able to bend with the times, to reshape its image to conform to the expectations and concerns of each successive audience as the viewers relish the format in their youth, discard it disdainfully in postadolescence, and return to it once again for the sake of simplicity and perhaps a bit of comfort in maturity and old age.

Thus the West and the Westerner grew to larger than life-size, and when touched by the talent of particularly gifted legend-makers the American Ulysses could match his epic adventures with any tradition however ancient of the already-ancient world. Without blinking an eye, the mythmakers spun a web of fantasy about the few and far-between facts of history and created a West whose story—as the prologue states in introducing *The Life and Times of Judge Roy Bean*—if it was not really this way, it should have been.

The Film Mythmakers:
The Way It Should Have Been

In so vast an array of films during a span of more than seventy years, what deliberate choices or serendipitous happenstances have provided memorable experiences for the film audience? And which film makers have set about to create significant works in the Western genre? Choices are always hazardous, critics' choices seriously so. There is danger of idolatry and iconoclasm, inclusion and omission in making any selection of directors or films to be examined in detail. The directors chosen for examination here have been selected with several views in mind: first, their combined work spans nearly the entire history of film making in America; second, both have produced a body of significant film products in the Western genre; and finally, each could represent in categorical terms a unique and highly successful approach to the Western myth and the Western hero—Ford, that of the romantic; Peckinpah, that of the realist-iconoclast.

John Ford and Sam Peckinpah have both contributed significantly to the film image of the Western hero. Like the Coopers, the numberless Beadle hacks, and the Ned Buntlines of the literary Western, each of these directors has consistently brought to his work a specialized view of the world of the film Western. Moreover, both film makers have played upon the character of the Man of the West while remaining within the boundaries that distinguish that character from the historical hero, the gangster, or the "good guy." Thus the Ford and Peckinpah approaches to the hero can be useful in illuminating facets of the Western genre itself. Whether his perspective is personal or historical, mythic or academic, most certainly each director's manner of handling form and content does indicate those facets of the myth that interest him enough to develop them through the persona of the hero. The approaches, themes, and development of these directors may be seen most clearly by looking closely at some representative films.

John Ford: The Hero Mythologized

It is only reasonable that a man who directed some one hundred and twenty-five films in his fifty-year career should exhibit a wide variety of themes and subject matter. Yet John Ford wanted to be remembered for his Westerns, and he consistently worked within a limited number of themes in developing them.

Director Sidney Lumet has been quoted as saying, "There's one general premise: almost anything that any one of us has done you can find in a John Ford film."[50] Most other film makers would probably agree. Beginning in 1914 as a stuntman and less-than-topnotch actor in his brother Francis'films, by 1917 John was directing the first of many Western heroes ranging from Harry Carey, Sr. to Duke Wayne. About half of his work was outside the Western genre, but the totality of the Ford film canon is warmly and romantically Americana.

Although Ford's Westerns all bear the hallmark of their maker, they do change in attitude toward the genre. This shift, however, is more reflective of Ford's changing perspective with the passing years than of the altered expectations of his audience. Two Ford Westerns, *My Darling Clementine* in 1946 and *The Man Who Shot Liberty Valance* in 1961 illustrate a reversal of attitude toward the Western myth. Situation and character types overlap, but the theme turns upon itself in the years between 1946 and 1961.

In 1946 William S. Hart died. That same year the world was gathering up the pieces after a war that was to end all wars. Americans, however, were on the winning side. The Allies had achieved terms of unconditional surrender; the world had been made safe for Democracy; the American Way had once more triumphed over its enemies. In many ways it was the classic heroic legend come to life again—a large-scale version of the nation's earlier victory over its own Western frontier enemies decades before. The hero's retaliation only after he had first been attacked by the villain, the triumph of good over evil, the preservation of the community's way of life, the defense of the weak and the innocent—all those themes dear to the American heart appeared not only on a worldwide scale but on movie screens throughout the land.

Mythmaker John Ford retold the tale in the visual terms he knew best; 1946 was also the year of *My Darling Clementine*. Not a jingoistic tract, not a vehicle for triumphalism, the film is reflective of the mood of the time yet stands on its own cinematic merit as an artwork whose appeal is not timebound. It is a fond and loving look at the Western myth with the sense of history that was uniquely Ford's own.

As *My Darling Clementine* epitomizes the early Ford hero, Henry Fonda epitomized the type of actor Ford used to portray that hero—tall, lean, with an air of innocence, and projecting a curious mixture of shyness and determination. But despite the director's comments to the contrary, neither Fonda's Wyatt Earp nor Ford's gunfight at the OK Corral is faithful to the facts of history. Both, however, are eminently faithful to the myth.

The Tombstone days of Wyatt Earp are framed within the two subtly different images of the West that open and close the film. The opening is on a wide expanse of the Arizona territory—uncharted, wild, and beautiful—and provides a backdrop for a straggling group of riders and cattle. The first image of the Earp brothers is in harmony with the terrain. They are bearded men; their clothes are rough and weather-stained; if anyone can survive in such country, these are the men who can. They are mountain men moving deeper into the wilderness.

The closing images of the film underscore the changes that have taken place in Wyatt Earp, in Tombstone, and by implication in the West as well. This is a picture that is more familiar to us today than the open range. The land seems to have become almost a meadow. A dirt road stretches out into the distance; a wooden fence marks the boundaries of "owned" land—a sure sign that the Garden has come. A buckboard is following the road. A girl is standing near the fence; a man on horseback is saying goodbye. But he is a different person from the Wyatt Earp who first rode into Tombstone. He has been touched by civilization and it has changed him both in physical appearance and in spiritual outlook, but the old ambivalence of the Western man remains. Earp is not settling down in Tombstone. He is moving on to California, but his parting words are, "Ma'am, I sure like that name—Clementine." His appearance is more genteel, more civilized (since his encounter with the Tombstone Tonsorial Parlor), yet he has just emerged from a gunfight having killed several men and is no doubt headed for more of the same. There is an indication of hard times to come in the natural, yet visually strong image of the rugged butte in the distance, rising up at what seems to be Wyatt's destination and imposing itself in the way. The wilderness, it seems to say, will continue to resist the Garden.

Between these opening and closing images, the film plays repeatedly upon human ambivalence toward the wilderness and the Garden in a manner more visual and subtle than the narrative explicitness of *The Man Who Shot Liberty Valance. Clementine* is more carefully constructed—as well as more carefully made—than *Liberty Valance,* and this is evident in the exquisite composition and development of its series of contrasting images. Some are vignettes; others are extended versions of the metaphor.

One of the first of these images depicts Wyatt Earp's initial glimpse of Tombstone. As they ride across the desert, the Earp brothers pause on a rise to look down upon the cluster of tiny wooden buildings. The sorry little town in the hollow of the valley is dwarfed by the majestic country that holds it. The only indications that this tiny thing is alive are pinpoints of light and the faint tinkle of the barroom piano drifting up into the hills. It is a good moment—vividly reflecting the tenuous hold that civilization has scratched upon the savage terrain that it ultimately expects (how brash, how foolish!) to conquer.

The images constantly move from attempts at civilization to reaffirmations of barbarism. When the Earp brothers return to their camp that night they find James, the youngest, murdered. There is a sternly but delicately composed shot of his head and shoulders as they discover him; a horse's hoof and a man's booted foot are in the frame; hands are reaching down to the body; a cactus is partially reflected in a pool of rain. The dark powers of the wilderness have touched the Earp family for the first time.

Much later in the film, and as part of a longer sequence, Ford juxtaposes two other facets of the conflict, with Earp directing and presiding over both. One is the attempt to save Chihuahua's life by a Doc Holliday who has regained his integrity; the other is the vengeful ride after her killer, Billy Clanton. Virg Earp, sent by Wyatt to get Billy, has never lost his integrity, but he does lose his life at the end of the chase. The arts of civilization are attempting to save one life while primitive urges seek to destroy another. The mourners of each death are presented in striking contrast as well: Doc, Wyatt, and Clementine in honest grief on one hand, and the treacherous Clantons luring Virg to his death on the other.

The two longest sequences illustrating the contrast and conflict between civilization and savagery are, of course, those of the Sunday morning in Tombstone and the gunfight at the OK Corral. Perhaps the most striking element of both is the perfect logic with which they fit into the narrative of the story, yet the symbolic weight that each carries in the positing of the myth of the West and the affirmation of the Western hero.

In the Sunday morning sequence, the composition of Wyatt's face framed by the barber's mirror; the barber's and Wyatt's faces framed in turn within the film itself; the uncomfortable gaze of one and the delighted smile of the other—all are natural reactions to the real situation, and yet they tell a great deal about the men they depict. Wyatt is somewhat disoriented; he sees himself as the same man yet somehow no longer the same. He has been changed by the scissors and scents of a world foreign to him. The barber, on the other hand, has deliberately set out to change Earp from a man of the wilderness to an acceptable member of the community. ("It's the latest thing from the East!") Furthermore, the little man is delighted with his part in touching up the myth a bit to make it more suitable to a genteel audience.

Then follows the slow, rhythmic movement of the central segment: Wyatt stepping out into the hazy sunlight, the Earp brothers easily and half-heartedly planning their day, family buckboards moving leisurely toward the site of the church. As the brothers recall home, Sunday scrubbings, and the scent of honeysuckle (Wyatt: "That's me. Barber."), we realize that these rough men really do have roots in the past, making the present and future all that more pleasant and important to them. The encounter with the heroine, the first moments of understanding between them, and the hero's second (after the barber's triumph) submission to the demands of civilization—these episodes move easily into his stiff but dignified walk to the church site, the lady on his arm. The third submission takes place at the church site and amid profusion of physical objects symbolizing the fledgeling community: the church floor, the bell scaffolding, the flag, the family wagons, the wooden store in the background, the towering butte in the distance. And again, both logically and symbolically correct, the song that is sung tells of a community gathering at nature's gift of water. The scene culminates in the solemn but joyous celebration of Wyatt's stiff and stately dance.

The directorial movement of the hero through this long and beautiful sequence underscores Ford's concern with a man who is poised between two ways of life—a man who knows it and can still move easily between the two. Thus the Sunday morning sequence both contrasts sharply with and leads inevitably into the gunfight at the OK Corral.

The fight sequence begins, not in the Tonsorial Parlor, but in a rough adobe shack with the skull of a steer over the door. Here, Wyatt and his handful of men are gathered awaiting sunup. The action moves from there, not to the sunlit porch of a hotel or to a church, but through dusty and deserted streets toward an animal pen. As in the Sunday morning sequence, the movement here is also slow and rhythmic, but the mood is tense rather than leisurely. Wyatt still carries some traces of Sunday morning with him, but this is another day. His clothes and those of his companions are suited to the work at hand, and now they are fully armed. What is left of the Earp family, with Doc Holliday now a member, begins to move slowly upon the Clanton family in the citadel of the corral. There is no music; this gathering will end in violence and death.

The images composing the battle scene are characteristic of Ford: shot from shadow and enclosure and opening out into space; darkness and silhouette framing image and light. Perhaps the most striking image of the sequence— again, logical for the narrative and symbolic for the myth—is a long shot looking down the street from the corral. The buildings of Tombstone are lined up along one side; wagons and cactus border the other. Wyatt Earp, protector of the town on the one hand and the embodiment of the transient life of the wilderness on the other, strides down the center of the street between the images of frontier and civilization. In *My Darling Clementine,* the hero is idealized as the man in the middle, but a man capable of mastering both the wilderness and the garden.

Fifteen years later, when Ford made *The Man Who Shot Liberty Valance,* time had left its mark on the director, the actors, and the sort of story that both could produce at that time in the Western formula mold. The basic characters and themes are the same; the attitude and execution are markedly different.

The opening image of *The Man Who Shot Liberty Valance* follows logically and symbolically upon the closing of *My Darling Clementine.* The wilderness, as Hallie says, has indeed become a Garden. The meadow of *Clementine* has been cultivated and has proved productive; the dirt road is now a stretch of iron rails; the buckboard and horse have been displaced by the whistling and chugging train; the rocky butte has disappeared and in its place are rolling hills.

This play upon the audience's expectations is continued (although not nearly so savagely or ironically as in *Ride the High Country* and *The Wild Bunch*) when the train reaches Shinbone. As in *Clementine,* the inanimate objects that comprise the town tell much about the coming of civilization. But whereas objects in *Clementine* were temporary, fragile, and poor, those in *Liberty Valance* are permanent, sturdy, and complex—like the community they stand for. The buildings seen behind the old marshal as he stands on the station platform are brick. The enthusiastic young newspaperman rings up the offices of the "Shinbone Star" on a telephone and wears, not a sombrero or a Stetson, but an impossible, foolish-looking straw hat. As the marshal tells Hallie and Ranse, the railroad has changed the town. But the railroad is only a symbol of what is and what will be, just as the cactus rose is a symbol of what was and will never be again.

There are other objects of importance in *Liberty Valance*—more, perhaps, than in other Ford films: the long wooden box in the cobwebs and dust in another corner; "Pilgrim's" law books and Liberty Valance's silver-handled whip; the sharp clarity of the front-page headlines of the newspaper and the shiny ribbons on Peter's citizenship certificate; Tom Doniphon's burned-out house as we first see it and then the same place in earlier times with the added room painted white and two rocking chairs on the tiny porch. But in this film, most of the objects speak more of what is now than of what was then. That—in *Liberty Valance*—is left to narrative and flashback devices that are at times less subtle than one would wish.

There are also in this film signs of growing age: Ford's disillusion with the once-fresh promise of the Garden and his nostalgia for the wilderness; the use of Wayne and Stewart as less believable rivals for the heroine than they would have been twenty years before; the one-dimensional portrayal of the villain; the usual Ford weakness for inserting strong comedy scenes which seem less appropriate here than in some of his other films. (He cannot resist, for example, the extended comic monologues and posturing of the editor and the rancher. But he uses well the parody of a western myth gone stale in the dandified cowboy whirling his lariat on the stage of the convention hall.) If *My Darling Clementine* is a better-made film, *The Man Who Shot Liberty Valance* comes full circle in Ford's final resignation to the fate of the Man of the West.

John Wayne, who remained the embodiment of the Ford hero until his death, does not give as good a performance in *Liberty Valance* as he does in *The Searchers* and some of the cavalry films, but by this time the Wayne myth works for the tough and inarticulate character of Tom Doniphon as the Stewart myth works for the bumbling, soft-spoken dude Ranse Stoddard. Beginning with the hero as the core of the film, it almost seems as though Ford followed with a series of questions beginning, "What if . . . ?" What if the hero is dead when the film begins? What if the West is no longer wild? What if the girl doesn't marry the hero in the end? What if the gunfighter's opponent is a dishwasher in an apron who can't shoot? What if the glory goes to the wrong guy? And finally, what if the hero's death is not only shorn of spectacle, but hardly noticed by anyone in the film? The possibilities are fascinating, and Ford explores them all. Through the character of Tom Doniphon, Ford plays variations upon the theme of the Western myth—reversed, developed contrapuntally, and attacked from a variety of viewpoints.

Consistent with this tangential approach to his material, Ford spends a great deal of time in the film developing the characters of Hallie and Ranse. Tom is less in visual evidence but he, without question, dominates the action. What we know of Tom we discover through Hallie's and Ranse's relationship to him—not merely in Ranse's story to the newsmen, but in the flashback depicting their younger days in Shinbone. Tom is consistently the Man of the West—silent, reticent, in command of person and nature until a foe appears that he cannot fight: civilization.

Civilization comes in the person of the "Pilgrim" with his books, his strange ideas of justice ("I don't want to kill him; I want to put him in jail."), and his Eastern enlightenment that captivate the town—and Hallie as well. Stoddard is all those things that Doniphon is not. When Ranse is brought to Hallie's home after the stage holdup, he is dazed, bewildered, totally confused by the efficient activity of those aiding him. In contrast, Tom (who has rescued him) is calmly overseeing the action as he drinks a cup of coffee.

The incapability of the Easterner to match the man of the West is emphasized throughout in Ranse's relation to Tom, but chiefly through situation and dialogue rather than through visual symbols. The dude is put to work washing dishes, and he's not very good at it. Furthermore, he cannot handle a gun. Ranse works better with his mind than with his hands. He is master of the situation in the little schoolroom but he quickly diminishes in stature when Tom, weary and travel-stained from the trail, interrupts the lessons to claim Pompey for neglected work on the ranch. As the rest of the pupils scatter from the schoolroom soon after, Ranse, defeated, turns to the blackboard and erases the day's axiom, "Education is the basis of law and order"—words written in careful script and enclosed in very straight lines.

Ranse is again no match for Tom in the sequence of shooting practice. At Hallie's request, Tom rides out after Ranse, who is on his way to rehearse for the inevitable showdown with Liberty Valance. Tom (on horseback) overtakes Ranse (riding in the "Shinbone Star" buckboard) and again proves himself superior to the Easterner, although he does it without malice. Ranse's surprising retaliation grounds Tom more than physically; he is genuinely amazed at what this dude can do when he puts his mind to it. It is then that Tom reminds Ranse that Hallie is—has always been—Tom's girl.

Hallie's attitude toward Tom from the first moments of the flashback indicates this. They seem to have known each other for a long time. Hallie is as natural and lovely as the cactus rose Tom presents to her. She has been able to blossom in this wild land, and the contrast between her later Eastern image and her youthful character serves to underscore the importance of the proper setting needed for a cactus rose to bloom.

Unlike Clementine, Hallie is a woman of the West. *Liberty Valance* represents a Ford film in which it is the woman who is at home in the wilderness and who mourns its passing. Yet as a young woman, Hallie succumbed to the great temptation represented by Ranse and his way of life. Her sympathy for Ranse when she meets him and her concern for him when he is humiliated, her desire to read and write, her ignorance of the genteel world (she has never seen a "real" rose)—all of these feelings play upon her as temptations to forbidden knowledge. In her simplicity and openness she does not realize that the attainment of such knowledge and the satisfying of such desires will result in both gain and loss. Finally, the myth of Ranse's heroism—*really* a myth— intensifies her fascination for him and turns it into love. Once she has made her decision, the man and the land that she first loved are both lost to her. She is not an unhappy woman in the end; she is simply wiser, resigned, and more than a little nostalgic for people and things that the passing years have told her can never return.

Hallie's physical presence in the film is not as strong as that of Ranse, nor is her interaction with Tom as frequent. But her spiritual presence is a motivating force for both men. Hallie's ambivalence toward the two is a strong symbol of the individual who cannot remain between two worlds as the Wyatt Earp of *Clementine* can; she must choose one or the other. Her love is divided between the two men who represent each world. They cannot change; therefore she must. Her decision is the decision of most of us, but that is of little comfort to a woman like Hallie. The Garden is indeed beautiful, she tells her Senator husband as the train takes them away from Shinbone and toward Washington; he should be proud. But, she adds, "My roots are here, my heart is here," and her love of the land remains with her love of the man of the land—buried with him beneath her cactus rose.

These two, Ranse and Hallie, provide the action in *Liberty Valance*. Tom's reactions to their distress, requests, and desires illuminate (again, through indirection in Ford's distinctive approach in this film) the character of Doniphon as the last of a dying breed. He *must* respond as he does, even though he begins to realize that each response will trigger a new situation, leading ultimately to an end for his own desires for the future.

The moment of the gunfight is the moment of truth for Tom, even though he is not one of the combatants. With careful composition, Ford frames the figures of Ranse and Liberty Valance between the silhouettes of Tom and Pompey. A rifle is tossed between the two shadows; it is raised and aimed. A true Man of the West, Tom Doniphon knows what he has to do and he does it. Ford's constant sense of the past and concern for the future imply in that moment that Tom has chosen to act and the consequences of the act will determine his future as a man who must remain alone.

The visual image of that future is most vivid in the beginning of the film, when the marshal and Hallie drive up to the burned-out house to see the cactus roses blooming amid the rubble that once was the new room. Then the old man climbs painfully out of the buckboard and trudges toward the overrun garden to fetch the rose that remains on the long wooden box at the end of the film. Legends, Ford seems to say, can survive only if they can fit the expectations of those who embellish and feed on them. The real heroes are left to die unsung, save by those few who knew and loved them.

Sam Peckinpah: The Hero Remythologized

John Ford has been accused of canonizing the Western myth; Sam Peckinpah has the reputation of seeking to destroy it. But in a curious and almost perverse manner, Peckinpah has succeeded not in demythologizing but in remythologizing the Western hero. The transformation is perfectly consistent with the audience expectation of the hero (or antihero) that began in the early sixties and is still evolving in the seventies: the present-day legend is existential, sardonic, and disillusioned. At the same time, however, there exists at the core of a Peckinpah hero a certain nobility and beauty that are the essence of the Ford tradition and perhaps even fostered by it.

Peckinpah, a Westerner by birth (the mining area of California near Fresno), became a maverick in reputation. After finishing a master's degree in drama at the University of Southern California he worked in theatre as an actor, director, and producer. He then became interested in film making, and one of his first jobs was as dialogue director with Don Siegel. When he fell into disgrace in the eyes of Hollywood, Peckinpah continued to develop his style and approach through work in television, scriptwriting and directing for several Western series and dramatic productions in other genres. Beginning in 1961, he began to develop what admirers and adversaries both agree is a unique approach to character and theme in whatever genre he produces. The character is antiheroic and the theme is violent.

In the early years of the seventies, Peckinpah's name became synonomous with cinematic violence. Literal and visual overkill in each of his films is the object of praise or blame, audience ecstasy or shock. But in the early sixties the

Peckinpah approach to violence was subtle and covert—directed more toward spiritual personality than physical person. The action focused upon the Westerner as a man no longer in control or even in the middle—a man totally outside, behind, and unnecessary to a civilization that Peckinpah felt lost its own soul when it lost its spiritual and geographical frontiers.

Like the heroes of other cinematic and literary genres of the sixties, the Peckinpah hero is a reflection of the man of his time. Gone is the assurance, the command, the cool moral certainty of the classical hero. He is now bewildered, confused, and beleagured by forces that he cannot even identify, much less control. Thus, *Ride the High Country* (1961) and *The Wild Bunch* (1969) circumscribe in cinematic parentheses the personal dilemmas and turbulent events of that decade. Taken together with the two other Peckinpah films of that period *The Deadly Companions* (1961) in which Peckinpah had little faith and *Major Dundee* (1964) in which he lost faith, *Ride the High Country* and *The Wild Bunch* also provide a glimpse of the director's developing approach to both character and theme.

Peckinpah's image of the hero, like Ford's image is evident in his choice of actors to play the roles. Major characters like Joel McCrea, Randolph Scott, William Holden, Ernest Borgnine; minor characters like Edmond O'Brien, Warren Oates, L.Q. Jones, Strother Martin—these older, rugged men are not the stuff of which the traditional hero is made. But it is not the traditional hero that interests Peckinpah.

Peckinpah's hero is an outsider, a character operating apart from the community and conventional society. It is only when the hero is outside the comunity that he can achieve any meaningful action, if meaningful action indeed exists. This man must play out his life in isolation. Even the community of his companions cannot solve the problems he must face; ultimately he must face them alone. This paradox of individual isolation in the midst of a group is perhaps the most interesting facet of the Peckinpah hero; it is a reflection of a contemporary paradox as well.

Steve Judd and Gil Westrum of *Ride the High Country* come close to the Wyatt Earp of *Clementine* (which Peckinpah greatly admires) in approaching an idealized image of the hero. Judd and Westrum also share Tom Doniphon's realization of the passing of the West, but like Hallie they face the change with peaceful resignation rather than despair. And like Ford in *Clementine,* Peckinpah in *Ride the High Country* pours out a profusion of images that add to the richness of an already good script as he tells the hero's story.

Here also, the opening and closing images of the film are a commentary on what happens in between. In the beginning, the camera swoops down upon a grotesque parody of a Western town. It is not Shinbone made civilized by the railroad or Tombstone made safe for the community. It is a nightmare of carnival booths, belly-dancers, careening cars, and racing camels. The people are unreal, insensitive, and could belong to no community on earth. In his own world of unreality, Steve Judd rides into town, nodding and smiling at the expectant crowd until he is forced off the street and sharply reprimanded by the uniformed policeman ("Watch out, old-timer!").

The camera then moves to another travesty of the Western myth: a crooked shooting gallery where Gil Westrum as the Oregon Kid ("tamer of Dodge and Wichita and member of the Omaha Gang") is dressed and bewigged as a horrendous Buffalo Bill figure and is bilking the townspeople attracted to his booth. Judd's approach to Westrum and the interplay of the two as they recognize one another establishes their relationship as old friends and serves as a reference point for Judd's later conflict when he realizes that Westrum intends to betray him. Through references to the past throughout the film, it becomes obvious that the two have shared both the good and the bad of many years together. In fact it becomes more and more clear that Judd and Westrum are but two faces of the same man; a man at odds with himself much of the time but reaching perfect harmony of mind and action at the end.[51] The splitting of the persona, however, provides a more detailed look at the final form of the Western hero that interests Peckinpah in the film. The playing off of the two against each other—provides the conflict between the two old comrades that is in reality a conflict within the individual himself. Judd's character is most clearly identified in terms of Westrum; Westrum becomes understandable in the light of Judd.

Much about Steve Judd (and, consequently, about the fading Western man) becomes evident in the opening sequences of the film. His entry into the town and his meeting with Westrum have been noted. The negotiations with the town bankers further serve to establish his character. Again, the images are logical, but also deeply symbolic. The bankers, ancient father and middle-aged son, expected a much younger man. "I used to be," says Judd. "We all used to be." And in excellent meeting of visual and verbal irony, the bankers remind him, "The days of the forty-niners have passed. The days of the sturdy businessman have arrived." Judd steps into the only room in the bank which affords any privacy, wipes his brow, and gingerly puts on a pair of spectacles to read the contract. Having examined it, he puts away his spectacles, flushes the toilet, and emerges to confront the bankers with a command that intimidates them into agreement. The sequence is well done, with dialogue that is brief but succinct enough to accompany the strong image of a man employing the bravura which will give him his last chance at restoring his honor.

Judd's search for his honor is the conscious and driving force of his character. It is also central to Westrum's character although Westrum is unaware of such forces until very near the end of the film. Heck and Elsa discover their honor as well, but it happens to them as a result of their experience in the mining camp of Coarse Gold. All four, however, must leave where they are and journey into the high country in order to find wholeness. The journey is both a logical and a metaphorical necessity to the film.

The first stop places the three men in the rarefied air and isolated world of the Knudsen farm. At the supper table, Judd matches proverbs with Joshua Knudsen on an almost esoteric plane while Westrum wryly cites scripture to apply to the situation at hand. This is one of the first indications that Westrum possesses the hard-nosed practicality and pliable morality that Judd will have need of before their journey brings them back to the confines of the Knudsen farm.

From this time on, the character of Westrum is fleshed out beyond the image of the stereotyped opportunist that he appears to be back in the town. Although Judd will enter the brothel and rescue Elsa from the Hammonds at gunpoint, it will be Westrum who takes the decisive action to save her from honoring the marriage contract. Judd, in his unbending rectitude, is reluctant but nonetheless willing to abide by the verdict of the miners' court of Coarse Gold. Westrum's practical vision sees farther than Judd's. Westrum knows that the verdict of such a judicial group will be as ethically obscene as the ceremony that same group witnessed the night before in the brothel.

The wedding ceremony itself is as surreal as the film's opening image in the town. Coarse Gold is another limbo through which the hero must pass before he can enter his house justified. The first sight of Coarse Gold confirms it as another world, and it is certainly not the other world that Elsa envisioned outside the fences of her father's farm. Her terror quietly increases from the moment that Heck reluctantly leaves her in the Hammond camp, through the bizarre ride to the ceremony with Elsa in the lead and wearing her mother's white wedding gown, during the curiously moving marriage homily of the dissolute judge, and culminating in Billy's striking her and the attempted rape by the two Hammond brothers. Again, there is little dialogue here, but the imagery is unforgettable. Finally, it is in the same room where Elsa's terror reached its peak that Westrum forces the corrupt judge to speak the lie that frees her.

Westrum's brand of action is beyond Judd at this point in the film. Elsa tells Judd later on that her father says there is only right and wrong, good and evil, nothing in between. But, she adds, it is more complex than this. Westrum already knows it; Judd has yet to find it out.

The trip back down to the Knudsen farm is the turning point for Heck Longtree, the cocky camel rider with the flashy red shirt, sheepskin vest, and pretty gun that he doesn't bother to keep clean. As he tells Westrum, he has seen something in the old man (Judd) back in Coarse Gold that he didn't realize was there, and he cannot bring himself to betray him. Westrum plays upon Heck's growing sense of honor, but in reverse. "The thing to remember is we made a deal," says Westrum. "Yes, sir," Heck replies, and they prepare to desert Judd and Elsa that night. But the attempted robbery fails. As Westrum and Heck move silently through the camp, the camera pans upward from Judd's feet, pauses at his no longer firm midsection where a still firm hand levels a gun, and then moves up to his face. There is a look of anger—almost rage—in his eyes. But at the same time there is a shadow of terror. Judd sees in Westrum's decision an image of his own determination. Westrum, too, is a man who will not be bent from his avowed purpose, even at the cost of deserting a friend.

The next day, the gun battle amid the rocky terrain of the high country confirms Heck's loyalty to Judd and precipitates Westrum's escape from the group that night. In a fine moment of the film, Westrum asks Judd to cut his hands loose for the night. Judd asks why. "Because," replies Westrum, "I don't sleep so good anymore." One of the many moments (like the conversation in underwear and the brief fight between Judd and Heck) of mutual understanding between the two old men, this brief exchange welds them together as extended background narrative could never do.

The final set of images begins to take shape near the Knudsen farm. As Judd, Elsa, and Heck approach the strangely quiet barnyard, they ride out of the frame and Westrum appears in the lower distance, tracking them from afar and visually uniting the group for the last time. The camera closes in on a tight shot of the black-and-white, speckled, and bright red hens fluttering nervously behind the wooden fence of the farmyard. The image is ominously reminiscent of the brightly colored women of Coarse Gold. The black raven, Henry Hammond's bird, is stalking among them, and then flies up to perch on his master's shoulder as the camera pans to the remaining Hammond brothers waiting in ambush in the barn.

Judd senses the danger too late, and Westrum regains his own honor and the respect of Heck and Elsa as he runs across the open yard and leaps into the ditch to join the group for the final battle. But there is no exhibitionism in Westrum's act or rashness in his decision. It is simply the natural thing to do. Friendship is more dear than gold, and the brief dialogue between the two old men in the lull before the battle unites the two faces of the Western man. "Partner," one says, "what do you think?" "Let's meet 'em head on," says the other, "like always." Then follows the triumphal march across the farmyard that is echoed in *The Wild Bunch,* with Judd and Westrum striding tall and as one man.

The Hammonds are killed, but Judd is dying. "I don't want them to see this," he tells Westrum, and Westrum waves Elsa and Heck away. Westrum promises to take care of things as Judd would. Judd replies: "Hell, I know that. You just forgot it for a while." Judd asks Westrum to leave him: "I'll go it alone." "See you later," Westrum says. He rises and moves away. The camera frames Judd from behind, leaning on one arm and looking off into the aspen-covered mountains of the high country blazing like a sunset with autumn gold. There is the pause of a heartbeat, and his body falls away and out of the frame. Only the mountains remain.

The closing image is the only logical conclusion to balance the opening of the film. This man could never die in that miserable town that he left behind when he started on his journey up into the high country. His death must be in the mountains and it must be alone.

On one level, it is only logical that *Ride the High Country* is set in the autumn of the year. Autumn provides the motivation for a harvest-time town fair. It underscored Elsa's restlessness at the prospect of another winter alone with her father on the farm. It urges the trip to Coarse Gold before the winter snows block access to the high country. But on another level, autumn is the right time for Judd and Westrum to meet again and to travel this journey together. It is a journey that changes both men, restoring the integrity of one and vindicating the other. It is the autumn of the old Western man as well as the autumn of the old West, and both—like the autumn—are immortalized in the midst of their dying.

The hero of *The Wild Bunch* is again, on the surface, a member of a group. And once more Peckinpah seems to split the persona of one man and to divide facets of it among the other members of the group, much as Cooper split the Leatherstocking persona. But although Dutch, Sykes, the Gorch brothers, and Angel are all reflections of Pike Bishop, it is Deke Thornton who is Bishop's true alter ego. Unlike Judd and Westrum of *Ride the High Country,* Bishop and Thornton do not set out on their journey as partners; on the contrary, one is the pursuer and the other the pursued. Yet they are drawn closer and closer together during the chase so that by the end they share the same sentiments, even though one dies and the other is not very far from the end of his days.

The opening images of *The Wild Bunch* play with our expectations—not of the West, but of such solid and realistic concepts as American soldiers, laughing children, and defenders of law and order. The children, however, are laughing at a scorpion being devoured by red ants. The soldiers are outlaws robbing a bank. The defenders of law and order are a pack of bounty hunters shooting down citizens who stand between them and their prey. The aftermath of the opening massacre finds the scorpion set on fire, the flames dissolving into an image of the scattered bodies on the streets, and this is followed shortly by the Wild Bunch straggling into their hideout only to discover that they have stolen metal washers instead of money. With this ghastly joke as the beginning, all that is left to the Bunch is to play out the game until the end.

At this point, however, Pike seems to be the only one in the Bunch who begins to sense this failure as the beginning of the end. "This was going to be my last," he says to Dutch of the bank job. But it was a failure, and Pike would like to "make one good score and then back off." "Back off to what?" asks Dutch, and Pike is silent.

It is 1914, and the West had been "civilized." It is not Hallie's Garden, however, but a hypocritical, greedy community that is rotten to the core. The

Western man of the old order is being continually forced back into a savage wilderness and a more savage mode of life in an attempt to survive outside the dehumanizing confines of such a civilization. Peckinpah puts his sympathy with the outlaw, excoriating the champions of law and order and painting them in even bloodier hues than the Wild Bunch. The Bunch, in fact, emerge as the only affirmation of any positive themes in the film—fellowship, loyalty to the group, faithfulness to one's word of honor. Yet following the final slaughter, even these attitudes seem buried beneath the riddled bodies of soldiers, citizens, peasants, and outlaws.

Pike Bishop is the heroic center of the film. He is not a Steve Judd or Gil Westrum, although they too were the Western man grown old. Pike bears even less resemblance to Wyatt Earp or Tom Doniphon. Bishop is a man who knows he is doomed from the start, but a man with a fatalistic panache that makes him determined to play out his hand to the end. When Dutch tells him that if the Bunch moves back across the border "They'll be waiting for us," Pike replies, "I wouldn't have it any other way." Yet, as leader of the Bunch, Pike finds it increasingly difficult to keep them together and maintain control. Pike's struggle for dominance on one level is a metaphor for his struggle with himself on another. His companions provide reflection of his own inner conflict; the final resolution is death to those other selves as well as to him.

The Gorch brothers repeatedly revert to a brutal and simple-minded childishness and represent the carefree lawlessness that might have been Pike's way of life in his younger days when the West still had a place for men like him. Angel, the idealistic patriot, reflects zeal for an honorable cause that has been subverted in Pike at this time in his life by the simple desire for survival. Angel's death, significantly, is far more tortured and inglorious—a direct result of his adherence to loyalties outside the Bunch. Sykes is a battle-scarred, near-useless old man who foreshadows what Pike would become were he to live to old age. Dutch, fiercely loyal to Pike and to the Bunch, mirrors the anarchistic, darker, and more mysterious side of Pike's character.

Deke Thornton, still a part of the Bunch in spirit if not in body, brings Pike Bishop closer to the Judd-Westrum persona of *Ride the High Country*. Here again are the aging heroes, both flawed and both burdened with an equivocal past. There is in each a deep understanding of what the other was and has become. Both are in the process of a physical as well as a spiritual journey. Something is driving them—something to which they are unwillingly but fatefully committed. Nothing else can take precedence, no matter how much each man may wish it.

There is also more than just a hint of nostalgic reminiscing of one with the other; their shared memories communicate across the barren wastes between the opposing goals to which each are committed. Thornton can anticipate Bishop's moves, even from afar; he has experienced Pike's thinking so often in the past that he knows him like his own hand. He warns his miserable band of scavengers, "We're after men; and I wish to God I was with them." Pike, on the other hand, is losing his grip through world-weariness and a mounting despair. He is frequently forgetful of Thornton's technique until its consequences are hard upon him. But Bishop's painful leg wound that refuses to heal is perhaps the most vivid symbol of his past relationship with Thornton. The memory of the old betrayal refuses to go away.[52]

The physical effects of this old wound provide at one point a strong cinematic statement about the Peckinpah hero. Ford's hero is one who leaps astride his horse and, together with his companions, rides off across an expanse of wild and beautiful country in pursuit of his goal. Peckinpah's Pike Bishop, on the other hand, falls to the ground in the attempt to mount. He calls to the Bunch to aid him; they stand immobile. Cursing, he struggles into the saddle and rides slowly away from the group. The wide-angle lens of the camera flattens his hunched shoulders as they gradually disappear beyond a sand dune, and he is gone.

Another sequence parallels the unreality of the wedding procession in *Ride the High Country* and adds to the mythic, dreamlike image of the Peckinpah hero. It is the departure of the Bunch from Angel's Mexican village home. The similarity between the two surrealistic scenes is, however, in structure only; the meanings are not the same. Elsa's procession preceded the crude wedding ceremony; the ride of the Bunch follows the celebration of Angel's community in showing their hospitality to the young man's friends. The Hammond brothers are raucously singing "When the roll is called up yonder we'll be there"; but there is a gentleness and melody in the voices of the Mexican villagers that adds to the almost mystical beauty of the scene in *The Wild Bunch*. Elsa is uneasy, for she is riding to disaster, but she will ultimately be saved. The Bunch is light-hearted; only Pike senses that this is the moment of peace before the final disaster. In this lovely sequence, however, the image of the Bunch is apotheosized to heroic stature.

The Bunch rides out of the Mexican village but, idyllic as the respite had been, Pike knows that neither he nor the others can be a part of this culture any more than they can be a part of the town they rode into at the beginning of the film. There is no possibility of turning back now; there is, in fact, nothing to turn back to. A way of life is dead. The old Mexican has told Pike the evening before, "We all dream of being a child again, all of us; perhaps even the worst of us." It is through the mist of that dream that the Wild Bunch rides out of the village and into the bloody denouement.

The final images of the film parallel those of the massacre at the beginning, but with a visual vengeance. The sequence is touched off by the last four of the Bunch marching abreast through the town to rescue Angel. The force of the scene lies in the Bunch's awareness that rescue is impossible but the gesture is necessary to preserve the meaning of whatever honor is left to them. They plan to die; they also plan to take many enemies with them.

When the massacre is finished, the survivors straggle out through the gate of the town. Sykes, still alive because he was too old to accompany the Bunch into the town, meets Thornton at the gate. Thornton's band of bounty-hunters are scrambling among the bodies inside, the image reminiscent of the tiny ants devouring the once-deadly but now harmless scorpion. And if the beginning of the film plays upon our traditional expectations, the ending satirizes our expectation of some notion of resolution. Sykes asks Thornton to join him. "It won't be like old times," Sykes says, "but it's something." Thornton agrees and the two men move off, their laughter mingled with that of the Bunch, whose laughing faces are superimposed upon the final frames.

The richness of image and complexity of statement in *The Wild Bunch* grow more compelling as one achieves distance from this sprawling film. Yet the ending, with its superimposed affirmation of the eternal vitality of the Bunch, is as ambiguous as much of the film. Perhaps Peckinpah is saying that there is no other response possible in the world his film has created than that of laughter, eternal childhood—or childishness—and final and meaningless gestures of nobility.

The Film Western: A Song of Arms and the Man

Both Ford and Peckinpah depict the Western hero as an outsider. Ford's Western man has a past and future. He also possesses a sense of community, even though he may not always be able to become part of a community. Peckinpah's hero has little love of the past and less hope for the future. He either does not understand the community or he rejects it, since it has consistently betrayed him.

Both directors, however, possess a strong sense of history, albeit strongly colored by their individual interests as portrayed in their films. The Beadle dime novels turned the history of the Man of the West into the reality of myth. Men like Ford and Peckinpah have embellished, renewed, and transformed the Beadle hero through their own visions into a myth acceptable to their own time and the expectations of their audience. They know the facts; they print the legend.

In *My Darling Clementine,* the historical Wyatt Earp is transformed into legend during the course of the film. The disillusioned, slightly bitter reversal of *The Man Who Shot Liberty Valance* prints the legend—but about the wrong man. *Ride the High Country* creates another kind of legend: the old Man of the West who can die like the autumn dies—fulfilled and justified. In *The Wild Bunch* the legend has become meaningless and can be justified only by playing it out to a senseless and brutal end.

Finally, both directors have chosen to look at the Western myth as more than a vehicle for a personality, an exciting bit of action, a cheap filler or quick money-maker while concentrating on more lavish projects. Rather, they have celebrated the land and the people who ventured and adventured there. Ford and Peckinpah tell an epic tale. They sing of arms and the man on a conceptual and visual scale that is larger than life. Moreover, while keeping within the rigid format of the Western, they wrestle with questions that are not limited to that genre but are questions that must be asked by anyone at any time. John Ford and Sam Peckinpah work within the limits of a traditional formula and at the same time speak to the concerns of an audience rapidly changing in its entertainment tastes and its social, political and ethical mores.

The Western films of Ford and Peckinpah may be about our pasts, but they are able also to illuminate our present and point toward our future. Their Western hero is the American Ulysses venturing out upon the open, darkly beautiful wilderness of the once-upon-a-time West as that ancient Ulysses set forth into the uncharted regions of the half-fantasy, half-real Mediterranean world. To the tellers of both ancient and present-day tales, it matters little whether the facts are true; it is the meaning of the man—the hero—that is important. His story bears upon our story; his ambivalence, his quest for both independence and community is ours; his struggle to attain and preserve his honor is our desire to enter our house justified.

4

Television: The Myth as Pastoral

Electronic Aesthetics: A Question of Identity

Like its elder sibling the moving picture, the phenomenon of television resulted from multiple experiments by the curious dabblers of several nations who investigated the potential of electronics. Names like John Logie Baird, Charles Francis Jenkins, Philo T. Farnsworth, and Vladimir Zworykin must be noted in marking the birth of the medium; but it is not within the scope of this historical summary either to sort out the achievements of each or to take sides in the argument of who is, indeed, the father of television. The fact is that the medium appeared—tentative in the thirties, suspended during the War—and by 1947 exploded upon the joyful and optimistic postwar population with an impact that brought programming into over 14,000 American homes.

Unlike the moving picture, however, television was heralded as something more than simply a toy. With the powerful backing of David Sarnoff and his RCA empire, first faltering experiments were considered mere steppingstones to the expansion of that empire into an industry that today outstrips its parent radio corporation's humble dreams of over fifty years ago. Born into a more complex age than that which produced film, television was less free to enjoy the naivete, intrepidity, and wild innocence of the cinema of early days. Nonetheless, the medium did enjoy a comparable age of innocence during the early and mid-fifties that is still considered a profusely creative, exuberantly innovative "Golden Age." Then, as wider possibilities began to develop in types of programming and approaches to content, the industry and art of television took on some of the characteristics of adolescence—that period of life in which one is in search of a mature identity but is often slipping in and out of role after role in the attempt to discover what that identity may be.

In many ways that struggle continues today. The question seems to be whether the young medium can find happiness as art, or entertainment, or fact-finder, or myth-spinner—or can it successfully be all things to all people of the twentieth and twenty-first centuries? The industry which created and sustained the medium has not yet been able to answer the question; critics who have brought principles derived from other disciplines to bear upon the study of electronic aesthetics have only begun the exploration.

But whatever investigation is in process, a facet of that study must include an examination of the many Westerns that populated the first frontiers of television and which are now fading from the first-run screen as their historical counterpart—the Westerner—disappeared from reality to reappear in legend.

The following review of television's development is focused upon the changing role of the Western throughout the years. With an incredibly voracious appetite, the medium had fed upon hundreds of thousands of stories structured more or less upon the Western formula and displayed with varying degrees of success in Western series.[1] With his persona multiplied and his size diminished, the mythic Western hero squeezed himself into the television tube at considerable cost. The story of Ulysses was transformed from epic to pastoral through the unique message of the new electronic medium.[2]

Transition to Television: Small-Scale Saga of the Hero Reborn

As the film industry struggled to fend off the encroachments of the interloper television in the middle and late forties, the studios turned toward large-scale, wide-screen, star-studded products. The humble B-Western, unable to withstand such formidable competition, found new life on the television screen. The first of the cowboy heroes to make his appearance on television was Gene Autry, whose real-life role as a shrewd businessman enabled him to realize considerable profit from the numerous products of his Flying A company. Besides the series in which he himself starred, Autry was responsible for developing several others: *Range Rider, The Adventures of Champion, Buffalo Bill, Jr.,* and *Annie Oakley.* But these were to come later. In 1947 Gene Autry rode the range as the sole cowboy, sharing the then-plentiful time with pioneer entertainers like Buffalo Bob and Howdy Doody and Kukla, Fran and Ollie with on-the-spot coverage of roller derbies and the World Series; and with nightly newscasts by Douglas Edwards. Autry developed an emphasis on action while toning down the musical element that had been predominant in his films. At the same time he became conscious of the unique needs of television for increased closeup work (as opposed to the unidentifiable images produced by long shots) and the requirements of time slots, commercial breaks, sponsor influence, numerous episodes to fill out the season, and ever-present budget restrictions. Nonetheless, the Gene Autry series lasted well into the fifties and the coming of the "adult Western."

In 1948 Hopalong Cassidy appeared on the television screens that were growing more numerous throughout the United States. Along with Hoppy came Uncle Miltie and Ed Sullivan, the beginning of game shows, and dramatic series in the form of Studio One and Philco Playhouse. Matching the foresight of Gene Autry, William Boyd had purchased the television rights to all his old Hopalong Cassidy films in the early forties. It was a shrewd long shot that paid off. By 1951 the series was running on 63 television stations as well as the allied media of 152 radio stations and 155 newpaper comic sections. In addition, the resurrection of Clarence Mulford's hero revived Boyd's flagging career and provided him with lucrative sidelines of promotional merchandise and personal appearances. In still another instance of the recreation of an original character into the image of the audience's preference, Fenin and Everson relate that

> all of Clarence E. Mulford's Hopalong Cassidy novels were reprinted and completely rewritten to tie in with the uncommon conception of Cassidy as an idealistic and gentlemanly Western hero. Mulford's excellent authoritative picture of the West was therefore completely distorted, to be presented anew on the level of a "B" Western.[3]

Boyd, who died in 1972, made over one hundred Hopalong Cassidy films that can still be viewed in syndication today.

The tiny 1948 television screens also displayed a cowboy hero who had been created by committee for a Detroit radio station sixteen years earlier. Turning to children's programming in a last-ditch effort to save his troubled Detroit station WXYZ, owner George W. Trendle hit upon a hero who would combine the qualities of Robin Hood with the authoritativeness of law and order. Staff discussions developed the concept and at last there emerged amid galloping hoofbeats and strains of the *William Tell Overture*[4] the character of the Lone Ranger. From that moment and well into the fifties, 224 radio stations carried the half-hour adventures of the Masked Man and his sidekick Tonto. Each episode began with the ringing voice of the announcer proclaiming:

> With his faithful Indian companion Tonto, the daring and resourceful Masked Rider of the Plains led the fight for law and order in the early western United States. Nowhere in the pages of history can one find a greater champion of justice. Return with us now to those thrilling days of yesteryear. From out of the past come the thundering hoofbeats of the great horse Silver. The Lone Ranger rides again![5]

Nowhere in the pages of history, indeed. The Lone Ranger was a man who could command his own destiny and as such he was also tailor-made to fulfill a need for fantasy and surrogate heroism in the minds of both children and adults caught in the throes of the Great Depression. Trendle conceived his character to appeal to children, but he was also aware that parents not only were interested in what their children heard on the radio but were in addition ultimately responsible for the purchase of any sponsor's product. The Lone Ranger is an example of myth and business in one more successful merger. On television, 130 films starring the Lone Ranger and Tonto (played by Clayton Moore and Jay Silverheels) ran from 1948 to 1961. Certainly better quality Western series have

existed, but the long life of both the radio and television versions of this concept
have unquestionably contributed to its status as one of the most identifiable and
beloved of the Western stories. What began as a gimmick to save an investment
endures as an international legend.[6]

For the next few years the television medium expanded in all directions—
some shows visual versions of their radio counterparts, others developed for the
new medium. New Westerns, however, were few. Instead, there were game
shows, family comedies, sports events, variety shows, "issue" programs, tales of
crime, suspense, and terror, distinguished dramatic series, and fine music. There
were, however, a few new culture heroes who appeared in other genres during
these years, namely: Captain Video; Martin Kane, Private Eye; Superman;
Buck Rogers; Tom Corbett, Space Cadet; Rocky King, Detective; and Ellery
Queen.

From 1951 to 1955 the number, if not the variety, of heroes increased.
While Americans watched the unfolding real-life investigation or organized
crime by the Kefauver committee in 1951 and the Army-McCarthy hearings in
1954, they could also thrill to the better-than-real adventures of *Mr. District
Attorney, Mark Saber, Racket Squad, Gangbusters, Boston Blackie*, and
Dragnet. Dick Tracy and Flash Gordon made the transition from strip to screen
in 1951. In 1954—seven years before Ben Casey and Dr. Kildare—Worthington
Miner produced *Medic*, featuring Richard Boone as the first in television's line
of doctor-heroes.

During the first half of the fifties, the few Westerns that were added to the
already-running Gene Autry, Hopalong Cassidy, and Lone Ranger series were:
The Cisco Kid (1951), *Roy Rogers* (1952), *Action in the Afternoon* (1953), and
Wild Bill Hickok (1954). *The Cisco Kid* was, of course, based upon the popular
O. Henry creation, developed and embellished beyond O. Henry's recognition
by the movies, and played with proper panache by Duncan Renaldo as Cisco
and Leo Carillo as the lovable dullard Pancho. The Rogers series, a syndication
product from the beginning, was short-lived and short-loved by an audience that
had at one time acclaimed Rogers as the king of the film cowboys.[7] The Hickok
series, also short-lived, was a totally mythical approach to the bad guy of history
starring the good guy of movie leading men, Guy Madison, with Andy Devine as
his faithful sidekick Jingles. *Action in the Afternoon* is probably the least well-
known of these series but is noteworthy as the first Western series to be telecast
live. Since *The Great Train Robbery* was shot in New Jersey, what better locale
for *Action in the Afternoon* than the outdoor Western set built by WCAU-TV in
the suburbs of Philadelphia, with Jack Valentine riding the empty lots every
afternoon from 3:30 to 4:00 EST Monday through Friday.

The year 1955 is generally designated as the beginning of the era of the
"adult western," although the full impact of the adult formula did not show up in
the ratings until two years later. There were three minor series added to the

Western roster in 1955 that merit naming, three others that are worth noting, and one more that has withstood the slings and arrows of the Nielsens from that year to this. The minor series were predictable for those early television years. *Sgt. Preston of the Yukon* was a television development from the radio series. *Tales of the Texas Rangers* covered the more than one hundred years of the history of that group. *Brave Eagle* featured the first television series with an Indian as the lead.

Of the three notable developments, the first came from a traditionally enterprising source. Walt Disney Studios and Disneyland displayed the Davy Crockett character in a highly romanticized but appealing three-part story that so popularized the historical Davy that he became synonomous with the image of Fess Parker. Furthermore, without extending into a series, the Davy Crockett segments introduced a lucrative line of merchandising that moved the young of America to idolize Davy (or rather, Parker) in dress, weapons, play, and song.

On the other hand, Hugh O'Brien as the hero of *The Life and Legend of Wyatt Earp* was provided with a sartorial splendor that would have stunned Davy with a kickback stronger than that of his long rifle. This second notable series was ABC's contribution to the adult format in 1955. Using Stuart Lake's sympathetic and overblown biography as a basis for the series, the hero was created in a suave, sophisticated, sure image. This image was then shrewdly presented to an evening audience while kid stars Hoppy, Autry, and Rogers were innocently running in the afternoon.

A third series of 1955 was possibly one of the best to be offered to the audience of that time. With a writing combination that would be hard to surpass—Friedkin and Fine—Worthington Miner produced a series of half-hour Western stories for NBC called *Frontier*.[8] A line of narration from this documentary-style creation indicates the possibilities for a more mature approach to the genre than had been previously realized on the television screen:

> There were other villains than Indians and cattle rustlers. There was space and wind and rain and cold. There was loneliness and isolation.[9]

Turning from space and wind and rain and cold, rejecting loneliness and isolation, CBS program developers looked toward the town, the marshal, and the age-old stock characters in creating *Gunsmoke* in 1955. Simply the endurance of this Western television series would qualify it for more detailed study. But, more importantly, its long life provides an opportunity to look more closely at the basic formula, the subtle changes through the years, and the product as it stands today. For the moment, let it be said that when *Gunsmoke* appeared on the television screen in 1955, Western watching ceased to be child's play.

The second half of the 1950s saw an incredible proliferation of television Westerns coming from a film industry that was discovering that if the enemy couldn't be licked, they had to be joined. Besides, as the adult Western captured its adult audience it also lassoed a sizeable chunk of the public for the show's sponsor, always a necessary element in the network economy. At the height of the genre's popularity on television, *Life* magazine reported the following statistics:

> one-third of nighttime network hours filled with Westerns; the 1957 fall season opened with 28 new Westerns and the 1959 season introduced 32 new ones; of the fifty shows canceled at the end of the 1956-57 season not one was a Western series.[10]

Among the many of these series which helped to develop—or further stereotype—the Western television formula were: *Cheyenne* (1956), with temperamental star Clint Walker and distinguished film Westerner L.Q. Jones; *Broken Arrow* (1956), based upon Elliot Arnold's novel *Blood Brother* with Michael Ansara playing Cochise; *Dick Powell's Zane Grey Theatre* (1957), a Western anthology series narrated by and sometimes starring Dick Powell; *Wagon Train* (1957), an internally troubled but successful story caravan that began under the leadership of wagon boss Ward Bond and scout Robert Horton; *The Rifleman* (1957), with Chuck Connors and Johnny Crawford; *Have Gun, Will Travel* (1957), Richard Boone's initiation as a television Westerner, albeit an unconventional one; *Maverick* (1957), a parody of the genre starring James Garner and Jack Kelly; *Bat Masterson* (1958), with Gene Barry lending gentlemanly elegance to the title role; *Wanted—Dead or Alive* (1958), providing Steve McQueen with a steppingstone into films and the audience with a hero of questionable morality; *The Deputy* (1959), with Henry Fonda attempting a first and unsuccessful venture into the medium of television.

The 1959 season also saw the premiere of the second longest-running Western to date. The saga of the Cartwright clan—headed by Pa Lorne Greene and with the strong support of his sons Pernell Roberts (until he left the show in 1965), Dan Blocker (until his death in 1972), and Michael Landon—seemed to provide the already Western-saturated audience with a family formula that worked. *Bonanza* worked so well that the series surpassed its rival *Gunsmoke* and from 1964 to 1967 commanded the highest average in the Nielsen audience rating of any show of the season. The growth, change, and demise of this show also deserve attention.

In the other time slots, television programming was dipping into an ever-expanding potpourri of fact and fantasy that had been brewing since the beginning of the medium's popularity. In 1956, Huntley and Brinkley became a team, Elvis (photographed from the waist up only) appeared on Ed Sullivan's show, and the newly introduced *Playhouse 90* presented Rod Serling's shattering *Requiem for a Heavyweight*. The following year witnessed a continuation of powerful dramatic presentations with distinguished casts. Jack Paar took over the hosting on *The Tonight Show* while hosts Dick Clark and Mike Wallace both moved into network versions of their shows—*American Bandstand* and *The Mike Wallace Interview.* Among the 1957 season series that developed the image of the American hero type were *The Thin Man, M Squad, Richard Diamond, Private Eye,* and the unbeatable barrister *Perry Mason.* Television viewers who were not busy being engaged over the exposure of the great quiz-rigging scandals of 1958 could view further developments of heroic adventure series in *Sea Hunt, Peter Gunn, Naked City,* and *77 Sunset Strip.* Locales and situations became more bizarre in 1959 with the advent of *The Untouchables, Hawaiian Eye, Adventures in Paradise, The Alaskans, The Detectives,* and *Tightrope!* The late fifties saw the development of the feud—not between the good guys and the bad guys—but between tough law enforcers, glamorous adventurers, and intrepid private eyes, with the now "adult" Westerner joining in. The battle was for the loyalty of the American television audience. It was a battle that the Westerner was to lose—with sporadic gains— during the sixties.

In the decade that in retrospect has been termed the era of awakening relevance, the Western—even the adult Western—was forced to reassess its hardening format and reshape its image. During the first few years of the sixties, however, the new series still adhered to the highly successful adult Western formula of the late fifties. With Eric Fleming as his trail boss, Clint Eastwood starred as the second in command in *Rawhide* (1960), a rather interesting series which began each season with the beginning of a new drive, following the adventures of the group on their journey, and finished the season at the end of the trail.[11] Each segment ended with Fleming's shout: "Head 'em up! Move 'em out!"—and on to a new adventure the following week. In 1961, *Whispering Smith* starring Audie Murphy was cited by the Senate committee investigating violence on television as a particularly offensive case in point. The series had been based on the character of the railroad detective in the novel of the same name and portrayed by Alan Ladd in a 1948 film. Another novel, Owen Wister's *The Virginian,* was the basis of television's first ninety-minute Western, beginning in 1962. With a fairly strong cast (James Drury and Lee J. Cobb— later replaced by Charles Bickford and then by John McIntyre) and a talented producer (Charles Marquis Warren in the beginning; Norman Macdonnell later) the series opened competing with the then top-rated *Wagon Train* but finished by outlasting its competitor by six years.[12]

In 1961 the actor who had portrayed the Virginian in 1929 appeared in a swan song production of NBC's *Project Twenty.* The special was called *The Real West,* and in it an ailing Gary Cooper attempted as narrator to demythologize the fantasy West that his own image as a Westerner had helped to create. It was indeed a paradoxical situation: Cooper, whose early career did not concentrate on Westerns, had come to the realization through the years that his taciturn manner, easy-going and pleasant style and acting abilities were best suited to the Western genre. His subsequent success and enduring popularity as the Man of the West created for him a persona that became his star identity. Yet is was still in the role of this make-believe cowboy that Cooper, attired in Western garb and poking a stick into the dust of a movie set ghost town, told the television audience that what they so often saw—and delighted in—in Western films and television was not the true story at all. And although *Project Twenty* told the history of the West through skillful kinestasis, the situation of the myth attempting to destroy his own mythic persona seemed a useless and unwarranted mission for this fading but noble Western film personality.

As Cooper attempted to change the audience's concept of the West, so too did the Western series adapt their concept to the changing tastes of the early sixties—the years that saw in factual programming the Great Debates, the tension of the Cuban missile crisis, the first faltering steps of the space program, the assassination of John F. Kennedy, Martin Luther King's march on Washington, and the beginning of coverage of the Vietnam war. These kinds of programming, many would later claim, contributed strongly to the protest movements of the middle and later sixties. Yet in 1961, Newton Minow took over the chairmanship of the Federal Communications Commission and declared that television was "a vast wasteland." A sampling of some of the entertainment programming either initiated or enjoying widespread popularity at the time would tend to support the accusation. *My Three Sons, Hazel, The Andy Griffith Show, The Beverly Hillbillies, My Favorite Martian, Let's Make A Deal, The Munsters, Bewitched, Gilligan's Island,* and *Gomer Pyle*—all these series were introduced in the early sixties and indicated the type of programming that produced, at least for a time, favorable ratings.[13]

The action and adventure series continued to develop the male hero in command of whatever situation he met. He was a doctor *(Ben Casey, Dr. Kildare, The Fugitive),* a lawyer *(The Defenders, Burke's Law),* a private eye *(Checkmate, Hong Kong, Surfside 6),* a soldier *(Combat, The Gallant Men),* or even a social worker *(East Side, West Side).* The super-spy character of *The Man from U.N.C.L.E.,* reflecting the popularity of Ian Fleming's James Bond, became a new category to be exploited into the seventies as the concept of the computer-age hero.

It is not surprising that the television Western developed a James Bond of its own in the person of Robert Conrad as Jim West in the 1965 series *The Wild Wild West.* As indicated by the title's double-talk play on the name of the hero and his locale, the series was designed as fantasy-comedy. The audiences, however, appreciated the diversion and even the syndicated reruns maintained a respectable popularity. Fess Parker returned as Daniel Boone in 1965, accompanied by singer Ed Ames as the Indian Mingo. That same year witnessed a matriarchal response to the males of *Bonanza.* Introduced by the musical theme first heard in the film *The Magnificent Seven,* Barbara Stanwyck presided over the Barclay spread and the Barclay children—Peter Breck, Richard Long, Lee Majors, and Linda Evans—in the story of *The Big Valley.*[14] Still another attempt to exploit the successful *Bonanza* format was *The High Chaparral* (1967), with a strong cast headed by Leif Erickson, Linda Cristal, and Cameron Mitchell. This series was created by the man responsible for *Bonanza*—David Dortort—but it did not achieve the same popularity; *Chaparral* was canceled in 1970. Finally, as a nod to the growing civil rights consciousness, a black cowboy who had been a slave (played by Otis Young) and a white Southerner (played by Don Murray) were teamed as *The Outcasts* in 1968 and set forth to roam the West after the Civil War. The series was not a success.

Meanwhile, the second half of the sixties provided television coverage of Vietnam, tension and violence in American cities, an explosive political convention in Chicago, moon landing countdowns and Super Bowl touch-downs. But although the late sixties seemed to be the era of live and lively coverage of unfolding events at home, abroad, and in space, 1966 marked Fred Friendly's resignation from his new post at CBS because the network substituted reruns of *I Love Lucy* for their live coverage of the Senate hearings on the escalation of bombing in Vietnam.[15] That same year Ronald Reagan withdrew as host of *Death Valley Days* to run for the governorship of California.

The television seasons from 1965 to 1969 had their share of new entertainment products that ran the gamut from innovative to insulting. Among them: *My Mother, the Car, Hogan's Heroes, Gidget, I Dream of Jeannie, Green Acres,* and game show *Supermarket Sweep,* all in 1965. In 1966: *The Dating Game* and *The Newlywed Game, The Monkees,* and *Dark Shadows,* a soaper with a vampire who became a wickedly fascinating male lead. The ill-fated Smothers Brothers took to television in 1967 as did Carol Burnett; that same year the *Flying Nun* took off for a mercifully brief time in and on the air. In 1968 *Laugh-In* exploited both the medium and the messages in a swift climb to success; the following year *Hee-Haw* produced a crass but regionally popular imitation. The closing years of the decade, however, provided viewers with an introduction to Jacques Cousteau, *Sesame Street,* the memorable British import *The Forsyte Saga,* and a marked increase in prime-time devoted to films and beginning with the successful airing of *The Bridge on the River Kwai.*

Of the roster of heroes in the second half of the sixties the early ones were super-spies, both in parody and in all seriousness. Among them: *Get Smart, I Spy, Secret Agent, Mission: Impossible,* and *The Avengers. The Fugitive* finally caught up with his wife's killer as sagging ratings caught up with the show in 1967. But there were always other heroes to take his breathless place. These replacements were varied in occupation but similar in focus on action: *Run For Your Life, Mannix, The FBI, Hawk, Ironside, Judd for the Defense, The Mod Squad, Hawaii Five-O, Adam 12, The Name of the Game, The Bold Ones,* and the *Survivors,* which did not survive for long. The fantasy heroes were still in evidence: *Tarzan,* for a brief period of time; *Batman,* played for the last shred of camp; and *Star Trek,* which is still viewed by many of its fans as one of the most significant allegorical commentaries upon contemporary living to come out of the television industry. With a passing nod to the educators in *Room 222,* the close of the decade must be noted by the increasing stature of doctor series: *Medical Center* premiered in 1969, as did *Marcus Welby, M.D.* which quickly achieved the rank of top network show the following season.

Of the "gimmick" or near-gimmick Westerns that appeared on television in the sixties, the following are some that run the gamut from inventive to ludicrous: *Tate,* whose smashed arm was preserved in a black rawhide sling—the unsuccessful forerunner of more successful "disabled" heroes like *Ironside* and *Longstreet; The Rebel,* an angry young man in the West: *Stoney Burke* and *Empire,* both attempts at contemporary Westerns; *Branded,* with Chuck Connors playing a Western version of *The Fugitive,* seeking those who wronged him; *F Troop* and *Laredo,* comedies about inept members of the U.S. Cavalry and the Texas Rangers, respectively; *Shane,* with David Carradine as a gunslinger with a sixties folk quality; *Cowboy in Africa,* lasting less that a season and with a title that tells why; and *Lancer,* another copy of *Bonanza.*

By the early seventies, ninety-five percent of American homes were equipped with television; thirty-nine percent of these were color sets. Now television audiences could watch the invasion of Cambodia and terror at the Munich Olympic games in living color. They could see Kenneth Clark relating mankind's history on *Civilization* and Alistair Cook telling us our own history in his *America* series with a wit, knowledge, and grace that we have yet to achieve. In the area of investigative reporting, CBS became embroiled in a lawsuit over its presentation of military public relations in *The Selling of the Pentagon* in 1971; correspondents wearily trailed the candidates in 1972; and within ten years of the McCarthy hearings daytime television was once again preempted[16] by what promised to be a long-running soap opera with a seemingly endless cast headed by Senator Sam Ervine. The show was called the Watergate hearings.

Public television provided some strong entries during the early seventies with *The Great American Dream Machine, The Electric Company, The Six Wives of Henry VIII,* and *Elizabeth R.* In 1970, *Flip Wilson, Mary Tyler Moore, The Partridge Family,* and *The Odd Couple* were entertainment staples. The following year, however, saw the beginnings of series that moved into ethnic topics, previously taboo dialogue and situations, and material that promised to have something for everyone in the area of mild shock, moderate insult, or downright rage. The shows were *All in the Family, M*A*S*H, Maude,* and

Bridget Loves Bernie, the last canceled at the end of the season amid denials that protests from religious groups had put pressure in places where it could not be withstood.

Numerous mystery-action-adventure series moved onto the television screen during this time, many of them appearing in rotation as a miniseries experiment to keep down production costs and prevent audience surfeit of too much of what creators hoped would be a good thing. These miniseries were realistic, gritty in dialogue and situation, and filled with action. Violence, since the inconclusive but foreboding Surgeon General's report published in early 1972, was kept to a minimum; killing, fighting, and other forms of mayhem were suggested rather than depicted for the most part. Some of the winners and the also-rans in the race for television survival were: *The Young Lawyers; The Senator* (which was awarded an Emmy as it was being canceled); *Columbo, McMillan and Wife,* and *McCloud* as the miniseries for NBC's Mystery Movie; *Longstreet; The Man and the City; Sarge; Cannon; Owen Marshall: Counselor at Law; Banacek; Search; Banyon; The Men; The Rookies;* and *The Streets of San Francisco. Me and the Chimp,* an attempt at a human playing second banana to a chimpanzee hero, met a sudden and deserved death.

The Western on television seemed to be dying as well. Gone were the dozens of entries of the late fifties and early sixties. The gimmick Westerns, when their formula wore thin, also slipped quietly away. It seemed the audience interest in the genre had all but disappeared.

During the 1970 season the single entry was a copy of the highly successful Paul Newman and Robert Redford combination in the film *Butch Cassidy and the Sundance Kid.* In *Alias Smith and Jones,* Ben Murphy and Pete Deuel played two reformed outlaws seeking amnesty. In the introduction to each segment, however, the narrator[17] dutifully reminded the audience that the two had merely—and no doubt, merrily—robbed trains and banks during their outlaw days; but they never killed anyone. The show was canceled in mid-1972 season a few months after the death of Deuel in December 1971.

The year for film stars attempting and failing at television series was 1971. Among the failures were two old Westerners: James Garner, who tried to recreate with *Nichols* the success of *Maverick;* and Glenn Ford, who with sidekick Edgar Buchanan lasted one season in a contemporary Western called *Cade's County.*

In 1972, two nonweekly series survived their first season and were renewed for 1973. The first of these, *Hec Ramsey,* was a rotating member of the NBC Mystery Movie and benefited from a generally strong line of scripts and the grizzled persona of Richard Boone in the lead as a turn-of-the-century peace officer. The second series successfully capitalized upon current interest in oriental philosophy. Termed by critics "an Eastern Western," *Kung Fu* made a star of David Carradine playing a pacifist trained from childhood in the deadly art of Kung Fu and the sometimes more deadly platitudes of its old monastic mentor.

Besides the renewal of *Hec Ramsey* and *Kung Fu,* other prospects for the genre in the 1973 fall season included a syndicated product called *Dusty's Trail,* and Raymond St. Jacques in *The Boomtown Band and Cattle Company.* Neither was successful.

The television cowboy, indeed, has been riding into the sunset. Old and worn, it is problematic whether he will see the dawning of a new day. His survival is contingent upon several factors. One is the ability of media creators to renew the ancient forms of the hero in a Westerner viable for contemporary audiences. Another is the ability to continually revitalize the ritual of the Western formula, a concept that is by its very nature prone to lapsing into stereotype. A look at the hero and at the formula can provide a basis for tentative conclusions.

Television Types: "Who Was That Masked Man?"

The four generic images of the Western man noted earlier—the mountain man, the soldier, the cowboy, the man with a gun—all appear in the television Western. Each persona, however, has been scaled down and simplified in order to conform to and be contained within the limits of the medium.

The mountain man faces the same difficulty he met and only partially overcame in Cooper's novels. The only way to make him attractive to a popular audience seems to be either to split him in two and give his commanding stature to a younger hero, or to allow him to accompany that younger hero as an able but often comedic sidekick.

The Western soldier usually appears as a comedy character as well, and most often in the company of a group.[18] Like his film counterpart, the television soldier seems to fill the role of martinet and, ultimately, foil for the hero.

The cowboy image in the broadest interpretations of the term has enjoyed the most success, since that image carries with it the heroic elements and the "leading man" glamor necessary to build and sustain a media persona. But whatever success the lone cowboy character enjoys, he consistently moves toward some degree of involvement with others. In the more successful series, that involvement is in the context of permanent relationships of close friends or family and usually carries with it some type of power and responsibility in the social milieu.

In this manner the cowboy image merges with that of the man with a gun, the gun being the symbol of power and authority even though the hero may rarely use it. Gunmen in the historical sense are relegated to the role of bad guy—at least as bad as any bad guy gets on the still-touchy medium of television. The implications of the gun as a symbol of socially sanctioned power, however, are far-reaching for audiences assenting to law and order control and at the same time rejecting show of force to keep control. This split response is an important factor in any assessment of the Western hero's role in mass media.

The specific role of the hero, however, becomes most clearly delineated in the context in which he operates. The kinds of stories and situational relationships that make up the various formulas of Western series both limit the hero to act in certain ways and enable him to establish a formulaic persona that the audience can find recognizable, comfortable, and comforting. The formulaic types might be categorized under the general headings of anthologies, loners, pardners, families, and parodies. Approaching the Western myth from different directions and with varying emphases, each of these clusters provides a certain kind of audience appeal that is worth noting.

Anthologies

Among the more enduring of the anthology series were *Death Valley Days, Frontier,* and *The Zane Grey Theatre.* The anthology (used during the fifties in other television genres as well) is a remarkably free format in which story usually take precedence over character. There is little time to develop character during the span of the half-hour show, but many of these series provided tight little stories that highlighted the sparkling talents of topnotch actors and actresses, both established and newly discovered by the medium. The nature of the anthology form also precludes the continuity of building a heroic image that will reappear from week to week, and as a result the only familiar face was that of the narrator who introduced each segment. If heroes were developed in anthology series, they perforce were the men who provided the framework for the story. Stanley Andrews as "The Old Ranger" did it for *Death Valley Days;*[19] Walter McCoy narrated and occasionally took part in *Frontier;* and Dick Powell (also president of the Four Star company that produced the series) provided the continuing introductions for *Zane Grey Theatre.*[20]

Variations on the basic anthology format also developed, moving the continuity and character identification to the stories themselves. Willard Parker and Harry Lauter were continuing figures in the *Tales of the Texas Rangers* series; Clint Eastwood as the ramrod and Gil Favor as the trail boss held together the many adventures of *Rawhide*'s seasonal cattle drive; Dale Robertson was the *Wells Fargo* troubleshooter; and Ward Bond and Robert Horton headed up *Wagon Train.*

Whether playing within or without the story framework itself, the Westerner in the anthology format provided a somewhat omniscient (and thereby, authoritative and powerful) viewpoint for the development of the tale. Involved, yet apart, these heroes could comment philosophically upon the actions of other characters bound within the emotional and situational entanglements of the story. Since most of these series were also journey tales, the hero never had to sink roots in a town or a ranch; yet his constant reappearance reinforced the familiarity factor for the audience. The anthology format—which might have within it the best of the Western theme elements because of its flexibility—seems to have had its heyday from the late fifties through the sixties. No pure anthology Western has appeared since that time.

Loners

The man alone in undoubtedly the classic image of the Westerner. In both film and television media, this concept provides the best of both worlds for creating and sustaining the heroic image and the series itself. The format is ever-ancient and ever-new: the hero, while possessing the freedom to move from story to story and place to place, is still able to sustain and develop his own personal image by reappearing in each segment. From Beadle versions of Kit Carson's adventures to video version of *Kung Fu*'s Caine, the wanderer is adventuresome and free yet comfortably familiar—a combination of qualities that proves delectably appealing to basic audience needs.

There are, of course, varieties and degrees of loners. Hugh O'Brien as Wyatt Earp and Gene Barry as Bat Masterson worked within the context of the town— as did Richard Boone in *Hec Ramsey*—yet remained aloof from the kind of involvement that creates a strong repertory cast. The loners who rejected the town as base and wandered each week in the more-or-less wilderness were men like scout Clint Walker in *Cheyenne,* bounty-hunter Steve McQueen in *Wanted—Dead or Alive,* angry young American Nick Adams in *The Rebel,* fugitive cavalry officer Chuck Connors in *Branded,* and ascetic David Carradine in *Kung Fu.* The basis of this type of loner series is a highly romantic and popular one—the concept of the questing knight who journeys, does battle when needed, and then moves on after having deeply affected those whom he leaves behind. The question, "Who was that Masked Man?" is spoken in some way by someone in each of the questing knight series.

The most mannered or capricious of the Western questers, however, was the incomparable Paladin, played by Richard Boone in *Have Gun, Will Travel.* A far cry from the classic loner, Paladin was a man of elegant and expensive tastes which interfered not a whit with his more serious business of disposing of dangerous persons. Shulman and Youman, in their view of television Westerns, summarize the career of this offbeat hero with a description that Paladin—and Boone—would pleasure in: "As Paladin, Richard Boone swiftly completed his appointed rounds with a unique combination of epicurean zest, Spartan valor, and existential ennui."[21]

As heroic image, the loner has remained highly successful in both Western series and related adventure genres. The potential for variety yet familiarity is too good for a commercial medium to pass up.

Pardners

His series title notwithstanding, the Lone Ranger was never a loner in the true sense. His relationship with his faithful Indian companion Tonto places him in the pardner category that moves from Hawkeye and Chingachgook *(Hawkeye),* to combinations like Cisco and Pancho *(The Cisco Kid),* Cochise and Tom Jeffords *(Broken Arrow),* Lucas and Mark McCain *(Rifleman),* and Hannibal Heyes and Kid Curry *(Alias Smith and Jones).*

The concept of the sidekick as alter ego, confidant, complement, and comic relief is a very important one in literature and, by extension, in films and television. Pardners in the Western format, moreover, reflect the reality of frontier history, when the physical and psychological pitfalls of being alone were overcome by companionship with another whose quest was the same or at least temporarily compatible.

The extension of the pardner type is, of course, the format in which the group acts as a unit. Series like *Rawhide, Laredo,* and *F-Troop* provided the camaraderie of the pardners while expanding the possibilities for variety by increasing the number of pardners involved. The group format, however, stresses much more than the pardner version the solidarity of relationship among the group members. Whether they are comic characters or serious men, there is a singleness of purpose that has brought them together and keeps them as a unit no matter what may befall, all for one and one for all. In a culture in which groups play an integral role, the societal values—loyalty, trust, companionship, reliability, mutual support—are both reflected and reinforced through group Westerns.

Families

The selective companionship of the group format is also closely related to the unit bound by familial ties, whether of blood or adoption. The family series is another staple in mass media story-telling, and though the format has its basis in Western history it lacks the color and freedom of types previously noted. Nonetheless, the family concept has produced some interesting series beginning with *Gunsmoke* and *Bonanza* and through the brief but successful histories of series like *The Virginian, The Big Valley,* and *The High Chaparral.*

The characters in these series are not all exclusively family units, yet they exhibit the characteristics of a family that tie them together in a manner different from the pardners or the groups. For example, the home (the ranch, the town) is the physical and social core of the format; the characters play the family roles of parent, child, adolescent, black sheep, scapegrace, in relation to the unit rather than independently; the familial values closely related to the group societal values of loyalty, mutual affection, and trust are often the primary focus of character motivation.

The family series, moreover, possesses some of the same advantages of other formats, since the family can include within itself a variety of characters—one of whom can be a loner, two of whom can be pardners, all of whom can form a cohesive group. There is room also for a variety of hero and heroine types: the mountain man, the cowboy, the cattle baron or landowner, the pioneer woman, the schoolmarm, the dance-hall girl. The gunman, however, is never part of the television Western family.

Thus, the Virginian and Trampas can strike out on their own adventures and return at the end to the bosom of their ranch "family." John and Victoria Cannon are able to look after each other and their respective relatives (Buck Cannon, Billy Blue Cannon, and Manolito Montoya) as they dwell in the rugged beauty of *The High Chaparral.* Land baroness and matriarch Victoria Barclay can provide wise advice and guidance for her grown children and from time to time enjoy an adventure or romance on her own. Pa Cartwright does the same for his sons on the Ponderosa, while each of them plays a role so far afield from a cohesive family unit that the explanation of the scriptwriters—that each son was born of a different mother—seems to be the only one possible, though it still remains improbable. The *Gunsmoke* "family" contains within it all the familiar roles from father figure Matt and mother-mistress Kitty to scapegrace child Festus and stolid elder brother Doc. Finally, the family format seems to possess an element of identification that audiences respond to in whatever television genre it appears.

Parodies

No art form is considered serious until it is parodied. The film Western came into its own in this respect through the work of the silent comedians; television Westerns had their first stab of satire in *Maverick,* which also seems to be the only Western parody with some degree of quality and responsibility in relation to its parent genre. Perhaps it was an unconscious reaction against the surfeit of adult Westerns that flooded the television channels during the latter half of the fifties; perhaps it was the ingenuousness of a boyish James Garner as the sly but lovable hero. Whatever the cause, *Maverick* worked for four seasons, while its reincarnation in *Nichols* ten years later never quite seemed to catch on. The popularity of superhero Robert Conrad in *The Wild Wild West* might also be attributed to television creators who could seize opportunity at the right moment; the James Bond fervor was too good to pass by. Other series (often syndicated rather than network offerings) verged on parody in their extreme attempts to create a format that would attract an audience. With offbeat characters and gimmicky plots these shows were often low-budget, short-lived, and near ludicrous. The parody format, however, allows the audience to look with a good-natured but critical eye at what it heretofore had viewed with a single-minded and worshipful gaze.

The anthologies, loner, pardners, families, and parodies of the Western stand as witness for both defense and prosecution in the genre on trial. These varied types attest to the flexibility of the format as it is offered by television; they also strain that flexibility at times in attempting to create Western heroes that will be all things to all audiences. The final judge in every case is, of course, that audience. Time and the Nielsens tell the tale.

The Saddle-Soap Formula: "Television Westerns Drive Me Nuts!"[22]

In November, 1953, then-President Eisenhower climaxed his acceptance of a civil rights award by throwing away his prepared speech and moving into a bit of homespun:

> I was raised in a little town of which most of you have never heard, but in the West it's a famous place! It's called Abilene, Kansas. We had as marshal for a long time a man named Wild Bill Hickok. If you don't know him, read your Westerns more. Now that town had a code, and I was raised as a boy to prize that code.[23]

The President went on to develop the code—facing up to one's enemies in a free society—as one of the ideals of this nation. This adlibbed speech (with its questionable philosophy expressing the right to be shot from the front as a civil right) used a down-home approach to age-old, searing questions. Perhaps in this simplistic version of frontier philosophy the President was urging the nation not to read but to see its Westerns more. A visual reflection of those expressed values—*Gunsmoke*—came into being within two years of Eisenhower's homage to Hickok and Abilene. Four years after *Gunsmoke* began, *Bonanza* joined the Western ranks. Together, these two series have outlasted all others in both total running time and widespread popularity. A closer look at some of their basic elements can provide insights into what formulas, heroes, and myths seem to have enduring resonance for the mass of Americans who still respond to the entertainment that *Gunsmoke* and *Bonanza* provide. As heroic myth scaled down, as epic become pastoral, these two series have achieved a formula for long-standing success; they are the saddle-soap operas of television.

Gunsmoke: The Days of Our Lives

Created by John Meston and Norman Macdonnell and with William Conrad providing the voice of Marshall Matt Dillon, *Gunsmoke* began as a radio program in 1952.[24] Three years later the show premiered on CBS television as a half-hour series directed toward an audience that producer-director Charles Marquis Warren noted "has grown to adulthood during the past two years."[25] Was Warren indicating that *Gunsmoke* offered an adult approach to the

Western genre, or did the statement simply mean that the show's prime time placement and quality production values salved the cultural consciences of adults who simply enjoyed Westerns? Most likely not even Warren himself knew for sure. But the fact is that *Gunsmoke* soon took over a goodly portion of comedian George Gobel's Saturday night audience and within two years had outstripped *I Love Lucy* in the Nielsen ratings. By January 1958 the adventures of Matt Dillon enjoyed a viewer following outranking any other show; the television sets in over seventeen million homes were tuned in weekly. Originally created by Filmaster production company at Columbia Studios, *Gunsmoke* was launched by topnotch professionals—Warren as producer-director and Robert Stabler as executive producer. Later the show was filmed at Paramount with star James Arness as producer and owner of the company. He also headed the *Gunsmoke* "family" of personalities.

A reluctant hero at the beginning, Arness was encouraged by John Wayne to take on the role of the Dodge City marshal, and Wayne himself provided the aura of mythic legitimacy to the opening show by introducing the first episode. Legend himself, Wayne helped to create a legend in Arness, whose six-foot-six-inch frame fit easily, comfortably, and successfully within the confines of the television screen. Arness had appeared earlier in films (for example, he menaced a group of God-fearing pioneers as the brutish outlaw in John Ford's *Wagonmaster* and had the dubious honor of playing the title role in Howard Hawks' *The Thing*) but had never achieved success in that medium. But physical stature, a rugged, not-handsome face, and a manner suited to the traditional image enabled him to build an eminently successful career as the television personification of the Western hero. That role can be best evaluated in relation to the other characters in the *Gunsmoke* company.

Gunsmoke's leading lady, Amanda Blake, matured gracefully in a role running the gamut of traditional female roles in the genre. As owner of the Long Branch Saloon, Miss Kitty's original character type suggested the seductress by implication but never by overt expression. Yet Kitty's (and Amanda Blake's) playing out of that character type added depth and complexity to what might have become mere stereotype. In her relationship with Matt, she played the role of an affectionate wife in a long-successful marriage. In her many and varied relationships with other members of both the repertory and guest casts, Kitty was sister and mother to those in need of either role. Finally, in an age of growing awareness of the liberated woman, Kitty remained her own person.[26]

Milburn Stone, who played "Doc" Adams, began his career as both good guy and bad guy in the Western films of the thirties. As town physician, Doc provided several images that are a reflection of the heroic persona—images that are slightly inappropriate or limiting for the hero but still embody certain values that need support for the audience. Doc played in turn the elder statesman, the mature friend, and the big brother, and came as close to a philosopher-clergyman as any continuing character in the series was allowed to do.

At the beginning of the 1973-74 season, James Arness, Amanda Blake, and Milburn Stone were the only survivors of the original *Gunsmoke* cast. Some characters (like Burt Reynolds as a half-Indian blacksmith for two seasons) appeared for a time and then vanished. Others (like Dennis Weaver as Chester Goode) were replaced by similar characters; for example, Ken Curtis provided facets of the Chester image but remained an irascible child in the part of Festus Haggen.[27] Still others appeared from time to time as needed, like Buck Taylor in the role of Newly O'Brien, the gunsmith.[28]

Taylor as Newly was a case in point of television's need to provide all things for all audiences. *Gunsmoke*'s executive producer, John Mantley, admitted that this character was specifically designed to play a wide range of roles, even substituting for Matt himself as the focus of segments that didn't seem quite right for the Dillon image, and practicing a bit of doctoring when Milburn Stone was absent recovering from a heart attack during the 1971 season. Furthermore, the Newly character was a younger man who could appeal to younger viewers. According to Mantley, "The four characters— Matt, Kitty, Doc and Festus—are a cross section. The one category we neglected was the young man who learns from his elders."[29] Rounding off the possibilites with characters like Newly, the *Gunsmoke* family seemed able to cover all bets.

Perhaps another reason for consistent drawing upon the Newly image was the fact that Matt Dillon, like John Wayne in the Hawks Westerns, was becoming less the traditional hero image and moving toward the role of head of the family—the father. In fact, the concept of *Gunsmoke* shifted in its nearly twenty-year life span from a series whose focus is that of a traditional hero-centered Western to a series that may be described more accurately as the continuing story of people we all know and love and who, although they are not a family, have become a family unit.

What then, has happened to the traditional heroic image of Western history, literature, and legend portrayed by James Arness as Matt Dillon? Furthermore, how does this image differ from that offered by the other mass media perpetuator of the myth—the Western film? Exploration of these two areas can provide some insights into the functions of mass media and the differing approaches of film and television to fulfill those functions for their audiences.

The Westerner in both history and myth has been viewed in this study through his interrelationship with other characters, physical setting, stock situations, and specific story. The marshal of Dodge City differs in some rather significant ways from the traditional hero in these respects.

Matt's position as "father" of the "family" has been established and reinforced throughout the years of the show and this role places restrictions upon him as hero that no traditional Westerner would or could endure. Even the historical or legendary lawman, bearing a certain community responsibility upon his shoulders, remained a free agent. The lawman of history and myth would at one time take the law and bend it. Another time he would enforce it by show of strength or skill with arms. At still another time he would simply move out of the town situation when it became incompatible, tiresome, or too civilized for the marshal of Dodge City. To whom would the characters turn in case of need? What radical (or even possible!) changes would have to be made in the lives of the other members of the family with the head gone? Furthermore, Matt is not only father of the nuclear family of his friends, he is also guardian and defender of the extended family of the town. In this role he is closer to the traditional Western hero, but he cannot loose that tie as easily as the traditional Westerner can. Matt has lost the personal liberty and control over environment that are at the core of the Western heroic character.

The historical and geographical setting of *Gunsmoke,* the visual iconography that is characteristic to the Western—all are altered from their traditional forms because of what the hero has become. The borrowed name of "Dodge City" attempts to preserve a loose connection with the historical reality, but there the similarity ends. The town had become the Garden; we are secure in its contemporaneity even though the facade resembles the rough-hewn structures of a hundred years ago. The security comes partly from the fact that the marshal is watching over it, partly from the knowledge that it must still be there for next week's episode, and partly from the realization that nothing very terrible can happen in prime time. It is a story town in a story West, with just enough of the romantic to make us feel adventurous and just enough of the familiar to recognize our town (or Somerset, or Bay City, or . . .). We see little of the wilderness; what we glimpse is only for the purpose of indicating travel to another familiar setting (a ranch house, another town). There is little of the magnificent panorama of the real Western terrain. There is no possibility for the purple—but occasionally beautiful—prose of a Zane Grey describing such majestic country. There are few episodes that concentrate on one of the iconographic staples of the Western in film—the journey tale. Production costs preclude extended emphasis upon the imagery of the outdoor West in *Gunsmoke;* but the comparatively small screen and lack of image clarity also contribute to keeping these elements to a minimum.

The financial and technical aspects of television introduce another facet of the medium which relates to how the total story—and specific situations within it—may be told. In television, the very nature of the medium shifts the emphasis to what that medium can do best—tell a compact, intimate story about a small group of people in a rigid time framework and mindful of specific and limiting guidelines. Certainly the history and legend of the West were never constrained in this manner; and the film medium, while subject to some of these limitations, is much more free to tell its story. The traditional elements of the Western which involve the hero—the stagecoach or horseback chase, the walkdown, the shootout, the hangings, scalpings, saloon fights (to say nothing of the gambling, wenching, and drinking)—are at best implied and generally omitted in *Gunsmoke* stories. Direct or indirect pressures by individuals and groups have brought a wariness into the lives of both sponsors and network executives that results in self-regulation in order to avoid censorship or cancellation. Thus, Matt Dillon will not engage in the aforementioned activities, nor will they be witnessed in any sustained or realistic manner by the audience. The result is a continuing, intimate story about a small group of people in situations that are nonthreatening to as wide an age and educational background range of audience as possible.

As the medium limits the specific situations within the story, so too it limits the kinds of story that may be told. In *Gunsmoke,* what happens must occur in or near the town and involve the primary characters in some way. Usually one of the characters is the focus of the episode, thus providing variety from week to week, giving the cast members opportunity for leaves of absence, and keeping the danger of character overexposure to a minimun. With the limits of the story world coinciding with the city limits of Dodge, there is little opportunity for the epic sweep that was available to literary historians and story-tellers recording the saga of the opening of the American West. Thus the mythic themes that accompany such stories—the search for meaning in life, the age-old struggle to triumph over evil, the birth and death and rebirth rhythm, the heroic persona brought low by a fatal flaw—all these epic elements must be fragmented, submerged, or omitted from the continuing episodes of life in Dodge City. The weekly, self-contained segment of story is costumed in myth but is really much closer to a condensed two weeks in the days of each of our lives. Even though we do not witness in our towns the specific incidents of modified mayhem that occur in Dodge City, the emphasis is not upon the incidents nor even upon the story itself, but upon its relationship to the familiar and lovable members of the family that we tune in week after week to see. We are less interested in the story as a Western—indeed, it is questionable whether it could be termed a Western at all in some cases. Rather, we have come to know and love the group—Matt and Kitty and Doc and Festus—and we immensely enjoy looking in on what they might be up to this week. Myth has become anecdote; epic has become episode.

In relation to the other characters, to the setting, and to the situation and the story, the image of Matt Dillon as Westerner has been scaled down to fit into the familial setting but has remained clothed in the trappings of the romantic myth of the West. As heroic image, Matt has long since relinquished the latter, but he need not worry since his audience would now accept him in no other way.

A once-established image is dangerous to tamper with in a successful Western series. When it becomes necessary to make some changes, the results can become disastrous. *Gunsmoke*'s long-term stablemate, *Bonanza*, is a case in point.

Bonanza: One Man's Family

On September 12, 1959, the Bonanzaland map spread its fiery image across the nation's television screens while the galloping rhythm of David Rose's theme introduced the new series to viewers. Created and produced by David Dortort,[30] *Bonanza* was filmed at the Paramount studios of NBC and sponsored by Chevrolet.[31] By 1962, the series was being aired in fifty-nine foreign countries and in five languages;[32] furthermore, the Cartwright family was providing a far more serious challenge to Matt Dillon and company than any of the bad guys who turned up weekly at the Long Branch Saloon. From 1964 to 1967 *Bonanza* enjoyed the highest average audience ratings in the Nielsen survey, even with the departure of the eldest of the Cartwrights, Adam (Pernell Roberts), in 1965. At the beginning of the 1967 season a new character named Candy (David Canary) was added to flesh out the plot possibilities in the person of a ranch hand with more negative qualities than would be allowed to the Cartwright boys. Canary left in 1970[33] but was back in the 1972 fall season when Dortort attempted to revamp the slipping series. In May, 1972, Dan Blocker died, leaving a void in the television family that the return of Canary or the introduction of Tim Matheson (as Griff) could not fill.[34]

The opening of the 1972 fall season saw the remaining two of the original "family"—Lorne Greene and Michael Landon—attempting to memorialize Blocker, recapture a straying audience, and provide a movie-of-the-week all in one. The story was the romance, marriage, and untimely death of Alice Cartwright, bride of Little Joe. The premiere segment, written and directed by Michael Landon, was originally intended to star Blocker as the bridegroom. The episode backfired emotionally, however, following too hard upon the death of Blocker. Another tragic loss—even a fictional one—was more than *Bonanza* fans could bear. Angry and hurt letters from viewers were written and Landon finally found himself defending the position of the show's creative staff in a response to those who protested the murder of the young bride.[35] In addition to its casting and scripting troubles, in the fall of 1972 the series was moved from its long-time Sunday night slot to Tuesday, a position opposite the new, popular, and highly controversial *Maude*. Whether the move proved to be the kiss of death or whether it was merely the last in a series of both unforeseen and network-planned incidents, *Bonanza* was struggling for its life when the 1972 season opened. In November the announcement was made that the January 23, 1973 show would be the final episode; at the time of the cancellation notice *Bonanza* was being shown in 90 countries to an audience of 400 million viewers. In the superlative numbers world of a volatile television industry, that record was not enough to save the series. Or perhaps, for the type of myth spun out on the Ponderosa, the handwriting was already on the wall.

At any rate, there was no close-out story on January 23. With a backlog of 430 color episodes[36] constantly being picked up for syndication, there is no reason to superimpose "The End" upon the closing credits of the last-filmed segment in the saga of the Cartwrights.

The *Bonanza* concept was built on a much-used formula but developed strength through the successful chemistry of its characters. Nestled in the breathtaking landscape of the Lake Tahoe area near Virginia City, the mythical Cartwright spread is the setting for the continuing story of Ben Cartwright, master of the Ponderosa, and his sons. As owner of the largest expanse of land in the post-Civil War Nevada territory, Pa Cartwright (called "Pa" in earlier episodes; later more respectfully referred to as "Ben") is also the benevolent guardian of quasihistorical Virginia City. It is the family formula Western all over again, compounded with the fragmenting of the heroic persona into as many segments as are needed for a multiplicity of plots and action.

The primary heroic persona of the series is Ben Cartwright, thrice-widowed patriarch of the clan. In the early episodes, Pa Cartwright displayed a God-fearing image that was similar to but more bland than the Bible-quoting Joshua Knudsen in Peckinpah's film *Ride the High Country*. Ruling the Ponderosa, overseeing the town of Virginia City, and "raising his boys," Pa operated with an iron hand gloved in soft leather and stern benevolence. Throughout its fourteen seasons, however, the image of *Bonanza*'s father figure has mellowed into an older, more sophisticated philosopher who plays the role of mediator rather than parent to his grown sons.

Like their father, the boys themselves were each endowed with a formulaic persona in the beginning. Like their father, they also had an opportunity through the years to refine and shade their characters to keep abreast—but not ahead—of the times. Pernell Roberts as Adam set to work developing the first-born son type, a role which would have seemed more at home in *The Big Valley* or on *The High Chaparral*. Perhaps a certain colorlessness in the initial concept of the character prevented Adam Cartwright from fitting into the *Bonanza* family. Perhaps Pa Cartwright's character was too close for comfort to that of the eldest son. At any rate, Roberts left the series in 1965 and the concept survived without him.[37]

Perhaps the most lovable of the *Bonanza* family is the character created by Texan and exschoolteacher Dan Blocker. Cheerfully admitting that he had "sold out" a varied acting career in favor of a continuing role in the series,

Blocker played and replayed the endearing "gentle giant" Hoss for thirteen seasons until his death in 1972.[38] In the beginning, the emphasis was on the simple-minded, comedic aspects of the character. As the series developed through the years, however, Hoss became a symbol of values dear to the heart of a democracy that had become sophisticated to the point of boredom—or desperation. Hoss—and, curiously enough, Blocker himself—came to represent the pure and homespun qualities of the uneducated man whose simple, wide-eyed, and eternally optimistic approach to life could be experienced only in fantasy by the jaundiced, disillusioned, and near-paranoid individual struggling to survive the complexities of contemporary American life. Audiences could also empathize with the hurt Hoss often experiences when other characters— friends or enemies—take advantage of his simplicity and good nature. Yet another aspect of his character, related to his physical size and direct approach to life, is his awesome stature as an opponent when roused. The age-old heroic quality of brawn conquering brain and goodness conquering all is evident in both the origins and developing of the character of Hoss Cartwright.

With his first film appearance in the title role of *I Was a Teenage Werewolf* in 1957, Michael Landon might easily have continued in a career direction that would lead down darker paths rather than up into the mountains of mythical Nevada. Cast in 1959 as Little Joe, the youngest of the Cartwrights, Landon began to work with a character that was initially a combination of the rascal and the foolish but lovable youth. As a teenager, Little Joe represents a facet of the heroic persona that can act immaturely and impulsively and still be acceptable because of his basic goodness. Joe, as well as the rest of the family, seems to possess this goodness as a given; the Cartwrights are good *because* they are Cartwrights. Other forms of behavior would be unrecognizable as family traits. During the life of the series, however, Joe has not only lost the "Little" from his name, he has also matured into a responsible and stalwart son. Now possessing some of the qualities originally assigned to Adam Cartwright, the older Joe has an advantage that Adam never had—a residual personality. The audience knew him when and fondly watched him grow.

In the same manner, the familiar residual personalities of the three Cartwrights enable them, even in the reincarnated afterlife of syndication, to remain appealing to a vast audience. *Bonanza* is an example of a family format, yet its all-male cast of principals illustrates the possibilities inherent in the old technique of splitting the hero's persona. Ben, Hoss, and Joe are all a part of that entity that might be labeled "Cartwright." The early loss of one facet of that entity—Adam—was eventually compensated for by both Ben and Joe. The loss of Hoss and the richness that his character provided, however, along with the gradual decline of the Westerner as television hero, proved more than *Bonanza* could sustain. By the end of 1972 the composite persona was shattered, and it was simply too difficult—or too much trouble—to pick up the pieces.

Besides the strength that the Cartwright character provided for the series, the story thread that unwound each week for fourteen seasons centered about a soap-opera (rather than Western) format so closely knit that it might have contributed to its own demise. The central concept linking the three characters together is, of course, the life and times of the blood-family unit—itself a slowly disintegrating aspect of American society. All stories center about the Cartwright personality and involve the Cartwright family, individually or as a group. This, in fact, is one of the prime requirements for writers of *Bonanza* scripts.[39] The plots of each episode, say Shulman and Youman, contain "less gunplay than horseplay and less action than wholesome drama with soap-opera overtones, the better to hook the entire family watching at home."[40]

Lorne Greene explains the secret of *Bonanza's* long-term popularity in another way: "One of the reasons is love. The Cartwrights happen to be a family that other families want to be like. Nobody wants to be a sonofabitch. He wants to be a nice guy. He wants to love and be loved. The Cartwrights love each other."[41] It is of such stuff that publicity articles are made, but Greene is nonetheless correct. When combined with the value of family of which Shulman and Youman speak, the need to be nice and the vicarious experience thereof can account for much of *Bonanza's* popularity. When the formula changed to a more dramatic, gritty, and existential tone in the fall 1972 season with the ill-received murder of Joe's bride, the series was in deep trouble. Richard Collins, who had been producing the show for five years prior to the closing season, discussed at that time the new direction in terms of network pressures, fate, and audience response:

> We can't do conventional Westerns any longer; since NBC owns the show, they apply the antiviolence thing especially strictly, and we're not very interested in doing shows like that anyway. So we have to move farther afield, into unexplored areas. All of which could help us get a whole new audience....
>
> Just as we personally suffered a loss [in the death of Blocker], so the audience suffered one too. Whether they'll do what families do—what we've done—which is to close ranks and go on, remains to be seen. Obviously, this year is a crucial one—and there's nobody who isn't curious to see if we can make it.[42]

When they didn't make it, Collins' statement became a summary of the reasons why. The antiviolence pressures, the audience response to moving "farther afield," and the fact of death all contributed to changes in an original concept that could not survive in altered form. Yet *Bonanza* in its prime (and in its syndication reruns) exemplifies the kind of saddle-soap formula that appeals to contemporary audiences.

Building upon Marshall McLuhan's analysis of the Western in *Understanding Media,* Marshall Fishwick identifies *Bonanza* values as important in easing the *angst* of the existential, alienated individual. *Bonanza,* he says, represents the kind of nostalgia that manifests itself in reconstructing new myths out of old:

> This kind of remythologizing is at the heart of any creative renaissance, perhaps, eventually, of survival. Faced with a new situation, we inevitably attach ourselves to the objects and the aura of the most recent past. In McLuhan's metaphor, "We look at the present through a rear-view mirror. We march backwards into the future. Suburbia lives imaginatively in Bonanzaland."
> Who says cowboys are kid stuff?[43]

Scarcely anybody says so anymore, least of all those who are deeply affected by the demise of a long-running, highly successful series like *Bonanza.*

Gunsmoke and *Bonanza,* then, provide an image of the Western compatible with the small and still-unclear image of the medium of television. At the same time, these two series display the Westerner in a role that draws upon the qualities of the traditional historical and adapted film hero, yet has domesticized him to the extent that he will not make the audience uncomfortable in their living rooms. Moreover, the images of Matt Dillon and of the Cartwrights reflect two aspects of that altered persona that the television medium itself has created out of the myth-size Western figure of history and film. The two aspects—the hero as loner and the hero as group—have been assessed by John Cawelti in an examination of the adult Western written in 1968.

At that time, Cawelti viewed Matt Dillon as an example of the "man in the middle"—a man "called upon to carry out a duty morally or emotionally repugnant to him."[44] This might indeed have been Matt's dilemma when he was first created in 1955, but he seemed later to be more and more comfortable with carrying out his duty. We seem to be more and more comfortable with accepting his unflinching judgment in the matter as well. We do not question Matt, and he does not question himself. There is little room for ambiguity; brightly colored television screens omit from their spectrum the shades of gray which create an uncomfortable dilemma for either hero or audience. This assurance, of course, is in keeping with one aspect of the Western hero, but in Matt's case singleness of purpose and clarity of judgment are characteristic not of the complex man in the middle, but of the complacent man in the midst. He is not the heroic colossus, straddling the two worlds of civilization and savagery. He is rather the beneficent landlord of the town, comfortable in its security and pleased with his own ability to keep it that way. There is no latent civilization-savagery conflict in Matt Dillon. He is at ease in the world that he has created and in which he has chosen to dwell.

The Cartwright character—with its triple facets of Ben, Hoss, and Joe—is developed through what Cawelti calls the antithesis of the man-in-the-middle story. Labeled the "group involvement" Western, the format is not really a Western at all. Rather, such series are "disguised forms of realist drama, conventionalized and slightly romanticized by the use of Western settings—most of them still have a recognizable thematic pattern."[45] This was unquestionably the case with *Bonanza* in its beginnings, and has remained basically the same throughout the years. Specifically, Cawelti details the thematic pattern of the format as a social situation familiar to the contemporary American:

> The Cartwright ranch is surrounded by a world of chicanery, violence, and treachery in almost the way the harmonious American middle-class suburb is threatened by the explosive forces of the expanding city. But the cohesiveness, mutual loyalty, and homogeneous adjustment of the Cartwright family always turns out to be capable of throwing back, or blunting the edge of, the invading forces.[46]

Viable perhaps in the Cold War era in which it was created, the *Bonanza* heroic myth could be sustained only insofar as it remained loyal to its family setting and family composition. With the exploration of themes foreign to that kind of cohesiveness, and with the death of one member of the family, the concept lost interest. The audience could find the same values in a setting less mythical and more relevant to their experience. While *Bonanza* was dying, *The Waltons* was being born.

The Electronic Mythmakers: God Has Not Permitted Us To Know What Will Sell[47]

Gunsmoke and *Bonanza* are specific examples of a formula that has grown and developed along with the medium of television itself. Like all artists, the electronic mythmakers must shape their themes and messages to the medium from which the work emerges. Whereas the story-tellers of classical legend and popular literature were the auteurs in the sense of controllers of their characters and themes, whereas in many of the best Western films the director with his company has been able to take on the auteur function in shaping the myth, in television both writer and director are nearly anonymous and nowhere near autonomous. Instead, the basic concept and the actor as personality (rather than star) become the controlling forces that rule out the possibility of writer or director as auteur.[48] Thus, the basic concept and the actor-personality impress themselves deeply upon the three elements of the television Western series. The elements are structure, character, and story—all of which are givens by the time the writer and director approach their tasks.[49]

The structure of the television show itself is dependent upon time and money. As a result, the established time frames of half-hour units and designated commercial breaks are far more limiting than those imposed upon the writer of either books or films. Not only must the structure be tied to the constant rhythm of a climax prior to each commercial break, but the beginning teaser must also catch and hold the viewer while the ending "kicker" or preview must keep the audience through the commercial break just preceding it. Even the selection and placement of scenes are dependent upon the coordination of financial outlay with time spent in production. The constraints that this coordination places upon the television writer's development of the story reflect the ever-present reality that this is a medium to which only solvent artworks need apply. For example, a weekly episode generally requires six days of shooting, with between eight and one-half to ten and one-half pages of the script being put onto film each day (the two-page range is accounted for by the difference in pacing of each director). If a particular scene is to be shot at the *Bonanza* ranch, for example, it should amount to approximately eight pages of script, since the expense of going on location would be prohibitive for a segment shorter than a day's shooting time.[50]

Restrictions of this kind tend to develop in the writer and director an acute consciousness of craft rather than art. The structural rules of the series game can thus increase the risk of turning the format into at best a comfortable routine, at worst a predictable and boring sterotype.

Added to the exigencies of structure are the necessities developing about the recurring characters in any series. These types must remain stable enough for audience identification and development of residual personality, yet they are also responsible for satisfying the constant demand for variety. Irwin Blacker indicates the problem of developing character as one of the difficulties of creating a classic Western in the television format. If the story is to have any significance, says Blacker, the people in it must change; yet in a Western series the hero cannot risk change.[51] The writer, therefore, must constantly use "guest" characters who are able to develop, change, or die within the context of the weekly episode while the hero functions as a catalyst in that action. This constraint, though preventing the series from developing into a significant drama, achieves a twofold purpose necessary to the continuing story: the variety of secondary plots and characters retains audience interest; the stability of the continually developing (but basically unchanging) residual personality of the hero sustains audience loyalty. Thus the value of stability and the need for change further test the writer's skill in creating characters for the television medium.

Together with the requirements of structure and character, the problem of story as the third element in the television series format introduces still another challenge for the electronic mythmaker. The story line of each weekly show must be believable yet provide fantasy and escape; it must be seriously realistic yet entertaining and relaxing. Such is the paradox of television as story-teller, the dilemma of writer as mythmaker. This schizophrenia is symptomatic of a deeper conflict that the medium suffers as it attempts to address the question of its very identity.

Is television an art form or an entertainment medium? Is it fact-finder or myth-spinner? Or all of these? Or something else? A viewer may accept Ben Cartwright to such a degree that he accosts Lorne Greene in a restaurant and tells him that his (the viewer's) ancestors owned the spread adjoining that of the Cartwrights' near Virginia City. Other viewers shed real tears and send hurt letters to the series when the Cartwright bride is murdered. On the other hand, the documentary reality of a demonstration, a poverty-ridden town, or a space shot has been imitated in art so often that the violence or drama seems only part of a story and not a recording of life. To the degree that factual programming in television takes on the aura of fantasy, series story-telling becomes grippingly real. In a mass medium that purveys both fact and fantasy, the lines between documentary and fiction tend to blur. Writers must be constantly mindful that they are creating stories that are far more real at times than the unfolding of a developing news event.

Thus the three elements in the television series format—structure, character, and story—provide constraints, challenges, and responsibilities for the electronic mythmaker. They are sharing with their print and film counterparts in perpetuating the heroic image of the American Westerner, but with a vision adapted—again, like their counterparts—to the medium in which they create.

The Television Western: At Home on the Twenty-Five-Inch Range

The scaling-down process that takes place in the television Western, then, turns the bold colors and vibrance of the epic form into the leisurely pastels of the pastoral mode.[52] Drama becomes soap opera and, as one writer of Westerns put it, the contrast can be illustrated in a distinction resembling the different between free verse and the sonnet.[53] The film medium lends itself to free form; television tells its story in a much more mannered fashion. The old myths are present, but in vestigial form. Deprived of the size and scope that are the luxury of print and film, television turns toward the homey and personal aspects of the hero that will endear him to his audience even without a panoramic backdrop.

The question asked, the problems faced in the television pastoral are smaller because both the medium and the audience's world are smaller in psychological, if not physical size. Yet the questions are relevant to an audience living in a culture that is not struggling for physical survival but rather is attempting to learn how to live with its neighbors in psychological harmony. It is not an audience stepping off into the wilderness to conquer a virgin land, but is oftentimes a community of isolates who need to explore the world outside their front doors. Perhaps the pastoral mode of the television Western, focusing as it does on an idealized life set in an artificial format, should capitalize upon its ability to complement rather than compete with Western literature and films.

Television must do what it can do best. If the medium continues to opt for documentary realism in its search for identity, then the Western as television audiences have known it will, at least for a time, fade from the screen. For the story of the Western hero is myth-spinning at the top of its tall-tale bent. This American legend is based in reality, but reality it surely is not. When the epic qualities of both the reality and the myth must of necessity be so diminished as to fit within the confines of the television screen, the vigor and fire of the epic form cool down to the warming nostalgia of the pastoral.

It is not surprising, then, that the Western television hero is riding wearily into the sunset. But when a new day dawns for him he will no doubt return at a gallop, armed to service deep-seated needs, and in the image of whatever values his audience holds most dear.

Conclusion

The story is told that in 1913, a stage actor approached an old roommate who had shared poorer days with him in New York. Both were now successful; the actor was on tour and the old roommate had become a motion picture producer. The actor, so the story goes, wanted to try a film Western. The producer, Thomas Ince, told his old friend Bill Hart that he was too late; every company was making Westerns because they were cheap to make, the movie houses were surfeited with them, and besides, they were on the way out. Ince gave Hart a chance, however, and put him into a film called *The Bargain,* which the neophyte critic of *The Moving Picture Herald* castigated as one of those old-fashioned Westerns: "a bold, I might even say a reckless attempt to revive a style of motion picture which we had hoped was a thing of the past."

Sixteen years later Wyatt Earp died. At that time the film industry was struggling with sound and the Western hero was once again fighting for its popular life. His old enemy—civilization and its technology—had produced a new kind of hero as real as Wyatt Earp had ever been. In April 1929, James R. Quirk published as editorial in the influential *Photoplay* magazine that squared off the adversaries in the showdown. Lucky Lindy, Quirk concluded, had replaced the cowboy as national hero, while Tom Mix, Hoot Gibson, and Ken Maynard would have to take to the skies or retire to an old actors' home. Sam Browne, the editorial ran, would now draw the adulation of little boys aspiring to heroic deeds as a result of Lindbergh's flight, for the "Western novel and motion picture have slunk away into the brush, never to return."

With the dates removed, these columns could be slipped appropriately into today's newspapers or magazine. The demise of the Western formula has been regularly announced for the past sixty years, yet the critics who have predicted imminent death for the genre have also been forced periodically to review a Western film or television production that pumps new blood into the traditional, hack-weary formula with astonishing results. There seems to be life in the old boy yet.

The dire predictions of *The Moving Picture Herald* and *Photoplay,* appearing as they did upon the threshhold of the William S. Hart and John Ford eras, are perhaps patterns in a recurring rhythm indicating a renaissance for the Western in the future. If by this time the computer-age superhero has almost had his day and the bewildered audience is ready to return to the simpler things of life, then the man of the land will also return. If the popularity of the Western genre is a cyclic phenomenon in mass culture, it is based upon a reaffirmation that there is something of basic value in the form. Not something that is worth preserving, but rather something that perhaps does not need preserving because it is still operative—something that reflects the vitality and stability of recurring themes of ancient myth.

The Western, of course, represents a way of life that was eclipsed at the time of the closing of the American frontier. Once the new Adam and Eve of symbol and story, today's Americans are less sure of their strength, less confident of success through their own efforts. At one time reborn of American idealism and hope for the future, we no longer feel we are in control of our environment, ultimate victors in the battle against evil. Both the land itself and the mastery of the land have become a memory and an impossible dream for technological society. We often feel now that we have little choice but to place our confidence and existential hope (if that is not a contradiction in terms) in the power of the machine.

The outer landscape of the contemporary American has been altered with the hardware of technology. It began with the first slim threads of barbed wire and telegraph wire crisscrossing the open spaces of the Western prairie. It continued with the blasts of steam from Fulton's engine and the rods of steel railroad track winding through dynamited mountain passes. Without doubt the machine has all but dispossessed nature.

More seriously, perhaps, the contemporary American's inner landscape has been befogged by shades of grey. No longer is the cause clearly and unmistakably good or evil; no longer can the good guys be recognized by their color, gentle birth, cleanliness of speech and dress, and courtesy to women and children. No longer do the bad guys receive their just deserts; on the contrary, more frequently they become the possessors of the earth while the heroes are outsiders—symbolic of anti- or nonheroism. Contemporary Americans, moreover, are less able to account for their own conflicting desires, motivations, and impulses. We have few and immediate goals, we often find striving for them futile, and it is increasingly difficult to see purpose in what we do or are.

Americans' outer and inner life has become surrounded by a network of technology that provides the arteries bringing heat, light, and bodily sustenance as well as intellectual food and emotional feasts. Cut off our technology and we are dead—at least until we can, after great agony of withdrawal, readapt and reorient in a new (or is it an old?) pattern. If American society is to continually rejuvenate itself, it must be done not by rejecting the reality of the present through withdrawal into the past, but by embracing the present with all its frustrations, ambiguities, and paradoxes. The present world is the only possible one to live in.

To not merely survive, but to fully live in the present, individuals need to keep in touch with their historical and mythical roots. For Americans, the Western genre has played a cyclic but consistent role in sustaining and enriching the cultural images growing from those roots. The Westerner's lead pony is continuing the journey of Ulysses' ship and Sigurd's spirited horse. The hero's moment of truth on a dusty street or in a cleared-out saloon is the eternal challenge of Osiris against death or David against Goliath or Gawain against the Green Knight. And if at the present moment the Westerner has been eclipsed by the computer-age hero, that mechanized man himself is still on the same heroic journey but in an Aston-Martin, a private jet, or a space capsule. He is still waging a one-man battle against the unbelievable odds of a criminal mastermind, a galactic corporation, or the mysteries of the universe itself.

And astonishing as it is, Ulysses continually wins. Sigurd, David, and Gawain win. The Westerner wins, as does the computer hero. The songs of arms and the man continue; the old myths are not dead but changed. The mystery of humanity's relationship to the gods of earth and sky continues to be told by the mythmakers of both ancient and new tradition. The heroic images of demigods and champions carved upon the old altars are replaced by electronic images sent mysteriously through the air. As the new theologians, the mythmakers have inherited the ancient tradition of retelling the hero's story with whatever tools nature and culture put at their disposal. Through the labors of these spinners of tales the American Westerner has become a part of the heroic tradition, moving from oral history to electronic image.

The story in whatever form still responds to our needs and represents our dreams. It is the ancient tale of the hero, his quest, his battle and ultimate victory over evil, and his apotheosis by the community as the reward of his herculean labors. It is of such stuff that myths have always been made. It is of such stuff that the hopes of the future will always be made—in whatever form—as long as there is a story to be told, a mythmaker to spin the tale, and someone to believe in the dream.

Appendix A

Television Westerns

The following is a listing of Western series that have appeared on television in the United States from 1948 to 1972.

Action in the Afternoon
Adventures of Champion, The
Adventures of Jim Bowie, The
Adventures of Kit Carson, The
Alias Smith and Jones
Annie Oakley
Bat Masterson
Big Valley, The
Black Saddle
Bonanza
Boots and Saddles—The Story
    of the Fifth Cavalry
Branded
Brave Eagle
Broken Arrow
Bronco
Buffalo Bill, Jr.
Cade's County
Californians, The
Cheyenne
Cimarron City
Cimarron Strip
Cisco Kid, The
Colt .45
Cowboy in Africa
Crusader, The
Dakota
Daniel Boone
Davy Crockett
Death Valley Days
Deputy, The

Dirty Sally
Dundee and the Culhane
Empire (later: Redigo)
F Troop
Frontier
Frontier Circus
Gabby Hayes
Gene Autry
Guns of Will Sonnett
Gunslinger
Gunsmoke
Have Gun, Will Travel
Hawkeye
Hec Ramsey
Hero, The
High Chaparral, The
Hondo
Hopalong Cassidy
Hotel De Paree
Iron Horse, The
Jefferson Drum
Johnny Ringo
Judge Roy Bean
Klondike
Kung Fu
Lancer
Laramie
Laredo
Law of the Plainsman
Lawman
Legend of Custer, The (or: Custer)
Legend of Jesse James, The
Life and Legend of Wyatt Earp, The
Lone Ranger, The
Loner, The
Mackenzie's Raiders
Man Called Shenandoah, A
Man from Blackhawk, The
Maverick
Nichols
Oklahoma Kid
Outcasts, The
Outlaws
Overland Trail
Pony Express
Range Rider
Rawhide
Rebel, The
Red Ryder
Restless Gun, The

Rifleman, The
Riverboat
Road West, The
Rodeo, U.S.A.
Rough Riders
Rounders, The
Roy Rogers
Sergeant Preston of the Yukon
Shane
Sheriff of Cochise, The
Shotgun Slade
Stagecoach West
Steve Donovan, Western Marshal
Stoney Burke
Sugarfoot
Sundance Kid, The
Tales of the Texas Rangers
Monroes, The
Tall Man, The
Tate
Texan, The
Tombstone Territory
Trackdown
Trails West
Travels of Jaimie McPheeters, The
Twenty-Six Men
U.S. Marshal
Virginian, The (later: The Men from Shiloh)
Wagon Train
Wanted—Dead or Alive
Wells Fargo
Westerner
Whispering Smith
Wichita Town
Wide Country, The
Wild Bill Hickok
Wild Wild West, The
Yancy Derringer
Zane Grey Theatre (or: Dick Powell's Zane Grey Theatre)
Zorro

Appendix B

Writer Guidelines for *Bonanza*

These "rules" for *Bonanza* writers appeared in Nancy Vogel, " 'Bonanza' Scripts," *Writer's Digest,* Vol. 48, No. 12 (December 1968), 62-64, 93, 95.

1. Absolutely no railroad stories, or yarns which require mine interiors, floods, blizzards or fires.

2. Because of the color requirements, exterior night shots should be avoided if possible, with the exception of the Ponderosa ranch house and barn, which are located on stage.

3. Stories must *always* deeply involve the Cartwrights. We do not want the Cartwrights "looking in" on the problems of someone else. At times we have used, and will continue to use, guest stars of considerable stature, but when we do the problem is still to be a Cartwright problem and the solution a Cartwright solution.

4. The Cartwrights must never be cast as "do-gooders." In other words, the problem should never become a Cartwright problem merely by having the Cartwrights push their way into it.

5. We often have a surfeit of Indian stories. Forget, too, any stories concerning a "wife" showing up, or someone claiming to own the Ponderosa, or the young, misunderstood rebel who regenerates because of the Cartwrights' tolerance and example.

6. We have many stories submitted in which the townspeople "turn against" the Cartwrights. Unless the story is truly unique and believable, this area should be avoided. The Cartwrights are too intelligent in their behavior, too respected and too prominent to have such a thing happen.

7. What we do want is Western action and Western adventure, concerning a worthy and dramatic problem for the Cartwrights, and strong opponents. We want human drama built around a specific locale and specific period in the country's history; simple, basic stories as seen through the eyes of Ben, Hoss, and Little Joe Cartwright, and Candy.

Notes

Chapter 1

1. The Homestead Act, says DeVoto, meant that "Uncle Sam bets you a hundred and sixty acres that you'll starve in less than five years. It was a safe bet." Bernard DeVoto, "The West: A Plundered Province," *Harpers Magazine,* Vol. 169 (August 1934), p. 362.

2. Russel B. Nye and J.E. Morpugo, *A History of the United States,* 2 Vols., 2nd ed., Baltimore: Penguin Books, 1964, p. 345.

3. Cited in Russel B. Nye, *The Cultural Life of the New Nation, 1776-1830,* New York: Harper and Brothers, Publishers, 1960, pp. 117-18.

4. John Francis McDermott (ed.), *The Frontier Re-Examined,* Urbana: The University of Illinois Press, 1967, p. 2.

5. Nye and Morpugo, *A History,* p. 351.

6. Ibid., p. 351.

7. Nye, *The Cultural Life,* p. 120.

8. DeVoto, "The West: A Plundered Province," p. 356-57.

9. Frederick Jackson Turner, *Frontier and Section: Selected Essays of Frederick Jackson Turner,* with an Introduction by Ray Allen Billington, Englewood Cliffs, N.J.: Prentice-Hall, Inc., 1961, p. 39.

10. John G. Cawelti, *The Six-Gun Mystique,* Bowling Green, Ohio: Bowling Green University Popular Press, n.d., p. 27.

11. Northrop Frye, *Anatomy of Criticism,* Princeton: Princeton University Press, 1957, p. 83.

12. This concept will reappear in the discussion of mythmakers in print, film, and television.

13. Notable in the expanding of resources in this area is the investigative, codifying, and evaluative study of anthropologists examining the culture of the native American.

14. In the legend of the Trojan war the tradition of the hero based in history and transformed into myth is particularly adaptable to analogy with the American Western hero.

15. Increased scholarship in biblical studies is presently enriching the Judaeo-Christian tradition and theological perspectives through correlation between archetypal studies and anthropomorphic approaches.

16. Joseph Campbell (ed.), *Myths, Dreams, and Religion,* New York: E.P. Dutton, 1970, pp. 138-75. See also Sam Keen, "Man and Myth: A Conversation with Joseph Campbell," *Psychology Today,* Vol. 5, No. 2 (July 1971), p. 35.

17. DeVoto, "The West: A Plundered Province," p. 356.

18. See the Introduction by DeVoto to Benjamin Albert Botkin (ed.), *A Treasury of Western Folklore,* New York: Crown Publishers, 1951, p.x.

19. James K. Folsom, *The American Western Novel,* New Haven: College and University Press, 1966, p. 204.

20. See Botkin, *A Treasury,* pp. 417, 165; Harry Schein, "The Olympian Cowboy," *The American Scholar,* Vol. 24, No. 3 (Summer 1955), pp. 316-19; John Williams, "The Western: Definition of a Myth," *The Nation,* Vol. 193, No. 17 (November 18, 1961), p. 405; Robert Warshow's essay on the Westerner in Robert Warshow, *The Immediate Experience,* Garden City: Doubleday & Co., Inc., 1962; David W. Noble, *The Eternal Adam and the New World Garden,* New York: George Braziller, 1968; and Henry Nash Smith, *Virgin Land: The American West as Symbol and Myth,* New York: Vintage Books, 1950.

21. Nonetheless, many writers will insist that any basic theme is adaptable to the Western format; see the discussion on writing for television in Chapter 4.

22. Cawelti, *Six-Gun Mystique,* p. 27.

23. Ibid., p. 31.

Chapter 2

1. Pauline Kael, "Circles and Squares," *Film Quarterly,* Vol. 16, No. 3 (Spring 1963), pp. 12-26; Andrew Sarris, "The Auteur Theory and the Perils of Pauline," *Film Quarterly,* Vol. 16, No. 4 (Summer 1963), pp. 26-33.

2. Jim Kitses, *Horizons West,* Bloomington: Indiana University Press, 1969, Chapter I.

3. Tom Ryall, "The Notion of Genre," *Screen,* Vol. 11, No. 2 (March-April 1970), pp. 23-26.

4. Edward Buscombe, "The Idea of Genre in the American Cinema," *Screen,* Vol. 11, No. 2 (March-April 1970), p. 34.

5. Ryall ascribes this view to André Bazin and Andrew Sarris: the application seems to misread the intentions of both critics. On the other hand, it is practically impossible to refrain from comparative statements in criticism. It would seem, in fact, that the measurement of the real against *some* kind of ideal is one of the characteristics that distinguishes criticism from description.

6. Buscombe, "The Idea of Genre," pp. 39-40.

7. Ibid., p. 43.

8. Richard Collins, "Genre: A Reply to Ed Buscombe," *Screen,* Vol. 11, Nos. 4-5 (August-September 1970), pp. 69-70.

9. Ibid., pp. 74-75.

10. Andrew Tudor, "Genre: Theory and Mispractice in Film Criticism," *Screen,* Vol. 11, No. 6 (November-December 1970), p. 35.

11. Ibid., pp. 37-39.

12. Ibid., p. 42.

13. Ibid., p. 43.

14. See: Kitses, *Horizons West;* Alan Lovell, "The Western," and Colin McArthur, "The Roots of the Western," both in Edward Buscombe (comp. and ed.), *The Western: Study Unit 12,* unpublished manuscript disseminated by the British Film Institute, September, 1971, pp. 51-66; Warshow, *Immediate Experience;* Frye, *Anatomy of Criticism;* Cawelti, *Six-Gun Mystique;* Ralph Willett, "The American Western: Myth and Anti-Myth," *Journal of Popular Culture, Vol. 4, No. 2 (Fall 1970), pp. 455-62;* André Bazin (Hugh Gray, ed. and trans.), *What Is Cinema?,* Vol. 2, Berkeley: University of California Press, 1971, pp. 140-57. These titles deal with literature or film or both. Any body of serious or memorable study of the medium of television is nonexistent.

15. However, the public still tends to limit genre to these few basic and somewhat traditional categories. A James Bond story has not yet achieved the stature of genre (if stature it is), but that is not to say that the day may never arrive when Fleming's creation becomes a genre category of itself. This may also be true of science fiction. Such a possibility simply reflects once again the strong element of cultural conventions and cultural consensus in the notion of genre.

16. Extract from an interview in *Films and Filming* (April 1966), cited in Buscombe, *The Western: Study Unit 12,* p. 37.

17. Certainly there are shades and degrees of opinion in both these approaches, as there are in still another view which totally rejects the existence of myth or symbol in the Western. This third position will not be treated here, since the presence of mythic force in the genre has already been established as a basic premise of this study. The argument that this third group presents is an interesting one, but is material for another investigation.

18. See in particular the writing C.G. Jung, Kenneth Burke, and the members of the archetypal school of literary criticism.

19. See Campbell's four functions of myth noted earlier.

20. Cawelti, *Six-Gun Mystique,* passim.

21. Cited in Richard MacCann, *Hollywood in Transition,* Boston: Houghton Mifflin, 1962, pp. 175-76. Gruber is an interesting example of a contemporary mythmaker in the field of popular literature and will be discussed in relation to others of this category.

22. Film and television directors, however, frequently arrange for mountain backgrounds to enhance the often monotonous terrain of some of these regions.

23. Generally, if the setting is the frontier (as the term is used here) the other elements will function consistently with it. There have been attempts—usually for the sake of comedy—in which one or more elements are used outside the frontier context. This seems to be the case in Douglas Fairbanks' *Manhattan Madness* (1916), where any Western element included was perhaps more an excuse to display Fairbanks' energetic talent than an example of the Western genre. Other films have been used in this manner, particularly those of comedy teams.

24. Cawelti, *Six-Gun Mystique,* pp. 46ff.

25. Ray B. Browne and Ronald J. Ambrosetti, *Popular Culture and Curricula,* Bowling Green: Bowling Green University Popular Press, 1970, p. 11.

26. Kitses, *Horizons West*, p. 27.

27. The creator seems less constrained by the fact-fiction problem; story-tellers take it for granted that they are also mythmakers rather than reporters or historians. The audience seems less aware of the fact-fiction ambiguity.

28. As the only new Westerner of the 1972 television season, Richard Boone's Hec Ramsey bears striking similarities to a man named Heck Thomas, an Oklahoma lawman who rode for Judge Parker around the turn of the century; see Ken Sobol, "The West: Authentic and Absurd," *The Village Voice* (October 12, 1972), p. 50. Leatherstocking was, of course, patterned after Daniel Boone. Making the world smaller still, Kit Carson's mother was a Boone and Richard Boone claims seventh-generation nephewship to Kentucky's first settler.

29. Kitses, *Horizons West*, p. 11.

30. See Williams, "Definition of a Myth," p. 405.

31. Smith, *Virgin Land*, p. 58.

32. Kent Ladd Steckmesser, *The Western Hero in History and Legend*, Norman, Okla.: The University of Oklahoma Press, 1965, p. 5.

33. Cecil B. Hartley, *Life and Times of Colonel Daniel Boone*, Philadelphia: G.G. Evans, 1860, p. 62, cited in Steckmesser, *The Western Hero*, p. 7. Steckmesser notes: "When the reader is referred to a novel for historical information, fiction becomes history."

34. Smith, *Virgin Land*, p. 68.

35. Ibid., p. 76.

36. Cited in Nye and Morpugo, *A History*, p. 290. This description, almost word for word, is also given of keelboater Mike Fink. The similarity indicates the unabashed borrowing that mythmakers practiced in developing their tall tales.

37. Walter Blair, "Six Davy Crocketts," *Southwest Review*, Vol. 25, No. 4 (July 1940), pp. 444-45.

38. The only exception to this general attitude was the intensely popular but comparatively short-lived Disney version of Davy Crockett on television and in promotional items during the 1950s.

39. Smith, *Virgin Land*, p. 88.

40. Today's traveler in the western half of the United States will encounter both tourist bait and historical markers tracing the steps and exploits of Fremont and Carson. It seems that they never stood still, perpetually crisscrossing the vast wilderness from the Dakotas to Old Mexico, from Nebraska to California.

41. Smith, *Virgin Land*, p. 92.

42. Ibid., p. 93.

43. J. Edward Leithead, "The Anatomy of Dime Novels," *Dime Novel Roundup*, Vol. 36, No. 2 (February 15, 1967), pp. 14-17.

44. Steckmesser, *The Western Hero*, p. 53.

45. Smith, *Virgin Land*, p. 97.

46. Ibid., p. 107.

47.   Gilbert Patten, "Dime Novel Days," *Saturday Evening Post,* Vol. 203, No. 35 (February 28, 1931), p. 129. In this article Patten recounts an anecdote about the first meeting between Wheeler and William H. Manning, another Beadle employee, on a New Jersey ferry:

> [Manning's] attention was drawn to a not-at-all-ferocious-looking man who was swaggering around the forward deck beneath a huge sombrero. Presently this person ranged up beside Manning, who was gazing at the massed buildings of lower Manhattan, and spoke in a soft, drawling voice.
>
> "Well, pard," said the stranger, "it sure enough is right good to see the old town again after quite a spell of roughing it out in Dakota. I allow I'm plenty glad to get back."
>
> "So you've been out in Dakota, have you?" said Manning. "For business or pleasure?"
>
> "Business, pard—business," was the answer. "One of my regular trips to pick up atmosphere and material for my novels. I'm Edward L. Wheeler, author of the Deadwood Dick stories."
>
> Manning smiled.... He introduced himself as a fellow writer for Beadle and Adams, and thereafter he saw the proud creator of Deadwood Dick a number of times.

What caution was needed by these intrepid mythmakers, who could never be sure whether the next person they attempted to gull might be a fellow-guller writing under the same roof but at the other end of the room.

48.   Smith, *Virgin Land,* p. 134.

49.   Jane is Dick's feminine counterpart, and figures in several of the Deadwood Dick stories. She is featured in *Deadwood Dick on Deck; or, Calamity Jane, the Heroine of Whoop-Up. A Story of Dakota.* Other of Dick's ladies were 'Shian Sal and Phantom Moll, the Girl Footpad, ibid., pp. 132-33.

50.   Ibid., p. 111.

51.   George Armstrong Custer, *My Life on the Plains; or, Personal Experiences with Indians,* New York: Sheldon and Company, 1876, p. 12. Italics in the original.

52.   Frederick Van DeWater, *Glory-Hunter: A Life of General Custer,* New York: The Bobbs-Merrill Company, 1934, p. 227.

53.   Cody, who did some fighting under Custer's command, was also linked with him in dime novels; e.g., *Buffalo Bill's Grip; or, Oath-Bound to Custer* and *Buffalo Bill's Big Four; or, Custer's Shadow,* both by Prentiss Ingraham. Such titles indicate that the Custer name was possibly being used to enhance the growing Cody reputation and legend.

54.   Two recent examples in the arts are Vine DeLoria's book *Custer Died for Your Sins* and Arthur Penn's film *Little Big Man.*

55.   General D.S. Stanley, *Personal Memoirs,* Cambridge, 1917, cited in Van DeWater, *Glory-Hunter,* p. 242.

56.   See: Jack Parks, *Who Killed Custer?,* New York: Tower Publications, Inc., 1971; and Stanley Vestal, "The Man Who Killed Custer," *American Heritage,* Vol. 8 (February 1957), pp. 9-12.

57.   Joe B. Frantz and Julian Ernest Choate, Jr., *The American Cowboy: the Myth and the Reality,* Norman, Okla.: University of Oklahoma Press, 1955, p. 13.

58.   Smith, *Virgin Land,* p. 123.

59.   Marshall W. Fishwick, "The Cowboy: America's Contribution to the World's Mythology," *Western Folklore,* Vol. 11, No. 2 (April 1952), p. 84.

60. These four newspaper accounts are cited in Clifford P. Westermeier (ed.), *Trailing the Cowboy,* Caldwell, Idaho: The Caxton Printers, Ltd., 1955, pp. 48ff.

61. John Baumann, "On a Western Ranche," *Fortnightly Review,* Vol. 47 (1887), p. 516.

62. Fishwick, "America's Contribution," p. 78.

63. Carey McWilliams, "Myths of the West," *North American Review,* Vol. 232 (November 1931), p. 428.

64. See McMurtry's essay, "Cowboys, Movies, Myths, and Cadillacs: Realism in the Western," in William R. Robinson (ed.), *Man and the Movies,* Baton Rouge: Louisiana State University Press, 1967, p. 52.

65. Larry McMurtry, however, feels that this basic plot is changing, particularly on television; ibid., p. 48.

66. At the time they rode with Quantrill, Frank James was twenty years old, Jesse seventeen. The Youngers ranged from Cole at twenty-one, to Jim at eighteen, and Bob at seventeen. For an account of these and other Kansas-Missouri gangs, see Harry Sinclair Drago, *Outlaws on Horseback,* London: John Long, 1965.

67. Walter Prescott Webb, *The Great Plains,* Waltham, Massachusetts: Blaisdell Publ. Co., 1959 (1931), p. 496.

68. Eugene Cunningham, *Triggernometry: A Gallery of Gunfighters,* Caldwell, Idaho: Caxton Printers, 1947, pp. 2-3.

69. Fitzroy Raglan, *The Hero: A Study in Tradition, Myth, and Drama,* London: Watts, 1949; Frye, *Anatomy of Criticism;* and Joseph Campbell, *Hero with a Thousand Faces,* 2nd ed., Princeton: Princeton University Press, 1968. On American heroes, see Marshall Fishwick, *The Hero, American Style,* New York: D. McKay Co., 1969.

70. Mody Boatright, et al. (eds.), *Mesquite and Willow,* Dallas: Southern Methodist University Press, 1957, pp. 97ff.

71. One zealous debunker lists the Kid's possible names as they would appear in a telephone book. They range from Austin Antrim to Michael McCarty, with eight other versions between. See Peter Lyons, *The Wild Wild West,* New York: Funk and Wagnalls, 1969, p. 118.

72. J.C. Dykes, *Billy the Kid: The Bibliography of a Legend,* Albuquerque: University of New Mexico Press, 1952. The Kid has also been a sympathetic character on television—even a star in his own series.

73. Lyons, *Wild Wild West,* p. 123.

74. Bernard DeVoto, "Brave Days in Washoe," *American Mercury,* Vol. 17, No. 66 (June 1929), p. 234.

75. Boatright, *Mesquite and Willow,* p. 103.

76. Hardin's own account of his capture in his autobiography differs considerably from other versions.

77. Joseph G. Rosa, *The Gunfighter: Man or Myth?,* Norman, Okla.: University of Oklahoma Press, 1969, p. 11.

78. Ibid., pp. 10-11.

79. The absence of the gunfighter hero on television—and his replacement by the urban and "computer" hero—will be noted again later in this study.

80. Alexander Miller, "The Western: A Theological Note," *Christian Century,* Vol. 74, No. 48 (November 27, 1957), p. 1409.

81. Bernard DeVoto, "Birth of an Art," *Harper's Magazine,* Vol. 211, No. 1267 (December 1955), passim.

82. Lyons, *Wild, Wild West,* p. 126.

83. Rosa, *The Gunfighter,* p. 125.

84. For an interesting account of Masterson and others, see Jack Parks, "They Died With Their Boots Off," *True,* Vol. 52, No. 415 (December 1971), pp. 51-56.

85. Rosa, *The Gunfighter,* p. 121.

86. One of Masterson's subjects was his old friend from Dodge City days, Luke Short. Luke had a reputation as "the undertaker's friend:" "He shot 'em where it didn't show." Ibid., p. 140.

87. Ibid., p. 133.

88. John Sturges attempted to convey this image of both Earp and Holliday by beginning his *Hour of the Gun* with the shootout and continuing with a documentarylike approach to the subsequent events.

89. Frantz and Choate, *The American Cowboy,* p. 91.

90. Charles F. Gross to J.B. Edwards, June 15, 1925; Manuscripts Division, Kansas State Historical Society; cited in Rosa, *The Gunfighter,* p. 120.

91. Lyons, *Wild, Wild West,* pp. 144-47.

92. The series shared time with other media heroes—*Hec Ramsey* was one of the alternating segments of the network "Mystery Movie" miniseries.

93. See Mody Boatright, "The American Myth Rides the Range," *Southwest Review,* Vol. 36, No. 3 (Summer 1951), pp. 157-63; also David D. Davis, "Ten-Gallon Hero," *American Quarterly,* Vol. 6, No. 2 (Summer 1954), p. 112.

94. Marshall Fishwick, *American Heroes: Myth and Reality,* Washington: Public Affairs Press, 1954, p. 229.

95. For an excellent biography of early chronicles see Irwin R. Blacker (ed.), *The Old West in Fact,* New York: Ivan Obolensky, Inc., 1962; for a colorful composite portrait of the mountain man see George F. Ruxton, *Adventures in Mexico and the Rocky Mountains,* New York: Harper and Brothers, 1848, pp. 241-46.

96. It was upon such erroneous hearsay that the ill-fated Donner party set off on what was reputed to be an easier route to the Sacramento Valley.

97. For example, see Baumann, "On a Western Ranche."

98. Daniel J. Boorstin, *The Americans: the National Experience,* New York: Random House, 1965, Chapter 37.

99. The robbery took place on January 31, 1874, on the St. Louis, Iron Mountain, and Southern Railroad in southeastern Missouri, See Drago, *Outlaws on Horseback,* p. 56.

100. Cited in Fishwick, *American Heroes,* p. 85.

101. John Hays Hammond, "Strong Men of the Wild West," *Scribner's Magazine*, Vol. 77, No. 2 (February 1925), pp. 115-25 and No. 3 (March 1925), pp. 246-56.

102. Sister Blandina Segale, *At the End of the Santa Fe Trail*, Milwaukee: Bruce Publishing Co., 1949. Segale's journal notes have been collected and edited by Sister Therese Martin.

103. William A. Keleher, *The Fabulous Frontier*, Santa Fe: The Rydal Press, 1945, p. 125.

104. Ibid., p. 126.

105. For example, Stuart Lake's adulatory biography of Wyatt Earp in 1931 was the basis for the 1955 television series starring Hugh O'Brian.

106. Helena Huntington Smith, "Sam Bass and the Myth Machine," *The American West*, Vol. 7, No. 1 (January 1970), p. 32.

107. Charles M. Harvey, "The Dime Novel In American Life," *The Atlantic Monthly*, Vol. 100 (July 1907), p. 42.

108. Francis Edward Hodgins, Jr., "The Literary Emancipation of a Region: The Changing Image of the American West in Fiction" (unpublished Ph.D. dissertation, English, Michigan State University, 1957), pp. 93-4.

109. Ibid., p. 85.

110. Patten, "Dime Novel Days" (February 28, 1931), p. 126.

111. Fishwick, *American Heroes*, pp. 102-3.

112. Patten, "Dime Novel Days" (March 7, 1931), p. 36.

113. Smith, *Virgin Land*, p. 119.

114. Douglas Branch, *The Cowboy and His Interpreters*, New York: Cooper Square Publishers, Inc., 1961 (1926), pp. 226-27. Branch's book was originally published in 1926.

115. Edward Charles Abbott ("Teddy Blue"), and Helena Huntington Smith, *We Pointed Them North*, New York: Farrar and Rinehart, Inc., 1939, pp. 60-61.

116. Fishwick, *The Hero, American Style*, pp. 118-19.

117. In Jean Renoir's film, *Rules of the Game*, a muddle-headed matron somehow equates primitive American art with the only thing she knows about America: "But of course! Buffalo Bill!"

118. For a critical look at Wister see: DeVoto, "Birth of an Art."

119. Russel B. Nye, *The Unembarrassed Muse: the Popular Arts in America*, New York: Dial Press, 1970, p. 296.

120. See for a criticism of Grey: Frank Gruber, *Zane Grey*, New York: The World Publishing Co., 1970; Branch, *The Cowboy and His Interpreters*; and Nye, *The Unembarrassed Muse*.

121. Gruber, *Zane Grey*, p. 108.

122. Nye, *The Unembarrassed Muse*, p. 298.

123. Cited in MacCann, *Hollywood in Transition*, pp. 175-76.

124. Lola Goelet Yoakem (ed. and comp.), *Television and Screen Writing*, Berkeley: University of California Press, 1958, pp. 39-40.

125.   Of these latter artists, Will James is a curious case of a man who created his own legend. Born Ernest Dufault in Canada, James established a new identity when he moved to the United States as Will James of Wyoming. Evidently feeling that a true Western image required Western ancestry, he kept his secret to his death. He was a flamboyant Hollywood cowboy who wrote Western fiction and the story of his own life, which turned out to be largely fiction as well. His true talent, however, is as an illustrator. For a melodramatic, exposé-style biography of James, see Anthony Amaral, *Will James: the Gilt Edged Cowboy,* Los Angeles, Westernlore Press, 1967.

126.   Orrin E. Klapp, "The Creation of Popular Heroes," *American Journal of Sociology,* Vol. 54, No. 2 (September 1948) p. 135. The summary outlines Klapp's analysis contained in this seminal treatment on the hero's creation.

127.   For example, note the hero of the "new" Western film.

128.   Klapp, "The Creation of Popular Heroes," p. 139.

129.   Steckmesser, *The Western Hero,* p. 250.

Chapter 3

1.   William K. Everson, *A Pictorial History of the Western Film,* New York: The Citadel Press, 1969, p. 14.

2.   George N. Fenin and William K. Everson, *The Western: from Silents to Cinerama,* New York: Orion Press, 1962, p. 53.

3.   Kalton C. Lahue, *Winners of the West,* New York: A.S. Barnes and Co., 1970, p. 26. Many of the early film stars following Anderson, however, relied upon their own skill and were allowed—often required—to do their own stunting.

4.   Frank James died in 1915; Cole Younger died a year later.

5.   Fishwick, *American Heroes,* p. 112.

6.   See Everson, *Pictorial History,* pp. 32ff. Zane Grey did, however, form his own film production company in 1919. After a brief and unsuccessful time Grey sold the company to Jesse Lasky, whose own company—Famous Players-Lasky—would soon expand into Paramount Pictures, with Adolph Zukor as Lasky's partner. See Gruber, *Zane Grey,* pp. 204-5.

7.   Fenin and Everson, *The Western,* p. 68.

8.   Everson, *Pictorial History,* p. 40. Hart also counted several historical Westerners among his friends, including Bat Masterson, Charlie Russell, William F. Tilghman, and Wyatt Earp. Hart served as pallbearer at Earp's funeral.

9.   Fenin and Everson, *The Western,* p. 116.

10.   Cited in ibid., p. 117. In other respects, however, Scott actually resembled Hart more than Mix.

11.   Everson, *Pictorial History,* p. 66; Branch, *The Cowboy and His Interpreters,* p. 233.

12.   This period was rich in names of both film and fact Westerners. Al Jennings, the former Oklahoma outlaw who became a film cowboy, worked as both actor and advisor in Hollywood; Will James spent much time at the Fat Jones riding stable helping to train horses for films and occasionally landing a small part; Wyatt Earp was a frequent visitor on film sets; and Emmett Dalton even wrote an occasional script.

13. Mix was also the first screen Western hero to connect his name and image with the merchandising of toys and clothing sold with the seal of "Approved by Tom Mix." He also was the first Western star to have a radio series (in which he did not participate) and the first to be portrayed in a comic strip. Richard Griffith and Arthur Mayer, *The Movies,* New York: Simon and Schuster, 1957, p. 168; see also Lahue, *Winners,* p. 251.

14. Griffith and Mayer, *The Movies,* p. 121.

15. Everson, *Pictorial History,* p. 70.

16. André Bazin (Hugh Gray, ed. and trans.), *What Is Cinema?,* Vol. 1, Berkeley: University of California Press, 1967, pp. 17-22.

17. Fenin and Everson, *The Western,* p. 175.

18. Alan G. Barbour, *The Thrill of It All,* New York: Collier Books, 1971, p. 33. Barbour is not a discriminating critic; his work is useful chiefly as an overall (but shallow) review of the B-Western.

19. Other Cisco Kids were Cesar Romero, Duncan Renaldo, and Gilbert Roland. Baxter also starred in the 1931 version (the third, by DeMille) of *The Squaw Man.*

20. In his role as hero in *The Painted Desert* (1930), Boyd squared off against a sullen young Clark Gable, who played the villain.

21. Everson, *Pictorial History,* p. 135.

22. Fenin and Everson, *The Western,* p. 208.

23. For example, Ken Maynard had made use of music in his films, and John Wayne's voice was dubbed by Smith Ballew in Wayne's role as Singin' Sandy, the first of a series of Bs released by Monogram in the thirties. See Barbour, *The Thrill of It All,* p. 33.

24. Both Autry and Rogers, however, were still making Westerns into the fifties.

25. Everson, *Pictorial History,* p. 147.

26. See Richard Whitehall, "The Heroes Are Tired," *Film Quarterly,* Vol. 20, No. 2 (Winter 1966-67), p. 13.

27. Compare the case of Clint Walker in television's *Cheyenne,* whose star temperament was ever wary of a replacement waiting in the wings.

28. John Wayne played the role of Stoney Brooke in a few of the Mesquiteer films, while the future Rita Hayworth appeared in one when she was still Rita Cansino.

29. This series was action-packed and fast-moving and provided acting opportunities for no fewer than five actors who portrayed the heroic Masked Man. They were: Lee Powell, George Letz (later Montgomery), Herman Brix (later Bruce Bennett), Lane Chandler, and Hal Taliaferro (formerly Wally Wales). Clayton Moore played the role in the television series and in two feature films.

30. Fenin and Everson, *The Western,* p. 234.

31. Everson notes that, dating from the Hart and Cooper portrayals, a "strange moral metamorphosis" occured in the heroic stature of Hickok until he became universally accepted as a complete villain by the 1950s. Everson, *Pictorial History,* p. 164.

32. Ibid., p. 173.

33. Sidney Lumet attributes that role to Ford. If Lumet is correct, *Stagecoach* did, indeed, set the scene for a whole new generation of directorial techniques as well as a whole new generation of Westerns.

34. In one instance, at least, the outlaw was far more appealing than the hero. The outlaw was Randolph Scott, the hero was Robert Young, the film was Fritz Lang's *Western Union* (1941). There were many more interesting film outlaws to come, who would create far better characterization balance than the two-dimensional badmen who had appeared in many of the Westerns of the thirties.

    The Lang film was advertised—through an arrangement with the Zane Grey estate—as "Zane Grey's *Western Union,*" although it had been written by a studio scriptwriter. The film generated such interest that a book based upon it was written and published under Grey's name, even though he had been dead for two years. See Fenin and Everson, *The Western,* p. 241.

35. Everson asserts that the Hawks film is—like so many other Westerns—a remake or transposition of a non-Western into the frontier setting. In this case the original is *Mutiny on the Bounty,* with the "same conflict betweeen the two men, the same floggings, the same mutiny—and cattle substituting for breadfruit trees." Everson, *Pictorial History,* p. 200.

36. Anthony Mann's *The Tin Star* (1957) treats the same theme.

37. This variation on the loner theme appeared in other genres as well, notably Kazan's *On the Waterfront* (1954).

38. Bazin, *What Is Cinema?,* Vol. 2, p. 157.

39. *Variety* headlined in 1947: "$30,000,000 in Tinted Oaters," indicating a new high in the number of color Westerns produced during that season. Meanwhile, John Huston chose to shoot *The Treasure of the Sierra Madre* in black and white.

40. The early fifties also saw a rather interesting—though not artistically successful—attempt to pour war hero Audie Murphy into the Western mold. Murphy made many Westerns in the fifties and early sixties, films generally low in both budget and quality. He attempted a television series (*Whispering Smith* in 1961) and at the time of his death in a plane crash ten years later he had already become a postwar memory.

41. Lawrence Alloway, *Violent America: The Movies 1946-64,* New York: New York Graphic Society, 1971, p. 25.

42. See Kitses, *Horizons West* and Stephen Farber, "Peckinpah's Return," *Film Quarterly,* vol. 23, No. 1 (Fall 1969), for a discussion of some problems of *Major Dundee.*

43. But once again, no one could take the risk of casting an Indian heroine; the role was pallidly portrayed by the badly miscast but currently popular Audrey Hepburn.

44. See Sarris' caustic but clever paragraph on "the David Miller cult" in Andrew Sarris, *The American Cinema,* New York: E.P. Dutton and Co., Inc., 1968, p. 261. Sarris gives the credit for *Lonely Are the Brave* to producer-star Kirk Douglas.

45. Marvin's unforgettable scene in which he solemnly prepares himself for the showdown (with himself!) is a fine parody of the ritual of the heroic encounter. The visual and musical overtones of the bullfight arena are particularly effective.

46. Another step in the round-robin borrowing process, this film was patterned after Western fan Akira Kurosawa's *Yojimbo.*

47. Clinging desperately to its last shreds of censorship, the television run of *True Grit* trimmed the Duke's challenge to a ludicrous and faintly ethnic "Fill your hand, you!"

48. This film depicted the concept of the West of writers like A.B. Guthrie and Willa Cather. The theme is adjustment to a vanished frontier.

49. *The Cowboys* concept became a television series during the 1973-74 season.

50. See Sidney Lumet, "Keep Them on the Hook," *Films and Filming,* Vol. 11, No. 1 (October 1964).

51. It is interesting that McCrea and Scott started the film cast in each other's roles. They switched, according to Peckinpah, during lunch hour one day. See John Cutts, "Shoot! Sam Peckinpah Talks to John Cutts," *Films and Filming,* Vol. 16, No. 1 (October 1969), p. 5.

52. The flashback story of this betrayal was one of the cuts imposed much against Peckinpah's desires.

Chapter 4

1. See Appendix A for a listing of most of these series.

2. The chief sources for the following historical summary are Arthur Shulman and Roger Youman, *How Sweet It Was,* New York: Shorecrest, Inc., 1966; and Arthur Shulman and Roger Youmann, *The Television Years,* New York: Popular Library, 1973.

3. Fenin and Everson, *The Western,* p. 312.

4. The music was chosen because it was in the public domain.

5. For a comprehensive study of *The Lone Ranger,* see: David Willson Parker, "A Descriptive Analysis of *The Lone Ranger* as a Form of Popular Art" (unpublished Ph.D. dissertation, Northwestern University, 1954).

6. After the phenomenal success of *The Lone Ranger,* Trendle developed the same formula in other genres with *Sgt. Preston of the Yukon,* and *The Green Hornet,* who was in reality playboy Brit Reid and (in a delightful touch of nepotism) also the great-grand-nephew of Dan Reid, the Lone Ranger!

7. Fenin and Everson attribute the Rogers' failure to a strange combination of a brutal approach to the action and an excessive "gospel-thumping" on the part of Rogers and his wife, Dale Evans. See Fenin and Everson, *The Western,* pp. 312-13.

8. Directing in this series, at least in the beginning, was by Don Siegel.

9. "Grownup Horse Opera," *Newsweek,* Vol. 46, No. 13 (September 26, 1955), p. 108.

10. "TV Goes Wild Over Westerns," *Life,* Vol. 43 (October 28, 1957), pp. 99-102.

11. With the canceling of this series in 1965, Eastwood became involved in the "spaghetti Westerns" of Italian filmmaker Sergio Leone, from which Eastwood emerged a Hollywood superstar of the seventies.

12. *Wagon Train* was canceled in 1964; *The Virginian* ran into the seventies.

13. Many of these shows are still aired in syndicated reruns during the early evening hours set aside by FCC ruling to provide local stations with the opportunity to develop innovative programming. Their continuation in the midseventies does not speak well for the creative capacities of the industry on a local level.

14. The series earned Miss Stanwyck her second Emmy award as Best Actress (her first had been for *The Barbara Stanwyck Show* in 1961).

15. In another unforgettable preemption, the final spectacular moments of a pro football game were cut off in order to begin a scheduled airing of *Heidi*. That error has not been repeated.

16. In an unprecedented act of internetwork cooperation, NBC, CBS, and ABC rotated in covering the sessions, thereby helping each to recoup sponsor losses and retain their daytime game-show and soap opera audiences. Public television repeated the hearings in the evening hours for the convenience of the working public.

17. The narrator, Roger Davis, inherited the role of Hannibal Heyes upon the death of Pete Deuel.

18. The comic soldiers format seems to hold up well in other television genres, ranging in degree of sophistication from *Gomer Pyle* to *M*A*S*H*.

19. As noted earlier, this series was also narrated by Ronald Reagan.

20. The quality and reputation of this series was such that a special rate was established in the Writers' Guild for creating Powell's introductions.

21. Shulman and Youman, *How Sweet It Was,* p. 308. The creators of Paladin, however, finished their appointed rounds with a lawsuit pressed by Victor DeCosta, who claimed that many aspects of the character had been "borrowed" from his own work.

22. Attributed to Gene Autry.

23. Cited in Erik Barnouw, *The Image Empire: A History of Broadcasting in the United States,* Volume III, New York: Oxford University Press, 1970, p. 18.

24. Macdonnell later produced the television series for a time and Conrad moved to law enforcement on the urban range in the television police series *Cannon.*

25. "Grownup Horse Opera," p. 111.

26. Her own person both on and off camera, Amanda Blake chose to retire from *Gunsmoke* at the end of the 1973-74 season.

27. Curtis, of the whining voice, once warbled as a member of The Sons of the Pioneers.

28. Taylor is the son of character actor Dub Taylor, who has appeared in so many Westerns that his face, if not his name, is instantly recognized.

29. Leslie Raddatz, "*Gunsmoke*'s Designated Hitter," *TV Guide,* Vol. 21, No. 9, Issue 1080 (December 8, 1973), pp. 17-18.

30. Dortort later moved to the position of executive producer, with Richard Collins as producer for the last five seasons of the series.

31. The phenomenon of a single sponsor for a weekly series is rare, almost nonexistent, because of prohibitive costs.

32. The experience of seeing Hoss facing up to a tough opponent while hearing the dialogue in Japanese is an experience that borders on the surreal.

33. During 1970 the filming of the series also moved from Paramount to Warners.

34. Matheson, a *Virginian* regular during the 1969-70 season, was cast in *Bonanza* as exconvict Griff King, paroled to the ranch through the influence of Ben Cartwright. Another character

expanding the "family" several years prior to that time was Mitch Vogel as adopted younger son, Jamie.

35. Landon explained:

> The loss of Dan Blocker was a tremendous blow to all of us who have been so close to him for 14 years. It was terribly difficult to go back to work and know he would not be there.
> We had to transfer our personal loss onto film. We needed to share our sorrow. It would have been impossible for us to begin work again on a happy project when we were so filled with sorrow.
> The loss of Alice Cartwright was our way of expressing the great loss of Dan Blocker. In other words, we needed to cry.

Clarence Petersen, "Bonanza's Landon Responds," *Chicago Tribune* (October 17, 1972), p. 11.

36. Reruns had already appeared under the title of *Ponderosa*.

37. Irwin Blacker, who has extensively researched the fact of the Old West and helped to create the fiction as a writer and story editor for Western series, indicates that the original formula often provides for more characters than are really needed. A process of natural selection usually follows. However, the reverse phenomenon also occurs, and "one-shot" appearances that provide audience appeal are often incorporated into the series as continuing characters. Blacker feels that a series is able to work well with only two or three continuing characters, but that creators often feel they need more. Irwin R. Blacker, Interview, Los Angeles, California, July 7, 1972.

38. Blocker did provide audiences with an opportunity to see him work in a role that moved out of the *Bonanza* mold. He produced a memorable performance as the lead in *Something for a Lonely Man* in the late sixties.

39. See the rules for *Bonanza* writers, Appendix B.

40. Shulman and Youman, *How Sweet It Was*, p. 311.

41. Judy Klemesrud, "The Man Who Struck It Rich With 'Bonanza,'" *The New York Times*, (October 8, 1972), p. 23.

42. Dick Adler, "The Cartwrights Carry On," *TV Guide*, Vol. 20, No. 41, Issue 519 (October 7, 1972), pp. 40, 42.

43. Fishwick, *The Hero, American Style*, p. 69.

44. Cawelti, "The Gunfighter and Society," *The American West*, Vol. 5, No. 2 (March 1968), pp. 30-35, 76-77.

45. Ibid., p. 34.

46. Ibid., p. 76.

47. A paraphrase of a statement attributed to Samuel Butler in Nye, *The Unembarrassed Muse*, p. 9.

48. Borrowing from the Western film genre is obvious here. The Cooper, Wayne, Fonda, Scott, and Eastwood images of the Westerner are reproduced in Arness, Greene, Blocker, Landon and others. The continuing adventures of the hero from film to film, however, are less common but the work of Autry and Rogers attests to the fact that this is possible. The films of

Ford, Peckinpah, Boetticher, and Leone repeat and embellish not the same hero in every case, but often the same actor-hero in similar stories and recurring thematic elements.

49. The producer, who often is also the creator, is closer to auteurism because he is closer to the original concept. The actor, although he receives the concept as a given, is able to impress his own personality upon the material because he is continually involved with the development of that concept over a period of time.

50. By the same token, a longer segment on location should extend into multiples of eight rather than fractions thereof; fewer than eight pages would mean a half day (and money) lost. Blacker, Interview.

51. Ibid.

52. For an interesting discussion of the pastoral mode in literature (with the figure of the cowboy as pastor), see the article by James E. Phillips, "Arcadia on the Range" in Ray B. Browne and Donald Pizer (eds.), *Themes and Directions in American Literature,* Lafayette, Indiana: Purdue University Press, 1969, pp. 108-29.

53. McMurtry refers to Robert Frost's definition of writing free verse: like playing tennis with the net down. See Larry McMurtry, "Films, TV, and Tennis" in Robinson, *Man and the Movies,* p. 103.

Bibliography

Books

Abbott, E.C. ("Teddy Blue"), and Smith, Helena Huntington. *We Pointed Them North.* New York: Farrar and Rinehart, Inc., 1939.

Alloway, Lawrence. *Violent America: The Movies 1946-64.* New York: New York Graphic Society, 1971.

Amaral, Anthony. *Will James: The Gilt Edged Cowboy.* Los Angeles: Westernlore Press, 1967.

Barbour, Alan G. *The Thrill of It All.* New York: Collier Books, 1971.

Barnouw, Erik. *The Image Empire: A History of Broadcasting in the United States,* Vol. 3. New York: Oxford University Press, 1970.

Bazin, André. *What Is Cinema?,* Vol. 1. Berkeley: University of California Press, 1967.

———. *What Is Cinema?,* Vol. 2. Berkeley: University of California Press, 1971.

Bellour, Raymond, et al. *Le Western: Sources—Thèmes—Mythologies—Auteurs—Acteurs— Filmographies,* 2nd ed., Paris: Le Monde en 10/18, Union Générale d'Editions, 1968.

Blacker, Irwin R., ed. *The Old West in Fact.* New York: Ivan Obolensky, Inc., 1962.

Boatright, Mody, et al., eds. *Mesquite and Willow.* Dallas: Southern Methodist University Press, 1957.

Bogdanovich, Peter. *John Ford.* Berkeley: University of California Press, 1968.

Boorstin, Daniel J. *The Americans: The National Experience.* New York: Random House, 1965.

Botkin, Benjamin Albert, ed. *A Treasury of Western Folklore.* New York: Crown Publishers, 1951.

Branch, Douglas. *The Cowboy and His Interpreters.* New York: Cooper Square Publishers, Inc., 1961 (1926).

Browne, Ray B., and Ambrosetti, Ronald J. *Popular Culture and Curricula.* Bowling Green, Ohio: Bowling Green University Popular Press, 1970.

Browne, Ray Broadus, and Pizer, Donald, eds. *Themes and Directions in American Literature.* Lafayette, Ind.: Purdue University Press, 1969.

Campbell, Joseph. *Hero With a Thousand Faces.* 2nd ed., Princeton: Princeton University Press, 1968.

———. ed. *Myths, Dreams, and Religion.* New York: E.P. Dutton, 1970.

Cawelti, John G. *The Six-Gun Mystique.* Bowling Green, Ohio: Bowling Green University Popular Press, n.d.

Cohen, Hennig, comp. *The American Experience.* Boston: Houghton Mifflin, 1968.

Corneau, Ernest N. *The Hall of Fame of Western Film Stars.* North Quincy, Mass.: The Christopher Publishing House, 1969.

Cunningham, Eugene. *Triggernometry: A Gallery of Gunfighters.* Caldwell, Idaho: Caxton Printers, 1947.

Custer, George Armstrong. *My Life on the Plains; or, Personal Experiences with Indians.* New York: Sheldon and Company, 1876.

DeVoto, Bernard. *The Year of Decision, 1846.* Boston: Little Brown and Company, 1943.

Drago, Harry Sinclair. *Outlaws on Horseback.* London: John Long, 1965.

Dykes, J.C. *Billy the Kid: The Bibliography of a Legend.* Albuquerque: The University of New Mexico Press, 1952.

Everson, William K. *A Pictorial History of the Western Film.* New York: The Citadel Press, 1969.

Eyles, Allen. *The Western: An Illustrated Guide.* New York: A.S. Barnes and Company, 1967.

Fenin, George N., and Everson, William K. *The Western: from Silents to Cinerama.* New York: Orion Press, 1962.

Fishwick, Marshall W. *American Heroes: Myth and Reality.* Washington: Public Affairs Press, 1954.

_____. *A Bibliography of the American Hero.* Charlottesville, Va.: Bibliographical Society of the University of Virginia, 1950.

_____. *The Hero, American Style.* New York: D. McKay Company, 1969.

Folsom, James K. *The American Western Novel.* New Haven: College and University Press, 1966.

Ford, Charles. *Histoire du Western.* Paris: Pierre Horay, 1964.

Frantz, Joe B., and Choate, Julian Ernest, Jr. *The American Cowboy: The Myth and the Reality.* Norman, Okla.: University of Oklahoma Press, 1955.

Frye, Northrop. *Anatomy of Criticism.* Princeton: Princeton University Press, 1957.

Griffith, Richard, and Mayer, Arthur. *The Movies.* New York: Simon and Schuster, 1957.

Gruber, Frank. *The Pulp Jungle.* Los Angeles: Sherbourne Press, Inc., 1967.

_____. *Zane Grey.* New York: The World Publishing Company, 1970.

Jarvie, Ian C. *Towards a Sociology of the Cinema.* London: Routledge and K. Paul, 1970.

Keleher, William A. *The Fabulous Frontier.* Santa Fe: The Rydal Press, 1945.

Kitses, Jim. *Horizons West.* Bloomington, Ind.: Indiana University Press, 1969.

Klapp, Orrin E. *Heroes, Villains and Fools: The Changing American Character.* Englewood Cliffs, N.J.: Prentice Hall, 1962.

Lahue, Kalton. *Winners of the West.* New York: A.S. Barnes and Company, 1970.

Lake, Stuart N. *Wyatt Earp: Frontier Marshal.* Boston: Houghton Mifflin Company, 1931.

Lyons, Peter. *The Wild, Wild West.* New York: Funk and Wagnalls, 1969.

MacCann, Richard Dyer. *Hollywood in Transition.* Boston: Houghton Mifflin Company, 1962.

McDermott, John Francis, ed. *The Frontier Re-Examined.* Urbana, Ill.: The University of Illinois Press, 1967.

Mast, Gerald. *A Short History of the Movies.* New York: Bobbs-Merrill Company, Inc., 1971.

Noble, David W. *The Eternal Adam and the New World Garden.* New York: George Braziller, 1968.

Nye, Russel Blaine. *The Cultural Life of the New Nation, 1776-1830.* New York: Harper and Brothers, Publishers, 1960.

_____. *This Almost Chosen People.* East Lansing, Mich.: Michigan State University Press, 1966.

_____. *The Unembarrassed Muse: The Popular Arts in America.* New York: Dial Press, 1970.

_____, and Morpugo, J.E. *A History of the United States* (2 vols.). 2nd ed., Baltimore: Penguin Books, 1964.

Parks, Jack. *Who Killed Custer?* New York: Tower Publications, Inc., 1970.

Raglan, Fitzroy. *The Hero: A Study in Tradition, Myth, and Drama.* London: Watts, 1949.

Rhodes, May Davison. *The Hired Man on Horseback.* Boston: Houghton Mifflin, 1938.

Rieupeyrout, Jean-Louis. *La Grande Aventure du Western (1894-1964): du Far West á Hollywood.* Paris: Les Editions du Cerf, 1964.

Robinson, William Ronald, ed. *Man and the Movies.* Baton Rouge, La.; Louisiana State University Press, 1967.

Rosa, Joseph G. *The Gunfighter: Man or Myth?* Norman, Okla.; University of Oklahoma Press, 1969.

Ruxton, George F. *Adventures in Mexico and the Rocky Mountains.* New York: Harper and Brothers, 1848.

Sarris, Andrew. *The American Cinema.* New York: E.P. Dutton and Company, Inc., 1968.

Segale, Blandina, Sister. *At the End of the Santa Fe Trail.* Milwaukee: Bruce Publishing Company, 1949.

Shulman, Arthur, and Youman, Roger. *How Sweet It Was.* New York: Shorecrest, Inc., 1966.

———. *The Television Years.* New York: Popular Library, 1973.

Siringo, Charles A. *A Texas Cowboy: or, Fifteen Years on the Hurricane Deck of a Spanish Pony.* New York: Sloane, 1950 (1885).

Smith, Henry Nash. *Virgin Land: The American West as Symbol and Myth.* New York: Vintage Books, 1950.

Steckmesser, Kent Ladd. *The Western Hero in History and Legend.* Norman, Okla.; University of Oklahoma Press, 1965.

Tailleur, Roger., et al., eds. *Le Western: Sources, Mythes, Auteurs, Actors, Filmographie.* Paris: Union Générale d'Editions, 1966.

Trapnell, Coles. *Teleplay.* San Francisco: Chandler Publishing Company, 1966.

Turner, Frederick Jackson. *Frontier and Section: Selected Essays of Frederick Jackson Turner,* with an introduction by Billington, Ray Allen. Englewood Cliffs, N.J.: Prentice Hall, Inc., 1961.

Van DeWater, Frederic. *Glory-Hunter: A Life of General Custer.* New York: The Bobbs-Merrill Company, 1934.

Warshow, Robert. *The Immediate Experience.* Garden City: Doubleday and Company, Inc., 1962.

Webb, Walter Prescott. *The Great Plains.* Waltham, Mass.: Blaisdell Publishing Company, 1959 (1931).

Wecter, Dixon. *The Hero in America: A Chronicle of Hero Worship.* Ann Arbor: University of Michigan Press, 1966 (1941).

Weiss, Ken, and Goodgold, Ed. *To Be Continued...* New York: Crown Publishers, Inc., 1972.

Westermeier, Clifford P., ed. *Trailing the Cowboy.* Caldwell, Idaho: The Caxton Printers, Ltd., 1955.

Wollen, Peter. *Signs and Meaning in the Cinema.* Bloomington, Ind.; Indiana University Press, 1969.

Wright, Charles Robert. *Mass Communication: A Sociological Perspective.* New York: Random House, 1959.

Yoakem, Lola Goelet, ed. and comp. *Television and Screen Writing.* Berkeley: University of California Press, 1958.

Periodicals and Newspapers

Adler, Dick. "The Cartwrights Carry On." *TV Guide,* Vol. 20, No. 41, Issue 519 (October 7, 1972), 38-42.

Barker, Warren J. "The Stereotyped Western Story." *Psychoanalytic Quarterly,* Vol. 24, No. 2 (April 1955), 270-80.

Baumann, John. "On a Western Ranche." *Fortnightly Review,* Vol. 47 (1887), 516-33.

Blair, Walter. "Six Davy Crocketts." *Southwest Review,* Vol. 25, No. 4 (July 1940), 442-62.

Bluestone, George. "The Changing Cowboy." *Western Humanities Review,* Vol. 14 (Summer 1960), 331-37.

Boatright, Mody. "The American Myth Rides the Range." *Southwest Review*, Vol. 36, No. 3 (Summer 1951), 157-63.

Buscombe, Edward. "The Idea of Genre in the American Cinema." *Screen*, Vol. 11, No. 2 (March-April 1970), 33-45.

Cawelti, John G. "Cowboys, Indians, Outlaws." *The American West*, Vol. 1 (Spring 1964), 29-35, 77-79.

_____. "The Gunfighter and Society." *The American West*, Vol. 5, No. 2 (March 1968), 30-35, 76-77.

_____. "Prolegomena to the Western." *Studies in Public Communication*, No. 4 (Autumn 1962), 57-70.

Collins, Richard. "Genre: A Reply to Ed Buscombe." *Screen*, Vol. 11, Nos. 4-5 (August-September 1970), 66-75.

Cutts, John. "Shoot! Sam Peckinpah Talks to John Cutts." *Films and Filming*, Vol. 16, No. 1 (October 1969), 4-8.

Davis, David D. "Ten-Gallon Hero." *American Quarterly*, Vol. 6, No. 2 (Summer 1954), 111-25.

DeVoto, Bernard. "Birth of An Art." *Harper's Magazine*, Vol. 211, No. 1267 (December 1955), 8-9, 12-16.

_____. "Brave Days in Washoe." *American Mercury*, Vol. 17, No. 66 (June 1929), 228-37.

_____. "The West: A Plundered Province." *Harper's Magazine*, Vol. 169 (August 1934), 355-64.

Dobie, J. Frank. "Andy Adams, Cowboy Chronicler." *Southwest Review*, Vol. 11, No. 2 (January 1926), 92-101.

Farber, Stephen. "Peckinpah's Return." *Film Quarterly*, Vol. 23, No. 1 (Fall 1969), 2-11.

Fishwick, Marshall W. "The Cowboy: America's Contribution to the World's Mythology." *Western Folklore*, Vol. 11, No. 2 (April 1952), 77-92.

Grohman, W. Baillie. "Cattle Ranches in the Far West." *Fortnightly Review*, Vol. 34 (1880), 438-57.

"Grownup Horse Opera." *Newsweek*, Vol. 46, No. 13 (September 26, 1955), 108, 111.

Hammond, John Hays. "Strong Men of the Wild West." *Scribner's Magazine*, Vol. 77, No. 2 (February, 1925), 115-25, and Vol. 77, No. 3 (March 1925), 246-56.

Harvey, Charles M. "The Dime Novel in American Life." *The Atlantic Monthly*, Vol. 100 (July 1907), 37-45.

Hirsch, Foster. "The Actor as Auteur." *Kansas Quarterly*, Vol. 4, No. 2 (Spring 1972), 31-38.

Kael, Pauline. "Circles and Squares." *Film Quarterly*, Vol. 16, No. 3 (Sping 1963), 12-26.

Kaufman, Michael T. "George W. Trendle Dies at 87; Creator of 'The Lone Ranger.' " *The New York Times*, May 12, 1972, p. 44.

Keen, Sam. "Man and Myth: A Conversation with Joseph Campbell." *Psychology Today*, Vol. 5, No. 2 (July 1971), 35-39, 86-91, 94-95.

Klapp, Orrin E. "The Creation of Popular Heroes." *American Journal of Sociology*, Vol. 54, No. 2 (September 1948), 135-41.

Klemesrud, Judy. "The Man Who Struck It Rich With 'Bonanza.' " *The New York Times*, October 8, 1972, p. 23.

Leithead, J. Edward. "The Anatomy of Dime Novels." *Dime Novel Roundup*, Vol. 36, No. 2 (February 15, 1967), 14-17.

Lumet, Sidney. "Keep Them On the Hook." *Films and Filming*, Vol. 11, No. 1 (October 1964).

McArthur, Colin. "Sam Peckinpah's West." *Sight and Sound*, Vol. 36, No. 4 (Autumn 1967), 180-83.

McWilliams, Carey. "Myths of the West." *North American Review*, Vol. 232 (November 1931), 424-32.

Miller, Alexander. "The Western: A Theological Note." *Christian Century*, Vol. 74, No. 48 (November 27, 1957), 1409-10.

Nussbaum, Martin. "Sociological Symbolism of the Adult Western." *Social Forces,* Vol. 39 (October 1960), 25-28.

Orcutt, Eddy. "Passed By Here." *Saturday Evening Post,* Vol. 211, No. 8 (August 20, 1938), 20-21, 48, 50-53.

Parks, Jack. "They Died With Their Boots Off." *True,* Vol. 52, No. 415 (December 1971), 51-56.

Patten, Gilbert. "Dime Novel Days." *Saturday Evening Post,* Vol. 203, No. 35 (February 28, 1931), 6-7, 125-30, and Vol. 203, No. 36 (March 7, 1931), 33-36, 52-60.

Peterson, Clarence. "Bonanza's Landon Responds." *Chicago Tribune,* October 17, 1972, p. 11.

Raddatz, Leslie. "Gunsmoke's Designated Hitter." *TV Guide,* Vol. 21, No. 9, Issue 1080 (December 8, 1973), 17-20.

Ryall, Tom. "The Notion of Genre." *Screen,* Vol. 11, No. 2 (March-April, 1970), 22-32.

Sarris, Andrew. "The Auteur Theory and the Perils of Pauline." *Film Quarterly,* Vol. 16, No. 4 (Summer 1963), 26-33.

Schein, Harry. "The Olympian Cowboy." *The American Scholar,* Vol. 24, No. 3 (Summer 1955), 309-20.

Seldes, Gilbert. "Television: Art or Craft?" *Film Culture,* Vol. 3, No. 4 (November 1957), 4-5.

Smith, Helena Huntington. "Sam Bass and the Myth Machine." *The American West,* Vol. 7, No. 1 (January 1970), 31-35.

Sobol, Ken. "The West: Authentic and Absurd." *The Village Voice,* October 12, 1972, p. 50.

Speed, F. Maurice, ed. and comp. *The Western Film and TV Annual* (from 1951 to 1956 published as *The Western Film Annual*). London: Macdonald and Company, Ltd.

Stegner, Wallace. "History, Myth, and the Western Writer." *The American West,* Vol. 4, No. 2 (May 1967), 61-62, 76-79.

Tudor, Andrew. "Genre: Theory and Mispractice in Film Criticism." *Screen,* Vol. 11, No. 6 (November-December 1970), 33-43.

"TV Goes Wild Over Westerns." *Life,* Vol. 43 (October 28, 1957), 99-102.

Ulph, Owen C. "Cowhands, Cowhorses, and Cows." *The American West,* Vol. 3, No. 1 (Winter 1966), 64-71.

Vestal, Stanley. "The Man Who Killed Custer." *American Heritage,* Vol. 8 (February 1957), 9-12.

Vogel, Nancy. "'Bonanza' Scripts." *Writer's Digest,* Vol. 48, No. 12 (December 1968), 62-64, 93, 95.

Weaver, John D. "Destry Rides Again, and Again, and Again." *Holiday,* Vol. 34, No. 2 (August 1963), 77-80, 91.

Whitehall, Richard. "The Heroes Are Tired." *Film Quarterly,* Vol. 20, No. 2 (Winter 1966-67), 12-24.

Willett, Ralph. "The American Western: Myth and Anti-Myth." *Journal of Popular Culture,* Vol. 4, No. 2 (Fall 1970), 455-62.

Williams, John. "The Western: Definition of a Myth." *The Nation,* Vol. 193, No. 17 (November 18, 1961), 402-6.

Unpublished Materials and Interviews

Blacker, Irwin R. Interview, Los Angeles, California, July 17, 1972.

Buscombe, Edward, ed. and comp. *The Western: Study Unit 12.* Unpublished manuscript disseminated by the British Film Institute, September 1971.

Cawelti, John G. Interview, Chicago, Illinois, December 11, 1972.

Hodgins, Francis Edward, Jr. "The Literary Emancipation of a Region: The Changing Image of the American West in Fiction." Unpublished Ph.D. dissertation, Michigan State University, 1957.

Parker, David Willson. "A Descriptive Analysis of *The Lone Ranger* as a Form of Popular Art." Unpublished Ph.D. dissertation, Northwestern University, 1954.

Index

Alamo, The (1967), 100
Anderson, Gilbert M., 81-82, 83
Arness, James, 142-45
Artists, 71-73. *See also* Mythmakers
Aryan, The (1916), 84
Autry, Gene, 90-92, 126, 128

Badman. *See* Gunman
Ballad of Cable Hogue (1970), 103-4
Bargain, The (1914), 83
Battle at Elderbush Gulch, The (1913), 82
Beadle (publishing company), 40, 44, 64-68
Bend of the River (1952), 97
Big Trail, The (1930), 89, 93
Billy the Kid. *See* Bonney, William
Billy the Kid (1930), 93
Billy the Kid (1941), 94
Biographers, 60-63. *See also* Mythmakers
Blocker, Dan, 146-51
Bonanza, 33, 130, 133, 134, 139, 141, 146-52
Bonney, William (Billy the Kid), 13, 48-49, 55-56, 61, 62, 69, 94
Bonnie and Clyde (1967), 100, 104
Boone, Daniel, 9, 12, 36-39
Bounty Hunters, The (1975), 82
Boyd, William, 49, 89, 90, 127, 128
Brand, Max. *See* Faust, Frederick
Broken Arrow (1950), 95
Bronco Billy. *See* Anderson, Gilbert M.
Bronco Billy and the Baby (1908), 81
Buck and the Preacher (1972), 105
Buffalo Bill. *See* Cody, William F.
Buffalo Bill (1944), 94
Buntline, Ned. *See* Judson, E.Z.C.
Butch Cassidy and the Sundance Kid (1969), 50, 103

Cahill, U.S. Marshal (1973), 105
Carson, Kit, 12, 39-40, 56
Cassidy, Butch, 49, 81

Cat Ballou (1965), 100
Cavalry. *See* Soldiers
Cheyenne Autumn (1964), 99
Chip of the Flying U (1914), 85
Chroniclers, 59-60. *See also* Mythmakers
Cimarron (1931), 93
Cimarron (1960), 97
Cinema: auteur theory, 21-27; beginnings of, 80-87; changing perspectives in, 99-107; characteristics of, 3; "Golden Age" of the Western, 93-96; history of Western in, 79-107; and sound, 88-93; and television, 96-99. *See also* Television; Western, the
Cody, William F., 39, 44, 55, 65-68, 80, 82, 94
Cooper, Gary, 29, 55, 89, 94, 96, 131-32
Cooper, James Fenimore, 37, 40, 51, 69
Covered Wagon, The (1923), 84, 87, 93
Cowboys, 44-47, 56
Cowboys, The (1972), 105
Cripple Creek Bar-room (1898), 80
Crockett, Davy, 38, 56, 82, 129
Custer, George Armstrong, 42-43, 69, 82, 94
Custer's Last Fight (1912), 82

Davy Crockett (1917), 82
Deadly Companions, The (1962), 99
Deadwood Dick, 40-41, 44, 55, 65
Destry Rides Again (1939), 94
Devil's Doorway (1950), 97
Dime Novelists, 64-66. *See also* Mythmakers
Dime novels, 33, 39-40, 41, 44, 46, 47, 64-66
Duel in the Sun (1946), 95

Earp, Wyatt, 13, 53-54, 55, 69, 97, 108-11, 129
Eastwood, Clint, 103, 105, 131

El Dorado (1967), 103

Far Country, The (1954), 97
Faust, Frederick, 66, 69
Fighting Blood (1911), 82
Film. *See* Cinema
Firecreek (1968), 102
Fistful of Dollars, A (1964), 103
Fonda, Henry, 70, 102, 108-11, 130
For a Few Dollars More (1966), 103
Ford, John, 33, 34, 43, 54, 59, 86, 87, 93,
    95, 97, 99, 108-15
Fort Apache (1948), 43
Fremont, John Charles, 39
Frontier. *See* West, the
Furies, The (1950), 97

Genre: basic elements of, 22-27; categories,
    19, 24, 27; as critical approach, 22, 26-
    27, 33; function of, 27, 33; and mass
    media, 34-35; and popular culture, 33-
    34; Western, 77, 155-57
Go West (1940), 94
Good, the Bad, and the Ugly, The (1967),
    103
Great Adventures of Wild Bill Hickok
    (1938), 92
Great K & A Robbery, The (1926), 85
Great Northfield Minnesota Raid, The
    (1972), 49, 105
Great Train Robbery, The (1901), 49, 81,
    83
Greene, Lorne, 146-51
Grey, Zane, 66, 69, 70
Gruber, Frank, 30, 33, 69, 70-71
Gunfight at the OK Corral (1957), 54, 97
Gunfighters. *See* Gunman
Gunfighter, The (1950), 51, 95
Gunman, 47-56
Gunsmoke, 55, 129, 130, 139, 141-46

Hart, William S., 46, 55, 81, 83-84, 86, 155
Hell's Hinges (1916), 84
Hero: and antihero, 57-59, 76, 101-5, 115-
    24; classic, 15, 56-59, 76, 138; creation
    of, 72-73, 75-77; cult of, 73, 75;
    origin of, 73-74; popular, 1-2, 3-4, 49,
    76, 155-57; western, 35-59, 132-34,
    136-41. *See also* Western hero
Hickok, James Butler, 13, 39, 52, 53, 54-
    55
High Noon (1952), 96
High Plains Drifter (1973), 105
Hired Hand, The (1971), 104
History: of cinema, 79-124; and genre
    study, 23-24; and myth, 13-16; roots

of the Western in, 30-31; of television,
    125-36; westerner in, 35-59, 59-63
Hombre (1967), 100
Hondo (1953), 97
Hopalong Cassidy. *See* Boyd, William
Hour of the Gun (1967), 54
How the West Was Won (1963), 100
Hud (1963), 31, 100

In Old Arizona (1929), 89
Indian. *See* Native American
Ingraham, Prentiss, 44, 65
Invitation to a Gunfighter (1964), 51
Iron Horse, The (1924), 84, 87, 89, 93

James, Jesse, 49, 50, 55, 61, 82
Jesse James (1911), 82
Jesse James (1939), 94
Jeremiah Johnson (1973), 105
Joe Kidd (1972), 105
Johnny Guitar (1951), 97
Journalists, 61-63. *See also* Mythmakers
Judson, E.Z.C., 33, 65-68
Junior Bonner (1972), 105

Landon, Michael, 146-51
Last Drop of Water, The (1911), 82
Last Frontier, The (1955), 97
Law and Order (1932), 93
Lawman. *See* Gunman
Leatherstocking, 35, 37, 38, 40, 51, 56, 69,
    70
Left-Handed Gun (1958), 50, 98-99
Legend of Nigger Charley, The (1972), 105
Life and Times of Judge Roy Bean (1973),
    105, 107
Little Big Man (1970), 104
Lone Ranger, 127
Lone Ranger, The (1938), 92
Lonely Are the Brave (1962), 100

McCabe and Mrs. Miller (1971), 105
McCrea, Joel, 93, 94, 116-23
Magnificent Seven, The (1960), 99
Major Dundee (1965), 99
Man from Laramie, The (1955), 96, 97
Man of the West (1958), 97
Man Who Shot Liberty Valance, The
    (1962), 59, 99, 109, 111-15
Marshal. *See* Gunman
Masterson, William Barclay ("Bat"), 53, 55
Misfits, The (1961), 31, 100
Miracle Rider, The (1935), 86, 92
Mix, Tom, 81, 84-86, 89
Mountain Man, 39-41, 48, 51
My Darling Clementine (1946), 33, 54, 94,
    102, 108-12

Mystery Mountain (1934), 92
Myth: and archetype, 13-16, 19, 29-30, 34, 123, 155-57; definition of, 13-14; and formula, 18-19, 26, 30, 151-53; function of, 16, 155-57; and history, 13, 17-18, 58-60; and the Western, 5, 26, 29-32, 35-36, 46, 48-49, 51-52, 58-59, 72-73, 108-14
Mythmakers: artists as, 71-73; chroniclers as, 59-60; dime novelists as, 64-68; in film, 107; journalists and biographers as, 61-63; novelists as, 69-71; in television, 151-53

Naked Spur, The (1952), 97
Native American, 15, 32, 42-43, 82, 93-94, 95-96, 129
Nevada Smith (1966), 102
Novelists, 69-71. *See also* Mythmakers

Once Upon a Time in the West (1969), 103
One-Eyed Jacks (1961), 99
Outlaw. *See* Gunman
Outlaw, The (1942), 95
Ox-Bow Incident, The (1942), 95

Pat Garret and Billy the Kid (1973), 105
Peckinpah, Sam, 99, 104, 105, 107, 115-24
Phantom Empire, The (1935), 92
Photography, 72-73, 79
Plainsman, The (1936), 55, 93
Professionals, The (1966), 102

Rainbow Trail, The (1931), 85
Rhodes, Eugene Manlove, 13, 44, 62
Ride the High Country (1962), 99, 112, 116-23
Riders of the Purple Sage (Grey), 70
Rio Bravo (1959), 97, 103
Rio Grande (1950), 43
Rio Lobo (1971), 103, 105
Rogers, Roy, 91-92
Rustlers of Red Dog, The (1935), 92

Scott, Randolph, 46, 85, 94, 98, 116-24
Searchers, The (1956), 97
Sergeant Rutledge (1960), 99
Shane (1953), 51, 57, 97, 100
She Wore a Yellow Ribbon (1949), 43
Sky High (1922), 85
Soldiers, 42-43
Sometimes a Great Notion (1971), 104
Spoilers, The (1930), 93
Stagecoach (1939), 93
Stewart, James, 28, 94, 96, 102, 112-14
Street and Smith (publishing company), 39, 64-68

Sutter's Gold (1936), 93

Television: and adult western, 128-29, 131; characteristics of, 3, 125; history of the Western in, 126-36; types of Westerns in, 129, 132-36, 137-41; western format in, 151-53. *See also* Cinema; Western, the
Texans, The (1938), 93
Texas Rangers, The (1936), 93
They Died With Their Boots On (1941), 94
Three Godfathers, The (1949), 95
3:10 to Yuma (1957), 96
Three Word Bond (1921), 84
Tin Star, The (1957), 97
Toll Gate, The (1920), 84
Train Robbers, The (1973), 105
Treasure of the Sierra Madre (1948), 95
True Grit (1969), 103
Tumbleweeds (1925), 84
Tumbling Tumbleweeds (1935), 90
Two Rode Together (1961), 99

Unforgiven, The (1960), 99
Union Pacific (1939), 93
Upson, Ash, 33, 62-63

Vanishing Legion, The (1931), 92
Virginian, The (Wister), 52, 69
Virginian, The (1929), 89
Viva Zapata (1952), 96

Wagonmaster (1950), 97
Wayne, John, 43, 75, 86, 89, 97, 100, 103, 105, 108, 112-14
Welcome to Hard Times (1967), 51, 102
Wells Fargo (1937), 93
West, the: definition, 4; geography of, 7-12, 16-17, 30-31, 47; migration to, 7-11; myth of, 6, 11, 13-14, 16; towns of, 9, 44-45, 48
Western, the: "adult," 99, 128-29; audience consensus on, 32; audience for, 33-34; changing perspectives in, 108-15, 115-24, 129-36; characters in, 32; conventions of, 25-26; definition of, 27-28; as epic, 77, 124; and genre study, 21-35, 77, 156; and mass media, 34-35; as pastoral, 126, 153; plot in, 29-30; setting of, 31-32; stock situations in, 30; television types of, 136-41; themes in, 35-39, 77, 98, 99, 108-15, 115-24; violence in, 105-6, 115; visual and verbal elements of, 28-29. *See also* Cinema; Television
Western hero: as antihero, 101-5, 115-24; characteristics of, 56-58; doubling of,

36-37, 51, 90, 92, 139; parallels with myth, 15-16, 49, 52, 72, 123-24; and popular culture, 2, 49, 155-57; transformation of, 3-4, 38, 40-41, 42-44, 46, 48-49; types, 4, 32, 35-59, 136-41. *See also* Hero
Westerner (1939), 94
Wheeler, Edward, 40-41, 65
When the Daltons Rode (1940), 94

Wild Bill Hickok. *See* Hickok, James Butler
Wild Bill Hickok (1923), 84
Wild Bunch, The (1969), 50, 104, 112, 116-23
Will Penny (1967), 102
Winchester 73 (1950), 97
Wister, Owen, 52, 69, 70

Yellow Sky (1948), 95